Contents

Published by CGP

Editors:
Helena Hayes
David Hickinson
Julie Wakeling
Sarah Williams

Contributors:
Mark A. Edwards, Judith Hayes, Jason Howell, Barbara Mascetti, John Myers,
Moira Steven, Pat Szczesniak.

With thanks to Katherine Craig for the proofreading.

ISBN: 978 1 84762 545 8

With thanks to Science Photo Library for permission to reproduce the photographs on pages 60 & 61

Data used to construct stopping distance diagram on page 77 from the Highway Code.
© Crown Copyright re-produced under the terms of the Click-Use licence

Website: www.cgpbooks.co.uk
Clipart source: CorelDRAW® and VECTOR
Printed by Elanders Ltd, Newcastle upon Tyne

Based on the classic CGP style created by Richard Parsons.

Theories Come, Theories Go

SCIENTISTS are ALWAYS RIGHT — or are they?

Well it'd be nice if that were so, but it just ain't — never has been and never will be.
Increasing scientific knowledge involves making mistakes along the way. Let me explain...

Scientists come up with **hypotheses** — then **test** them

1) Scientists try and <u>explain</u> things. Everything.

2) They start by <u>observing</u> or <u>thinking about</u> something they don't understand — it could be anything,
    e.g. planets in the sky, a person suffering from an illness, what matter is made of... anything.

3) Then, using what they already know (plus a bit of insight),
    they come up with a <u>hypothesis</u> (a <u>theory</u>) that could
    <u>explain</u> what they've observed.

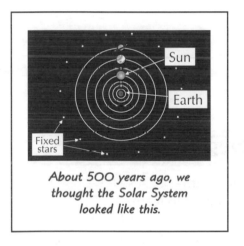

*About 500 years ago, we
thought the Solar System
looked like this.*

> Remember, a hypothesis is just a <u>theory</u>, a
> <u>belief</u>. And <u>believing</u> something is true doesn't
> <u>make</u> it true — not even if you're a scientist.

4) So the next step is to try and convince other scientists that
    the hypothesis is right — which involves using <u>evidence</u>.
    First, the hypothesis has to fit the <u>evidence</u> already
    available — if it doesn't, it'll convince <u>no one</u>.

5) Next, the scientist might use the hypothesis to make a <u>prediction</u> — a crucial step. If the hypothesis
    predicts something, and then <u>evidence</u> from <u>experiments</u> backs that up, that's pretty convincing.

> This <u>doesn't</u> mean the hypothesis is <u>true</u> (the 2nd prediction, or the
> 3rd, 4th or 25th one might turn out to be <u>wrong</u>) — but a hypothesis
> that correctly predicts something in the <u>future</u> deserves respect.

A hypothesis is a good place to start
You might have thought that science was all about facts... well, it's not as cut and dried as
that — you also need to know about the process that theories go through to become accepted,
and how those theories change over time. Remember, nothing is set in stone...

Theories Come, Theories Go

Other scientists will **test** the hypotheses too

1) Now then... <u>other</u> scientists will want to use the hypothesis to make their <u>own predictions</u>, and they'll carry out their <u>own experiments</u>. (They'll also try to <u>reproduce</u> earlier results.) And if all the experiments in all the world back up the hypothesis, then scientists start to have a lot of <u>faith</u> in it.

2) However, if a scientist somewhere in the world does an experiment that <u>doesn't</u> fit with the hypothesis (and other scientists can <u>reproduce</u> these results), then the hypothesis is in trouble. When this happens, scientists have to come up with a new hypothesis (maybe a <u>modification</u> of the old theory, or maybe a completely <u>new</u> one).

3) This process of testing a hypothesis to destruction is a vital part of the scientific process. Without the '<u>healthy scepticism</u>' of scientists everywhere, we'd still believe the first theories that people came up with — like thunder being the belchings of an angered god (or whatever).

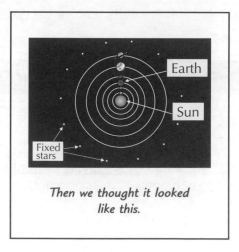

Then we thought it looked like this.

If **evidence** supports a hypothesis, it's **accepted** — **for now**

1) If pretty much every scientist in the world believes a hypothesis to be true because experiments back it up, then it usually goes in the <u>textbooks</u> for students to learn.

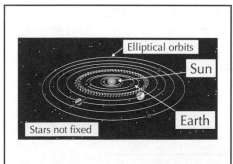

Now we think it's more like this.

2) Our <u>currently accepted</u> theories are the ones that have survived this 'trial by evidence' — they've been tested many, many times over the years and survived (while the less good ones have been ditched).

3) However... they never, <u>never</u> become hard and fast, totally indisputable <u>fact</u>.

You can never know... it'd only take <u>one</u> odd, totally inexplicable result, and the hypothesising and testing would start all over again.

You expect me to believe that — then show me the evidence...

If scientists think something is true, they need to produce evidence to convince others — it's all part of <u>testing a hypothesis</u>. One hypothesis might survive these tests, while others will be disproved — i.e. shown not to be true. So, you see... not everything scientists say is true. <u>It's how science works</u>.

Your Data's Got to Be Good

<u>Evidence</u> is the key to science — but not all evidence is equally good.
The way that evidence is <u>gathered</u> can have a big effect on how <u>trustworthy</u> it is.

Lab experiments *are better than* *rumour* *or* *small samples*

1) Results from <u>controlled experiments</u> in <u>laboratories</u> are <u>great</u>. A lab is the easiest place to <u>control</u> variables so that they're all kept <u>constant</u> (except for the one you're investigating).

 This makes it easier to carry out a <u>fair test</u>.

 It's also the easiest way for <u>different</u> scientists around the world to carry out the <u>same</u> experiments. (There are things you <u>can't</u> study in a lab though, like climate.)

2) Old wives' tales, rumours, hearsay, 'what someone said', and so on, should be taken with a <u>pinch of salt</u>. They'd need to be tested in controlled conditions to be genuinely scientific.

3) Data based on samples that are too small don't have much more credibility than rumours do.

 A sample should be <u>representative</u> of the <u>whole population</u> (i.e. it should share as many of the various <u>characteristics</u> in the population as possible) — a small sample just can't do that.

Evidence is only *reliable* *if* *other people* *can* *repeat it*

Scientific evidence needs to be reliable (or reproducible). If it isn't, then it doesn't really help.

> **<u>RELIABLE</u>** means that the data can be <u>reproduced by others</u>.

Example: Cold Fusion

In 1989, two scientists claimed that they'd produced '<u>cold fusion</u>' (the energy source of the <u>Sun</u> — but <u>without</u> the <u>enormous temperatures</u>).

It was huge news — if true, this could have meant energy from <u>sea water</u> — the ideal energy solution for the world... forever.

However, other scientists just <u>couldn't</u> get the <u>same results</u> — i.e. the results weren't <u>reliable</u>. And until they are, 'cold fusion' isn't going to be generally accepted as <u>fact</u>.

Reliability is really important in science

The scientific community won't accept someone's data if it can't be repeated by anyone else. It may sound like a really fantastic new theory, but if there's no other support for it, it just isn't reliable.

Your Data's Got to Be Good

Evidence also needs to be *valid*

To answer scientific questions, scientists often try to <u>link</u> changes in <u>one</u> variable with changes in <u>another</u>. This is useful evidence, as long as it's <u>valid</u>.

<u>**VALID**</u> means that the data is <u>reliable</u> AND <u>answers the original question</u>.

Example: Do power lines cause cancer?

Some studies have found that children who live near <u>overhead power lines</u> are more likely to develop <u>cancer</u>. What they'd actually found was a <u>correlation</u> between the variables "<u>presence of power lines</u>" and "<u>incidence of cancer</u>" — they found that as one changed, so did the other.

But this evidence is <u>not enough</u> to say that the power lines <u>cause</u> cancer, as other explanations might be possible.

For example, power lines are often near <u>busy roads</u>, so the areas tested could contain <u>different levels</u> of <u>pollution</u> from traffic. Also, you need to look at types of neighbourhoods and <u>lifestyles</u> of people living in the tested areas (could diet be a factor... or something else you hadn't thought of).

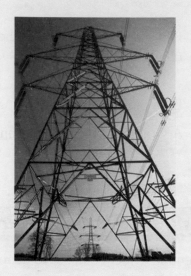

So these studies don't show a definite link and so don't <u>answer the original question</u>.

Controlling all the variables is *really hard*

In reality, it's <u>very hard</u> to control <u>all the variables</u> that might (just might) be having an effect.

You can do things to help — e.g. <u>choose</u> two <u>groups</u> of people (those near power lines and those far away) who are <u>as similar as possible</u> (same mix of ages, same mix of diets, etc). But you can't easily rule out every possibility.

If you could do a <u>properly controlled lab experiment</u>, that'd be better — but you just can't do it without cloning people and exposing them to things that might cause cancer... <u>hardly ethical</u>.

Does the data really say that?

If it's so hard to be <u>definite</u> about anything, how does anybody ever get convinced about anything? Well, what usually happens is that you get a <u>load</u> of evidence that all points the same way. If one study can't rule out a particular possibility, then maybe another one can. So you gradually build up a whole <u>body of evidence</u>, and it's this (rather than any single study) that <u>convinces people</u>.

Bias and How to Spot it

Scientific results are often used to make a point, but results are sometimes presented in a biased way.

You don't need to lie to make things biased

1) For something to be misleading, it doesn't have to be untrue. We tend to read scientific facts and assume that they're the 'truth', but there are many different sides to the truth. Look at this headline...

> **1 in 2 people are of above average weight** *Sounds like we're a nation of fatties.*

2) But an average is a kind of 'middle value' of all your data. Some readings are higher than average (about half of them, usually). Others will be lower than average (the other half).

So the above headline could just as accurately say: **1 in 2 people are of below average weight**

3) The point is... both headlines sound quite worrying, even though they're not. That's the thing... you can easily make something sound really good or really bad — even if it isn't. You can...

---

① ...use only some of the data, rather than all of it:

"Many people lost weight using the new SlimAway diet. Buy it now!!"

"Many" could mean anything — e.g. 50 out of 5000 (i.e. 1%). But that could be ignoring most of the data.

② ...phrase things in a 'leading' way:

90% fat free!

Would you buy it if it were "90% cyanide free"? That 10% is the important bit, probably.

③ ...use a statistic that supports your point of view:

| The amount of energy wasted is increasing. | Energy wasted per person is decreasing. | The rate at which energy waste is increasing is slowing down. |

These describe the same data. But two sound positive and one negative.

Think about why things might be biased

1) People who want to make a point can sometimes present data in a biased way to suit their own purposes (sometimes without knowing they're doing it).

2) And there are all sorts of reasons why people might want to do this — for example...

- Governments might want to persuade voters, other governments, journalists, etc. Evidence might be ignored if it could create political problems, or emphasised if it helps their cause.
- Companies might want to 'big up' their products. Or make impressive safety claims, maybe.
- Environmental campaigners might want to persuade people to behave differently.

3) People do it all the time. This is why any scientific evidence has to be looked at carefully. Are there any reasons for thinking the evidence is biased in some way?

- Does the experimenter (or the person writing about it) stand to gain (or lose) anything?
- Might someone have ignored some of the data for political or commercial reasons?
- Is someone using their reputation rather than evidence to help make their case?

Scientific data's not always misleading, you just need to be careful. The most credible argument will be the one that describes all the data that was found, and gives the most balanced view of it.

Science Has Limits

Science can give us amazing things — cures for diseases, space travel, heated toilet seats...
But science has its limitations — there are questions that it just can't answer.

Some questions are unanswered by science — so far

1) We don't understand everything. And we never will. We'll find out more, for sure
   — as more hypotheses are suggested, and more experiments are done.
   But there'll always be stuff we don't know.

> For example, today we don't know as much as we'd like about
> climate change (global warming). Is climate change definitely
> happening? And to what extent is it caused by humans?

2) These are complicated questions, and at the moment scientists don't all agree on the answers.
   But eventually, we probably will be able to answer these questions once and for all.

3) But by then there'll be loads of new questions to answer.

Other questions are unanswerable by science

1) Then there's the other type... questions that all the experiments in the world won't
   help us answer — the "Should we be doing this at all?" type questions.
   There are always two sides...

> The question of whether something is morally or ethically right
> or wrong can't be answered by more experiments — there is
> no "right" or "wrong" answer.

2) The best we can do is get a consensus from society — a judgement that most people are more or
   less happy to live by. Science can provide more information to help people make this judgement,
   and the judgement might change over time. But in the end it's up to people and their conscience.

To answer or not to answer, that is the question...

It's official — no one knows everything. Your teacher/mum/annoying older sister (delete as applicable)
might think and act as if they know it all, but sadly they don't. So in reality you know one thing they
don't — which clearly makes you more intelligent and generally far superior in every way. Possibly.

Science Has Limits

People have **different opinions** about **ethical questions**

1) Take the <u>atom bomb</u>. After hearing the <u>Nazis</u> were trying to build a nuclear bomb, the <u>Allies</u> began their own research, and got there first. The whole thing was <u>top secret</u> — but even amongst the people in the know, there were questions over whether they should use it...

- President Truman said it was <u>necessary</u>... it could <u>force Japan to surrender</u>, and <u>end the war</u> quickly. If they didn't use the bombs, then the <u>lives of countless American soldiers</u> might be lost in the continuing war with Japan. And the targets were justifiable as they were the sites of <u>military bases</u>.

- Some scientists said they should <u>not be used</u>... they said that there would be <u>no limit</u> to the <u>destructive power</u> of this new development, and that using the bombs in warfare would "open the door to an <u>era of devastation</u> on an <u>unimaginable scale</u>".

2) As we know, the bombs <u>were used</u> — that can't be changed. But the original discussions are still <u>relevant</u>. Should we develop <u>more powerful</u> nuclear bombs? Right now, <u>some countries</u> think not, and have signed a <u>treaty</u> not to. But <u>other countries</u> may have reason to think otherwise.

Loads of other **factors** can **influence decisions** too

Here are some other factors that can influence decisions about science, and the way science is used:

Economic factors

- <u>Companies</u> very often won't pay for research unless there's likely to be a <u>profit</u> in it.

- Society can't always <u>afford</u> to do things scientists recommend without <u>cutting back elsewhere</u> (e.g. investing heavily in alternative energy sources).

Social factors

- Decisions based on scientific evidence affect <u>people</u> — e.g. should fossil fuels be taxed more highly (to invest in alternative energy)? Should alcohol be banned (to prevent health problems)? <u>Would the effect on people's lifestyles be acceptable...</u>

Environmental factors

- Genetically modified crops may help us produce more food — but some people say they could cause <u>environmental problems</u>.

Science is a "real-world" subject...

Science isn't just done by people in white coats in labs who have no effect on the outside world. Science has a massive effect on the real world every day, and so real-life things like <u>money</u>, <u>morals</u> and <u>how people might react</u> need to be considered. It's why a lot of issues are so difficult to solve.

Heat Transfer

Heat energy tends to flow away from a hotter object to its cooler surroundings.

Heat *is* transferred *in* three different ways

1) Heat energy can be transferred by radiation, conduction or convection.

2) Thermal (infrared) radiation is the transfer of heat energy by electromagnetic waves (see below).

3) Conduction and convection involve the transfer of energy by particles.

4) Conduction is the main form of heat transfer in solids. See p11 for more on conduction.

5) Convection is the main form of heat transfer in liquids and gases. See p12 for more on convection.

6) Emission of thermal radiation occurs in solids, liquids and gases. Any object can both absorb and emit heat radiation, whether or not conduction or convection are also taking place.

7) The bigger the temperature difference, the faster heat is transferred between a body and its surroundings.

Thermal *radiation* involves *emission* of *electromagnetic waves*

Heat radiation can also be called infrared radiation, and it consists purely of electromagnetic waves of a certain range of frequencies. It's next to visible light in the electromagnetic spectrum (see page 37).

1) All objects continually emit and absorb heat radiation. An object that's hotter than its surroundings emits more radiation than it absorbs (as it cools down). And an object that's cooler than its surroundings absorbs more radiation than it emits (as it warms up).

2) The hotter an object gets, the more heat radiation it emits.

3) You can feel this heat radiation if you stand near something hot like a fire or if you put your hand just above the bonnet of a recently parked car.

(recently parked car)

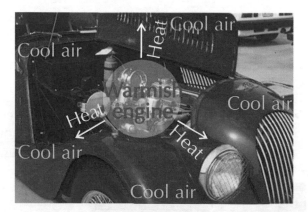

(after an hour or so)

If it wasn't for infrared radiation we'd all be pretty cold

Of the three heat transfer methods, radiation is the only one that works through a vacuum — since it doesn't rely on there being any particles about. And that's how we can get heat from the Sun across the great vacuum of space — which is good news for us.

Heat Radiation

The amount of heat **radiated** and **emitted** depends on...

1) Surface area

1) Heat is radiated from the surface of an object.

2) The bigger the surface area, the more waves can be emitted from the surface — so the quicker the transfer of heat.

3) This is why car and motorbike engines often have 'fins' — they increase the surface area so heat is radiated away quicker. So the engine cools quicker.

4) It's the same with heating something up — the bigger the surface area exposed to the heat radiation, the quicker it'll heat up.

Cooling fins on engines increase surface area to speed up cooling.

2) Colour and texture

1) Dark matt surfaces absorb heat radiation falling on them much better than bright glossy surfaces, such as gloss white or silver. They also emit much more heat radiation (at any given temperature).

2) Silvered surfaces reflect nearly all heat radiation falling on them.

There are lots of **experiments** to **demonstrate** this...

Here are two examples:

Leslie's cube

The matt black side emits most heat, so it's that thermometer which gets hottest.

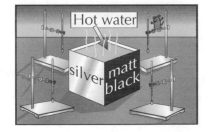

The **melting wax** trick

The matt black surface absorbs more heat, so its wax melts first and the ball bearing drops.

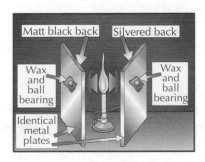

Heat Radiation

In reality that means you get black solar panels
and silver survival blankets

Making sure heat gets in — e.g. solar hot water panels

1) Solar hot water panels contain water pipes under a black surface (or black painted pipes under glass).

2) Heat radiation from the Sun is absorbed by the black surface to heat the water in the pipes.

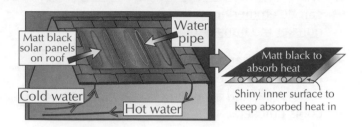

Matt black solar panels on roof

Water pipe

Cold water

Hot water

Matt black to absorb heat

Shiny inner surface to keep absorbed heat in

Making sure heat doesn't get in — e.g. coolbags

1) In coolbags you want to keep the heat out — obviously.

2) To minimise heat radiating in, the bag is lined with shiny silver or white material.

3) Probably most important though is the insulation to stop conduction (see p11).

4) Thermos®flasks (see p13) also have silver inner surfaces to keep heat in or out, depending on whether it's storing hot or cold liquid.

Making sure heat gets out — e.g. stoves

1) The whole point of a wood-burning stove is to heat up its surroundings.

2) Painting it matt black means it'll radiate as much heat as possible.

Making sure heat doesn't get out — e.g. survival blankets

1) If someone gets injured halfway up a big snowy hill, it can be crucial to keep them as warm as possible till help arrives.

2) A silver coloured blanket helps to stop their body heat radiating away — and could save their life.

3) Likewise after a marathon you get a silver blanket to stop you cooling down too quickly and getting hypothermia.

Confusingly, radiators transfer most of their heat by convection

The main thing to learn here is that heat radiation is strongly affected by the colour and texture of surfaces. In the exam thermal radiation questions often ask you why something's painted silver, or what you could do to reduce the heat wasted by some device or other.

Heat Conduction

Conduction of heat — occurs mainly in solids

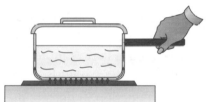

Heat carries on conducting through metal pan handle

Heat conducts through pan to water

CONDUCTION OF HEAT is the process where VIBRATING PARTICLES pass on their EXTRA KINETIC ENERGY (see p16) to NEIGHBOURING PARTICLES.

This process continues throughout the solid and gradually some of the extra kinetic energy (or heat) is passed all the way through the solid, causing a rise in temperature at the other side of the solid. And hence an increase in the heat radiating from its surface.

Metals conduct heat better than plastic or wood...

Metal's a great conductor — handle gets hot quickly

Wood's a poor conductor — handle takes much longer to warm up

Plastic's a poor conductor — handle takes much longer to warm up

...and it's because of their free electrons

Heat carried in metals by colliding free electrons

1) Metals "conduct" so well because the electrons are free to move inside the metal.

2) At the hot end the electrons move faster and collide with other free electrons, transferring energy. These other electrons then pass on their extra energy to other electrons, etc.

3) Because the electrons can move freely, this is obviously a much faster way of transferring the energy through the metal than slowly passing it between jostling neighbouring atoms.

4) This is why heat travels so fast through metals.

Also note that conduction is more efficient through a short, fat rod than through a long, thin rod. It all comes down to how far the electrons have to transfer the energy.

Copper is a great conductor

...which is why people make saucepan bottoms out of it.

Conduction is a bit like pass the parcel

Each particle passes the heat on to its neighbour. They can't chuck heat across the room or anything like that — that's just not playing fair. Each particle vibrates — the more energy a particle has, the faster it vibrates — and passes energy on to its neighbours.

Heat Convection

Gases and liquids are usually free to slosh about — and that allows them to transfer heat by convection, which is a much more effective process than conduction.

Convection of heat — liquids and gases only

CONVECTION occurs when more energetic particles
MOVE from a HOTTER REGION to a COOLER REGION —
AND TAKE THEIR HEAT ENERGY WITH THEM.

This is how immersion heaters in kettles and hot water tanks and (unsurprisingly) convector heaters work. Convection simply can't happen in solids because the particles can't move.

The immersion heater example:

In a bit more detail:

1) Heat is transferred from the heater coils to the water by conduction (particle collisions).

2) The particles near the coils get more energy, so they start moving around faster.

3) This means there's more distance between them, i.e. the water expands and becomes less dense.

4) This reduction in density means that the hotter water tends to rise above the denser water.

5) As the hot water rises it displaces (moves) the colder water out of the way, making it sink towards the heater coils.

6) This cold water is then heated by the coils and rises — and so it goes on. You end up with convection currents going up, round and down, circulating the heat through the water.

Fast-moving particles collide with slow-moving particles & transfer heat

Less dense water rises — Water cools and becomes more dense

Hot water less dense — Denser water sinks again

Water heats

Water (and heat) circulates by convection

Heater coils

Almost no conduction

Water stays cold below the heater

Note that convection is most efficient in roundish or squarish containers, because they allow the convection currents to work best. Shallow, wide containers or tall, thin ones just don't work quite so well.

Also note that because the hot water rises (because of the lower density) you only get convection currents in the water above the heater. The water below it stays cold because there's almost no conduction.

CONVECTION CURRENTS are all about CHANGES IN DENSITY.

And it's exactly the same process in any liquid or gas, of course.

There's a great experiment with purple crystals to show this

You stick some potassium permanganate crystals in the bottom of a beaker of cold water, then heat it gently over a Bunsen flame. The potassium permanganate starts to dissolve and make a lovely bright purple solution that gets moved around the beaker by the convection currents as the water heats.

Useful Heat Transfers

GCSE Science is all about getting you to <u>understand how science works</u> in the real world — for example you can use your knowledge to do things like <u>improving efficiency</u> or <u>saving energy</u>.

So <u>in the exam</u>, you might be asked to explain how a device controls the transfer of heat, or improve the efficiency of some device or other. Maybe a solar panel or a television or a pan.

There's usually **more than one type** of **heat transfer**

The Thermos® flask — the ultimate in **insulation**

1) The glass bottle is <u>double-walled</u> with a <u>vacuum</u> between the two walls.
   This stops <u>all conduction</u> and <u>convection</u> through the <u>sides</u>.

2) The walls either side of the vacuum are <u>silvered</u> to keep heat loss by <u>radiation</u> to a <u>minimum</u>.

3) The bottle is supported using <u>insulating foam</u>.
   This minimises heat conduction to or from the outer glass bottle.

4) The <u>stopper</u> is made of <u>plastic</u> and filled with <u>cork or foam</u> to reduce any <u>heat conduction</u> through it.

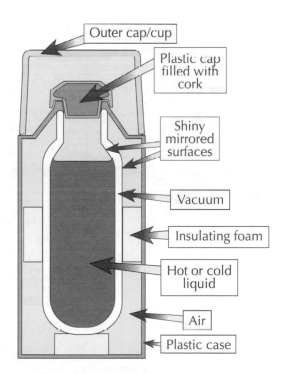

Outer cap/cup

Plastic cap filled with cork

Shiny mirrored surfaces

Vacuum

Insulating foam

Hot or cold liquid

Air

Plastic case

In <u>exam questions</u> you must <u>always</u> say which form of heat transfer is involved at any point, either <u>conduction</u>, <u>convection</u> or <u>radiation</u>.
"<u>The vacuum stops heat getting out</u>" will get you <u>no marks at all</u>.

Useful Heat Transfers

Here's a method that'll work for any 'improving efficiency' questions, whether they're just heat transfer or whether there are other energy transfers going on.

Another example where there's **more than one** heat transfer...

A pan

Heat conduction through the bottom of a pan to its contents is useful — you're trying to heat them up. Heat radiation out of the sides of the pan is NOT useful. It's the food you're trying to heat up, not the air around it.

You have to analyse what transfers are taking place, and work out which bits you can improve.

1) List the main types of heat transfer and where they're happening.

2) Write down if each transfer is useful or not.

3) For each transfer that's not useful, you want to reduce it.

4) For each transfer that is useful, you want to increase it.

5) Remember to make sensible suggestions — e.g. wood is a good insulator but it doesn't go well with steam and you don't want it getting too hot because it's flammable.

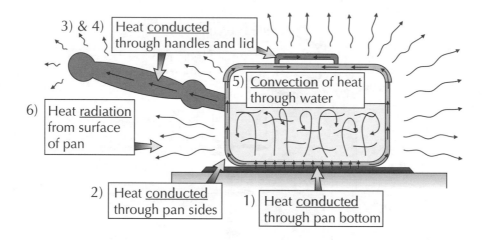

3) & 4) Heat conducted through handles and lid

5) Convection of heat through water

6) Heat radiation from surface of pan

2) Heat conducted through pan sides

1) Heat conducted through pan bottom

TYPE OF HEAT TRANSFER	USEFUL?	SUGGESTED IMPROVEMENTS
1) conduction through pan bottom	useful	use more conductive material — e.g. copper
2) conduction through pan sides	not useful	use less conductive material — e.g. steel
3) conduction through pan lid	not useful	use less conductive material — e.g. glass
4) conduction through handles	not useful	use less conductive material — e.g. wood or plastic
5) convection through liquid in pan	useful	not much you can do to improve
6) radiation from pan surface	not useful	paint the surface — e.g. shiny silver or white

Something else useful would be to learn all the steps above

See the pan example above — do the same for a solar panel. And then a wood-burning stove.

Warm-Up and Exam Questions

Here are a few questions for you to try — do the warm-up ones first, then when you think you're ready, have a go at the exam questions. If there's anything you can't do, make sure you go back and check on it.

Warm-Up Questions

1) Heat radiation can also be called thermal radiation. What is another name for it?
2) Give two ways the nature of a surface could be changed so that the surface emits more heat radiation.
3) Describe the process of heat transfer by conduction.
4) Explain why heated air rises.

Exam Questions

1 Which of the following would be a useful heat transfer for a pan?

    A   Conduction through the pan sides

    B   Conduction through the pan lid

    C   Radiation from the pan surface

    D   Convection through liquid in the pan

(1 mark)

2 Mandy wants some blinds for her new conservatory so that it doesn't get too hot on very sunny days. Which ones should she choose?

    A   matt, black blinds

    B   matt, white blinds

    C   shiny, black blinds

    D   shiny, white blinds

(1 mark)

3 The diagram shows a solar heating panel which is used to heat cold water in a house.

(a) Describe how heat is transferred:

    (i)   from the Sun to the solar heating panel.

          (1 mark)

    (ii)   from the hot water in the pipe to the colder water in the tank.

          (1 mark)

    (iii) throughout the water in the tank.

          (1 mark)

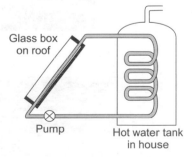

(b) Explain why the pipes in the heating panel are painted black.

          (1 mark)

Energy Transfer

Learn these **nine types** of energy

You need to know all the <u>types of energy</u> in this list <u>from memory</u>, including the examples:

1) <u>ELECTRICAL</u> Energy..................................... — whenever a <u>current</u> flows.
2) <u>LIGHT</u> Energy.. — from the <u>Sun</u>, <u>light bulbs</u>, etc.
3) <u>SOUND</u> Energy.. — from <u>loudspeakers</u> or anything <u>noisy</u>.
4) <u>KINETIC</u> Energy, or <u>MOVEMENT</u> Energy..... — anything that's <u>moving</u> has it.
5) <u>NUCLEAR</u> Energy...................................... — released only from <u>nuclear reactions</u>.
6) <u>THERMAL</u> Energy or <u>HEAT</u> Energy.............. — <u>flows</u> from <u>hot objects</u> to colder ones.
7) <u>GRAVITATIONAL POTENTIAL</u> Energy........ — possessed by anything which can <u>fall</u>.
8) <u>ELASTIC POTENTIAL</u> Energy...................... — possessed by <u>springs</u>, <u>elastic</u>, <u>rubber bands</u>, etc.
9) <u>CHEMICAL</u> Energy.................................... — possessed by <u>foods</u>, <u>fuels</u>, <u>batteries</u>, etc.

> The <u>last three</u> above are forms of <u>stored energy</u> because the energy is not obviously <u>doing</u> anything, it's kind of <u>waiting to happen</u>, i.e. waiting to be turned into one of the <u>other</u> forms.

There are two types of "**energy conservation**"

Try and get your head round the difference between these two:

1) "<u>ENERGY CONSERVATION</u>" is all about <u>using fewer resources</u> because of the damage they do and because they might <u>run out</u>. That's all <u>environmental stuff</u> — which is important to us, but fairly trivial on a <u>cosmic scale</u>.

2) The "<u>PRINCIPLE OF THE CONSERVATION OF ENERGY</u>", however, is one of the <u>major cornerstones</u> of modern physics. It's an <u>all-pervading principle</u> which governs the workings of the <u>entire physical Universe</u>. If this principle were not so, then life as we know it would simply cease to be.

The **principle of the conservation of energy** can be stated thus:

> <u>Energy</u> can never be <u>created nor destroyed</u>
> — it's only ever <u>converted</u> from one form to another.

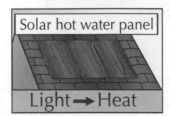

Solar hot water panel

Light → Heat

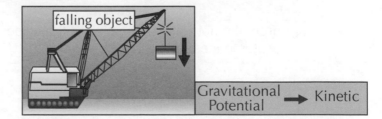

falling object

Gravitational Potential → Kinetic

Another <u>important principle</u> which you need to <u>learn</u> is this one:

> Energy is <u>only useful</u> when it can be <u>converted</u> from one form to another.

Efficiency of Machines

An open fire looks cosy, but a lot of its heat energy goes straight up the chimney, by convection, instead of heating up your living room. All this energy is 'wasted', so open fires aren't very efficient.

Machines *always* waste *some* energy

1) Useful machines are only useful because they convert energy from one form to another. Take cars for instance — you put in chemical energy (petrol or diesel) and the engine converts it into kinetic (movement) energy.

2) The total energy output is always the same as the energy input, but only some of the output energy is useful. So for every joule of chemical energy you put into your car you'll only get a fraction of it converted into useful kinetic energy.

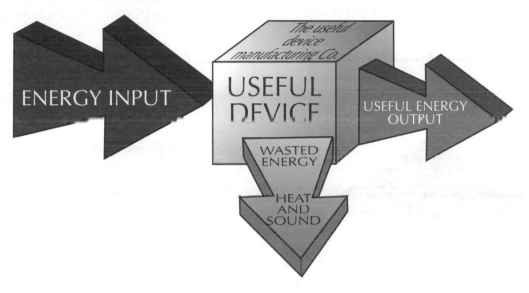

3) This is because some of the input energy is always lost or wasted, often as heat. In the car example, the rest of the chemical energy is converted (mostly) into heat and sound energy. This is wasted energy.

4) The less energy that is wasted, the more efficient the device is said to be.

The **efficiency** of a machine is defined as...

$$\text{Efficiency} = \frac{\text{USEFUL Energy OUTPUT}}{\text{TOTAL Energy INPUT}}$$

The useful energy output is ALWAYS less than the input energy

Efficiency is all about what goes in and how it comes out. The principle of the conservation of energy means that however much energy you put into a machine, you'll get that same amount out. The tricky bit is working out how much comes out usefully.

PHYSICS 1a — ENERGY AND ELECTRICITY

Efficiency of Machines

How to **use** the **efficiency formula** — *nothing to it*

1) To use the <u>formula for efficiency</u> (see page 17) you need to:
   - find how much energy is <u>supplied</u> to a machine. (The Total Energy <u>INPUT</u>.)
   - find how much <u>useful energy</u> the machine <u>delivers</u>. (The Useful Energy <u>OUTPUT</u>.) An exam question either tells you this directly or tells you how much it <u>wastes</u> as heat/sound.

2) Either way, you get those <u>two important numbers</u> and then just <u>divide</u> the <u>smaller one</u> by the <u>bigger one</u> to get a value for <u>efficiency</u> somewhere between <u>0 and 1</u> (or <u>0 and 100%</u>). Easy.

3) The other way they might ask it is to tell you the <u>efficiency</u> and the <u>input energy</u> and ask for the <u>energy output</u> — so you need to be able to swap the formula round. In comes the formula triangle...

The efficiency formula triangle:

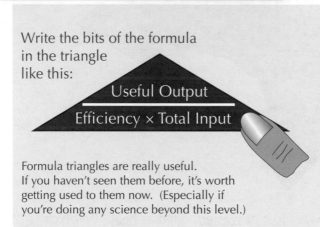

Write the bits of the formula in the triangle like this:

$$\frac{\text{Useful Output}}{\text{Efficiency} \times \text{Total Input}}$$

Formula triangles are really useful. If you haven't seen them before, it's worth getting used to them now. (Especially if you're doing any science beyond this level.)

1) Put your <u>finger</u> over the thing you're <u>trying to find</u>.

2) <u>Read off what's left</u> — that's how you work out your answer.

3) E.g. cover up <u>Total Input</u> and you're left with $\frac{\text{Useful Output}}{\text{Efficiency}}$.

4) So that's how you work it out: $\text{Total Input} = \frac{\text{Useful Output}}{\text{Efficiency}}$

5) <u>Magic</u>. You just need to <u>learn that triangle</u>.

For any <u>specific example</u> you can give <u>more detail</u> about the <u>types of energy</u> being <u>input</u> and <u>output</u>, but <u>remember this</u>:

> <u>No</u> device is 100% efficient and the <u>wasted energy</u> is always <u>dissipated</u> as <u>heat</u>.

<u>Electric heaters</u> are the <u>exception</u> to this. They're <u>100% efficient</u> because <u>all</u> the electricity is converted to "<u>useful</u>" heat. What else could it become? Ultimately, <u>all</u> energy <u>ends up as heat energy</u>. If you use an electric drill, it gives out <u>various types</u> of energy but they all quickly end up as <u>heat</u>. That's an important thing to realise.

Efficiency questions are all more or less the same

Some new appliances (like washing machines and fridges) come with a sticker with a letter from A to G on, to show how energy-efficient they are. A really well-insulated freezer might have an 'A' rating. But if you put it right next to the oven, or never defrost it, it'll run much less efficiently than it should.

Efficiency of Machines

We call it **wasted heat** because we **can't do anything useful** with it

1) Useful energy is concentrated energy. As you know, the entire energy output of a machine, both useful and wasted, eventually ends up as heat.

2) This heat is transferred to cooler surroundings, which then become warmer. As the heat is transferred to cooler surroundings, the energy becomes less concentrated — it dissipates (spreads out).

3) According to the Principle of Conservation of Energy, the total amount of energy stays the same. So the energy is still there, but it can't be easily used or collected back in again.

Some **devices** are more **efficient** than others...
...but that's **not all** that **matters**

You nearly always have a choice of devices to use for any particular situation.
E.g. you could play your CD on a little portable CD player with mini-speakers attached, or you could play it through a great big fancy stereo system and annoy all the neighbours.

As far as energy use goes it's pretty easy to say which is better — the more efficient one. But in reality, there are loads of factors you think about when choosing a device:

1) INITIAL COST
2) RUNNING COST (including energy efficiency)
3) How often will it need REPAIRING/REPLACING?
4) EASE of use, SUITABILITY for the job
5) LOOKS

If you're asked to compare two different devices in an exam, then they'll be looking firstly for energy efficiency, but you also need to think about the other stuff too. You should also be able to suggest reasons for people not wanting to use the most efficient product.

Example: light bulbs

1) For the same light output, a low energy bulb is about 4 times as efficient as an ordinary light bulb.
2) Energy efficient light bulbs are more expensive to buy but they last much longer.
3) Lampshades are designed for ordinary bulbs, which are a different shape and size.
4) Energy efficient bulbs take a little while to get to full brightness, which can be inconvenient.

Loss of energy is always the same thing
It always disappears as heat and sound, and even the sound ends up as heat pretty quickly. So when they ask, "Why is the input energy more than the output energy?", the answer is always the same.

Energy Transformations

They like giving **exam questions** on **energy transfers**

In the exam, they can ask you about <u>any device</u> or <u>energy transfer system</u> they feel like.
So it's no good just learning the examples on this page — you need to <u>understand the patterns</u>.

<u>ELECTRICAL DEVICES</u> CONVERT <u>ELECTRICAL ENERGY</u> INTO SOUND, LIGHT, HEAT, ETC.

(and, of course, a bit of wasted heat)

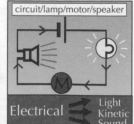

<u>BATTERIES</u> CONVERT <u>CHEMICAL ENERGY</u> TO <u>ELECTRICAL</u> TO RUN ELECTRIC DEVICES

(and, of course, there's a bit of wasted heat)

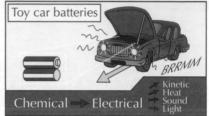

<u>ELECTRICITY GENERATION</u> ALWAYS INVOLVES CONVERTING OTHER FORMS OF ENERGY INTO <u>ELECTRICAL ENERGY</u>

(and guess what — there's a bit of wasted heat)

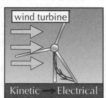

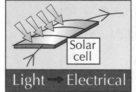

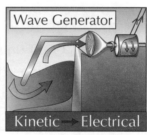

<u>GRAVITATIONAL AND ELASTIC POTENTIAL ENERGY</u> ALWAYS GET CONVERTED INTO <u>KINETIC ENERGY FIRST</u>

(... and there's a bit of wasted heat)

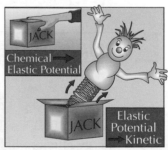

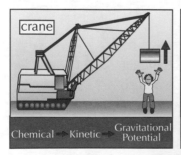

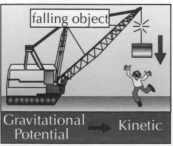

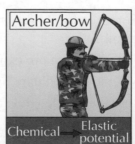

And <u>DON'T FORGET</u> — <u>ALL</u> types of ENERGY are measured in <u>JOULES</u>

Energy Transformation Diagrams

The idea of energy transformation (Sankey) diagrams is to make it <u>easy to see</u> at a glance how much of the <u>input energy</u> is being <u>usefully employed</u> compared with how much is being <u>wasted</u>.

The <u>thicker the arrow</u>, the <u>more energy</u> it represents — so you see a big <u>thick arrow going in</u>, then several <u>smaller arrows going off</u> it to show the different energy transformations taking place.

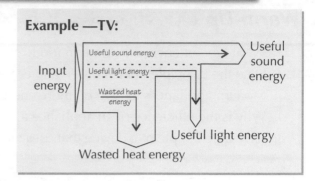

Example —TV:

Sankey diagrams can help you judge **efficiency**

You can have either a little <u>sketch</u> or a properly <u>detailed diagram</u> where the width of each arrow is proportional to the number of joules it represents.

Example — sketch diagram for a simple motor:

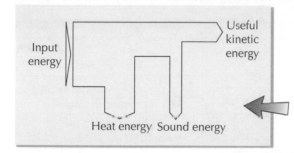

With sketches, they're likely to ask you to <u>compare</u> two different devices and say which is <u>more efficient</u>. You generally want to be looking for the one with the <u>thickest useful energy arrow(s)</u>.

You don't know the actual amounts, but you can see that most of the energy is being <u>wasted</u>, and that it's mostly wasted as <u>heat</u>.

Example — detailed diagram for a simple motor:

In an exam, the most likely question you'll get about detailed Sankey diagrams is filling in one of the numbers or <u>calculating the efficiency</u>. The efficiency is straightforward enough if you can work out the numbers (see page 17 and 18). ✳

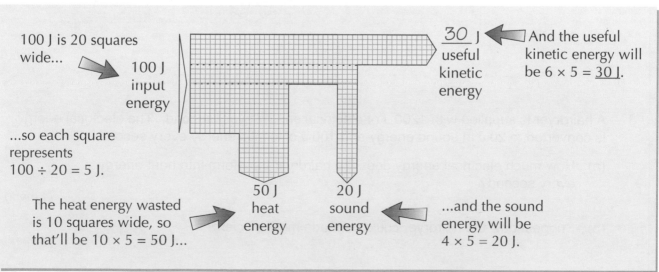

Warm-Up and Exam Questions

It's no good learning all the facts in the world if you go to pieces and write nonsense in the exam.
So you'd be wise to practise using all your knowledge to answer some questions.

Warm-Up Questions

1) What type of energy is stored in food?
2) State the principle of the conservation of energy.
3) Modern appliances tend to be more energy efficient than older ones. What does this mean?
4) Why is the efficiency of an appliance always less than 100%?
5) Give an example of a device that uses elastic potential energy.

Exam Questions

1 A motor is supplied with 200 J of energy to lift a load.
The load gains 140 J of potential energy.
What is the efficiency of the motor?

A 60 J

B 70%

C 0.3

D 1.43

(1 mark)

2 Paul is testing the efficiency of four
different light bulbs. He finds that the
'Brightlight Ecobulb' is 15% efficient.
Which of the Sankey diagrams on
the right could represent this bulb?

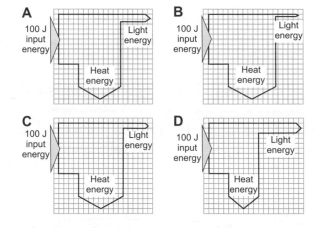

(1 mark)

3 A hairdryer is supplied with 1200 J of electrical energy every second. The electrical energy
is converted to 20 J of sound energy and 100 J of kinetic energy every second.

(a) How much electrical energy does the hairdryer transform into heat energy
every second?

(1 mark)

(b) Suggest how the hairdryer could be made more efficient.

(1 mark)

The Cost of Electricity

All the electricity you use has to be paid for. Your electricity meter counts how many units of electricity you use and the electricity company uses this to work out your bill.

Kilowatt-hours (kWh) are "UNITS" of energy

1) An electricity meter counts the number of "UNITS" used.
2) A "UNIT" is otherwise known as a kilowatt-hour, or kWh.
3) A "kWh" might sound like a unit of power, but it's not — it's an amount of energy.

> A KILOWATT-HOUR is the amount of electrical energy used by a 1 kW appliance left on for 1 HOUR.

4) Make sure you can turn 1 kWh into 3 600 000 joules like this:
"E = P × t" = 1 kW × 1 hour = 1000 W × 3600 s = 3 600 000 J   (= 3.6 MJ) ✳

(The formula is "Energy (in joules) = Power (in watts) × Time (in seconds)", and you must convert to those units first.)

The two easy formulas for calculating the cost of electricity

| No. of UNITS (kWh) used = POWER (in kW) × TIME (in hours) | | Units = kW × hours ✳ |

| COST = No. of UNITS × PRICE per UNIT | | Cost = Units × Price ✳ |

EXAMPLE: An electricity supplier charges 11p per unit.
Find the cost of leaving a 60 W light bulb on for: a) 30 minutes   b) one year.

ANSWER: a) No. of units = kW × hours = 0.06 kW × ½ hr = 0.03 units.
Cost = units × price per unit (11p) = 0.03 × 11p = 0.33p for 30 mins.

b) No. of units = kW × hours = 0.06 kW × (24 × 365) hr = 525.6 units.
Cost = units × price per unit (11p) = 525.6 × 11p = £57.82 for one year.

> N.B. Always turn the power into kW (not watts) and the time into hours (not minutes)

NOTE — the cost is usually 10 or 11p per unit...

...but they'll tell you the amount in the question.

EXAMPLE 2:   Each unit of electricity costs 11p. For how long can a 6 kW heater be used for 11p?
A 6 hours
B 1 hour
C 10 minutes
D 7 hours

ANSWER 2:   The cost of 1 unit is 11p. So for 11p you can use 1 unit.
UNITS = POWER × TIME,
so TIME = UNITS ÷ POWER = 1 ÷ 6 = 0.167 hours = 10 minutes

500 kWh doesn't mean much to anyone — £55 is far more real

In reality most electricity suppliers have complicated formulas for working out the cost of electricity, but using a cost per unit of 11p gives you a reasonable estimate of what you're spending.

Energy Efficiency in the Home

There are lots of things you can do to <u>save energy</u>, but some are <u>more effective</u> than others. And some are <u>better for your pocket</u> than others. The most obvious examples are in the <u>home</u>, but you could apply this to <u>any situation</u> where you're trying to save energy.

Insulating your home saves energy and money

1) To save energy, you need to <u>insulate</u> your home. It <u>costs money</u> to buy and install the insulation, but it also <u>saves</u> you money, because your <u>heating bills</u> are lower.

2) Eventually, the <u>money you've saved</u> on heating bills will <u>equal</u> the <u>initial cost</u> of installing the insulation — the time this takes is called the <u>payback time</u>.

3) <u>Cheaper</u> methods of insulation are usually less effective — they tend to save you less money per year, but they often have <u>shorter payback times</u>.

4) If you <u>subtract</u> the <u>annual saving</u> from the <u>initial cost</u> repeatedly then <u>eventually</u> the one with the <u>biggest annual saving</u> must always come out as the winner, if you think about it.

5) But you might sell the house (or die) before that happens. If you look at it over, say, a <u>five-year period</u> then a cheap and cheerful <u>hot water tank jacket</u> wins over expensive <u>double glazing</u>.

Loft insulation

Fibreglass 'wool' laid across the loft floor reduces <u>conduction</u> through the ceiling into the roof space.

Initial Cost: £200
Annual Saving: £100
Payback time: <u>2 years</u>

Hot water tank jacket

Lagging such as fibreglass wool reduces <u>conduction</u>.

Initial Cost: £60
Annual Saving: £15
Payback time: <u>4 years</u>

Cavity walls & insulation

Two layers of bricks with a gap between them reduce <u>conduction</u>. <u>Insulating foam</u> is squirted into the gap between layers, trapping pockets of air to minimise <u>convection</u>.

Initial Cost: £150
Annual Saving: £100
Payback time: <u>18 months</u>

The exact costs and savings will depend on the house — but these figures give you a rough idea.

Double glazing

Two layers of glass with an air gap between reduce <u>conduction</u>.

Initial Cost: £2400
Annual Saving: £80
Payback time: <u>30 years</u>

Draught-proofing

Strips of foam and plastic around doors and windows stop hot air going out — reducing <u>convection</u>.

Initial Cost: £100
Annual Saving: £15
Payback time: <u>7 years</u>

Thick curtains

Reduce <u>conduction</u> and <u>radiation</u> through the windows.

Initial Cost: £180
Annual Saving: £20
Payback time: <u>9 years</u>

Thermostatic radiator valves are another money saving method

These handy valves can be fitted to radiators to prevent a house being over-warmed.

Warm-Up and Exam Questions

Take your time with these questions — and don't miss out the tricky-looking parts.
If any of them baffle you, it's not too late to take another peek over the section.

Warm-Up Questions

1) What is a "unit" of electricity otherwise known as?
2) Give the formula for calculating the number of units of electricity used.
3) Give three methods of insulating a house.
4) What is meant by "payback time"?

Exam Questions

1 James's washing machine has a power rating of 1200 W. His electricity company charges
14p per kWh. How much will the electricity for a 1 hour 15 minute cycle cost?

  A 2.1p

  B 21p

  C 1.93p

  D 19.3p

  (1 mark)

2 Which of the following would have the shortest payback time?

	Method	Initial cost (£)	Annual saving (£)
A	Double glazing	2700	90
B	Hot water tank jacket	80	20
C	Loft insulation	240	120
D	Thick curtains	200	20

  (1 mark)

3 The diagram shows the heat losses from Tom's house. Tom estimates that £300 of his
annual heating bill is wasted on heat lost from the house.

(a) How much money does Tom waste every year
in heat lost through the roof?
(1 mark)

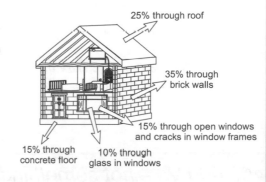

(b) Tom decides to insulate the loft. This costs him
£350, but reduces the amount he spends on
wasted heat to £255 per year.
Calculate the payback time for fitting loft
insulation in Tom's house.
(2 marks)

Electricity and the National Grid

The <u>National Grid</u> is the <u>network</u> of pylons and cables that covers <u>the whole of Britain</u>, getting electricity to homes everywhere. Whoever you pay for your electricity, it's the National Grid that gets it to you.

Electricity gets around *via the* National Grid...

1) The <u>National Grid</u> takes electrical energy from the <u>power stations</u> to just where it's needed in <u>homes</u> and <u>industry</u>.

2) It enables power to be <u>generated</u> anywhere on the grid, and then be <u>supplied</u> anywhere else on the grid.

3) To transmit the <u>huge</u> amount of <u>power</u> needed, you need either a <u>high voltage</u> or a <u>high current</u>.

4) The <u>problem</u> with a <u>high current</u> is that you <u>lose loads of energy</u> through <u>heat</u> in the cables.

5) It's much <u>cheaper</u> to <u>boost the voltage</u> up <u>really high</u> (to 400 000 V) and keep the current <u>very low</u>.

...with a little help from **pylons** and **transformers**

1) To get the voltage to 400 000 V to transmit power requires <u>transformers</u> as well as <u>big pylons</u> with <u>huge insulators</u> — but it's <u>still cheaper</u>.

2) The transformers have to <u>step</u> the voltage <u>up</u> at one end, for <u>efficient transmission</u>, and then bring it back down to <u>safe, usable levels</u> at the other end:

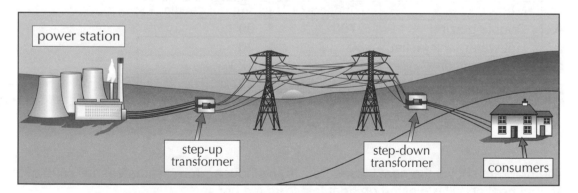

power station

step-up transformer

step-down transformer

consumers

3) The <u>voltage</u> is <u>increased</u> ('<u>stepped up</u>') using a <u>step-up transformer</u>.

4) It's then <u>reduced</u> again ('<u>stepped down</u>') at the consumer end using a <u>step-down transformer</u>.

You don't need to know the details about exactly what transformers are and how they work — just that they increase and decrease the voltage to minimise power losses in the National Grid.

400 000 V — not something you'd want to fly your kite into

If you have your own solar cell or wind generator, you can sell back any surplus electricity to the National Grid. So if you don't use much electricity, but you generate a lot of it, you can actually make money instead of spending it. Nice trick if you can do it. Shame solar cells cost a fortune...

Non-Renewable Energy Resources

There are various different types of <u>energy resource</u>.
They fit into <u>two broad types</u>: <u>renewable</u> and <u>non-renewable</u>.

Non-renewable energy resources will *run out* one day

The <u>non-renewables</u> are the <u>three FOSSIL FUELS</u> and <u>NUCLEAR</u>:

1) <u>Coal</u>

2) <u>Oil</u>

3) <u>Natural gas</u>

4) <u>Nuclear fuels</u> (<u>uranium</u> and <u>plutonium</u>)

> a) They will <u>all 'run out'</u> one day.
> b) They all do <u>damage</u> to the environment.
> c) But they provide <u>most of our energy</u>.

There are **environmental problems** *with* **non-renewables**

1) All three <u>fossil fuels</u> (coal, oil and gas) release CO_2. For the same amount of energy produced, coal releases the most CO_2, followed by oil then gas. All this CO_2 adds to the <u>greenhouse effect</u>, and contributes to <u>climate change</u>. We could stop some of it entering the atmosphere — by 'capturing' it and <u>burying</u> it underground, for instance — but the technology is too <u>expensive</u> to be widely used yet.

2) Burning coal and oil releases <u>sulfur dioxide</u>, which causes <u>acid rain</u>.
This is reduced by taking the sulfur out <u>before</u> it's burned, or cleaning up the <u>emissions</u>.

3) <u>Coal mining</u> makes a <u>mess</u> of the <u>landscape</u>, especially "<u>open-cast mining</u>".

4) <u>Oil spillages</u> cause <u>serious environmental damage</u>. We try to avoid them, but they'll always happen.

5) <u>Nuclear power</u> is <u>clean</u> but the <u>nuclear waste</u> is <u>dangerous</u> and difficult to <u>dispose of</u>.

6) But non-renewable fuels are generally <u>concentrated</u> energy resources, <u>reliable</u>, and <u>easy</u> to use.

Learn about the non-renewables — before it's too late

There's lots more info about the various power sources over the next few pages. But the point is that <u>none</u> of them are <u>ideal</u> — they all have pros <u>and</u> cons, and the aim is to choose the least bad option overall. Unless we want to go without heating, light, transport, electricity... and so on.

Renewable Energy Resources

Renewable energy sources are often seen as the energy sources of the future — they're more friendly to the environment and won't run out like the non-renewables, but they do have problems of their own.

Renewable energy resources will never run out

The <u>renewables</u> are:

1) <u>Wind</u>
2) <u>Solar</u>
3) <u>Hydroelectric</u>
4) <u>Waves</u>
5) <u>Tides</u>
6) <u>Geothermal</u>
7) <u>Biomass</u>

a) These will <u>never run out</u>.
b) Most of them do <u>damage the environment</u>, but in <u>less nasty</u> ways than non-renewables.
c) The trouble is they <u>don't provide much energy</u> and some of them are <u>unreliable</u> because they depend on the <u>weather</u>.

Wind farms — lots of little wind turbines

1) Wind power involves putting lots of wind turbines up in <u>exposed places</u> — like on <u>moors</u>, around the <u>coast</u> or <u>out at sea</u>.

2) Wind turbines convert the kinetic energy of moving air into electricity. The <u>wind</u> turns the <u>blades</u>, which turn a <u>generator</u>.

3) Wind turbines are quite cheap to run — they're very <u>tough</u> and reliable, and the wind is <u>free</u>.

4) Even better, wind power doesn't produce any <u>polluting waste</u> and it's <u>renewable</u> — the wind's never going to run out.

5) But there are <u>disadvantages</u>. You normally need a couple of thousand wind turbines to replace one coal-fired power station. Some people think that wind farms spoil the view and the spinning blades cause noise pollution.

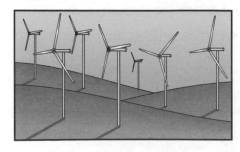

6) Another problem is that sometimes the wind isn't <u>strong enough</u> to generate any power. It's also impossible to increase supply when there's extra demand (e.g. when Coronation Street starts).

7) And although the wind is free, it's <u>expensive</u> to <u>set up</u> a wind farm, especially <u>out at sea</u>.

Renewable Energy Resources

*You can **capture** the Sun's energy using **solar cells***

1) <u>Solar cells</u> (<u>photocells</u>) generate <u>electricity directly</u> from sunlight. They generate <u>direct current</u> (DC) — the same as a <u>battery</u> (not like the <u>mains electricity</u> in your home, which is AC — alternating current).

2) Most solar cells are made of <u>silicon</u> — a <u>semiconductor</u>. When sunlight falls on the cell, the silicon atoms <u>absorb</u> some of the energy, knocking loose some <u>electrons</u>. These electrons then flow round a circuit.

3) The <u>power output</u> of a photocell depends on its <u>surface area</u> (the bigger the cell, the more electricity it produces) and the <u>intensity of the sunlight</u> hitting it (brighter light = more power). Makes sense.

Solar cells — expensive to install, cheap to run

1) Solar cells are very <u>expensive initially</u>, but after that the energy is <u>free</u> and <u>running costs</u> are almost <u>nil</u>. And there's <u>no pollution</u> (although they use a fair bit of energy to manufacture in the first place).

2) Solar cells can only <u>generate</u> enough <u>electricity</u> to be useful if they have <u>enough sunlight</u> — which can be a problem at <u>night</u> (and in <u>winter</u> in some places). But the cells can be linked to <u>rechargeable batteries</u> to create a system that can <u>store energy</u> during the day for use at <u>night</u>.

3) Solar cells are often the best way to power <u>calculators</u> or <u>watches</u> that don't use much energy. They're also used in <u>remote places</u> where there's not much choice (e.g. deserts) and in satellites.

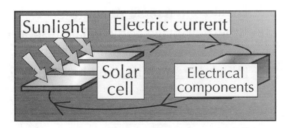

Passive solar heating — no mechanical stuff

Solar panels

Solar panels are much less sophisticated than photocells — basically just black water pipes inside a <u>glass</u> box. The <u>glass</u> lets <u>heat</u> and <u>light</u> from the Sun in, which is then <u>absorbed</u> by the black pipes and heats up the water.

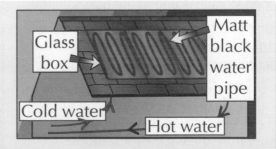

Unfortunately it's not too reliable here in Britain

And you can reduce the energy needed to <u>heat</u> a building if you build it sensibly in the first place — e.g. face the <u>windows</u> in a suitable direction. That's another example of passive solar heating.

PHYSICS 1a — ENERGY AND ELECTRICITY

Renewable Energy Resources

Here are another couple of renewables — learn the advantages and disadvantages. They both use water, but hydroelectricity generates electricity, whereas pumped storage only stores it. The clues are in the names — so don't mix them up.

Hydroelectricity uses *water* to produce *electricity*

1) Hydroelectric power often requires the flooding of a valley by building a big dam.

2) Rainwater is caught and allowed out through turbines.

3) The movement of the water turns the turbine, which turns a generator and produces electricity.

4) There is no pollution from the running of a hydroelectric scheme.

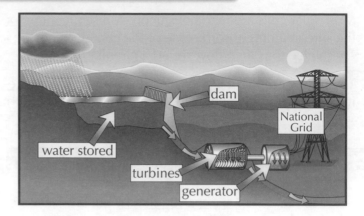

Hydroelectricity has an impact on the *environment*

1) Hydroelectricity has a big impact on the environment due to the flooding of the valley (rotting vegetation releases methane and CO_2) and possible loss of habitat for some species.

2) The reservoirs can also look very unsightly when they dry up. Location in remote valleys tends to avoid some of these problems.

3) A big advantage is immediate response to increased demand, and there's no problem with reliability except in times of drought.

4) Initial costs are high, but there's no fuel and minimal running costs.

Pumped storage gives *extra supply* just when it's *needed*

1) Most large power stations have huge boilers which have to be kept running all night even though demand is very low. This means there's a surplus of electricity at night.

2) It's surprisingly difficult to find a way of storing this spare energy for later use.

3) Pumped storage is one of the best solutions.

4) In pumped storage, 'spare' night-time electricity is used to pump water up to a higher reservoir.

5) This can then be released quickly during periods of peak demand such as at teatime each evening, to supplement the steady delivery from the big power stations.

6) Remember, pumped storage uses the same idea as hydroelectric power but it isn't a way of generating power — but simply a way of storing energy which has already been generated.

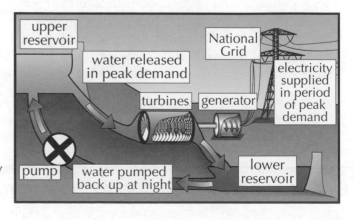

Renewable Energy Resources

Wave power and tidal power are two more fab renewable energy resources you need to know about.

Wave power — lots of little wave converters

Don't confuse wave power with tidal power — they're completely different.

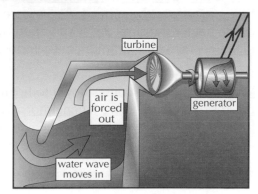

1) For wave power, you need lots of small wave converters located around the coast. As waves come in to the shore they provide an up and down motion which can be used to drive a generator.

2) There's no pollution. The main problems are spoiling the view and being a hazard to boats.

3) It's fairly unreliable, since waves tend to die out when the wind drops.

4) Initial costs are high but there are no fuel costs and minimal running costs. Wave power is unlikely to provide energy on a large scale but it can be very useful on small islands.

Tidal barrages — using the Sun and Moon's gravity

1) Tidal barrages are big dams built across river estuaries, with turbines in them. The source of the energy is the gravity of the Sun and the Moon. As the tide comes in it drives the turbines and fills up the estuary to a height of several metres. This water can then be allowed out through turbines at a controlled speed.

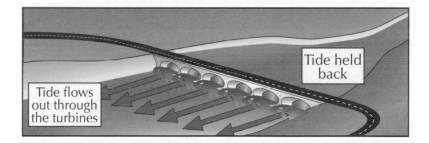

2) There's no pollution. The main problems are preventing access by boats, spoiling the view and altering the habitat of the wildlife.

3) Tides are pretty reliable, but the height of the tide is variable so lower tides will provide less energy than higher ones.

4) Initial costs are moderately high, but there's no fuel costs and minimal running costs.

Don't get wave power and tidal power confused

I do hope you appreciate the big big differences between tidal power and wave power. They both involve salty sea water, sure — but there the similarities end. Smile and enjoy. And learn.

Renewable Energy Resources

Well, who'd know it — there's yet more energy lurking about in piles of rubbish and deep underground.

Geothermal energy — heat from underground

1) This is only possible in certain places where hot rocks lie quite near to the surface. The source of much of the heat is the slow decay of various radioactive elements including uranium deep inside the Earth.

2) Water is pumped in pipes down to hot rocks and returns as steam to drive a generator. This is actually brilliant free energy with no real environmental problems. The main drawback is the cost of drilling down several km.

3) Unfortunately there are very few places where this seems to be an economic option (for now).

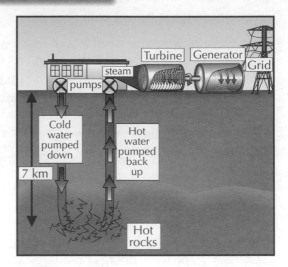

Biomass is waste that can be burnt — plant waste and animal poo

1) Biomass is the general term for all manner of organic 'stuff' that can be burnt to produce electricity. This can be anything from farm waste, animal droppings and landfill rubbish to specially-grown forests.

2) The waste material is burnt in power stations to drive turbines and produce electricity. Or sometimes it's fermented to produce other fuels such as 'biogas' (usually methane) or ethanol.

3) The plants that grew to produce the waste (or to feed the animals that produced the dung) would have absorbed carbon dioxide from the atmosphere as they were growing. When the waste is burnt, this CO_2 is re-released into the atmosphere. So it has a neutral effect on atmospheric CO_2 levels. (Although this only really works if you keep growing plants at the same rate you're burning things.)

4) Set-up and fuel costs are generally low, since the fuel is usually waste, and the fuels can often be burnt in converted coal-fired power stations.

5) This process makes use of waste products, which could be great news for our already overflowing landfill sites. But the downside of using unsorted landfill rubbish, rather than just plant and animal waste, is that burning it can release nasty gases like sulfur dioxide and nitrogen oxide into the atmosphere.

Where there's muck there's gas

Biomass isn't the nicest of things — dead plants, rubbish and poo. But it could be a good way of sorting out our energy problems as there's lots of the stuff about already.

Power Stations

Most of our electricity gets generated in <u>power stations</u>...

Most **power stations** use **steam** to drive a **turbine**

<u>Most</u> of the electricity we use is <u>generated</u> from the four <u>NON-RENEWABLE</u> sources of energy (<u>coal</u>, <u>oil</u>, <u>gas</u> and <u>nuclear</u>) in <u>big power stations</u>, which are all <u>pretty much the same</u> apart from the <u>boiler</u>. <u>Learn</u> the <u>basic features</u> of the typical power station shown here and also the <u>nuclear reactor</u> below.

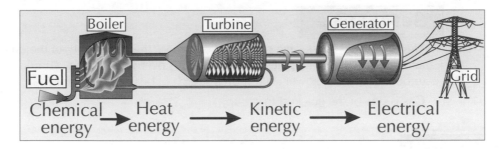

Nuclear reactors are just **fancy boilers**

1) A <u>nuclear power station</u> is mostly the same as the one above, where <u>nuclear fission</u> produces <u>heat</u> to make <u>steam</u> to drive <u>turbines</u>, etc. The difference is in the <u>boiler</u>, as shown here.

2) Nuclear power stations take the <u>longest</u> time of all the power stations to start up. <u>Natural gas</u> power stations take the shortest time.

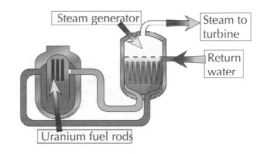

Setting up a **power station**

Because coal and oil are running out fast, many old <u>coal- and oil-fired power stations</u> are being <u>taken out of use</u>. Mostly they're being <u>replaced</u> by <u>gas-fired power stations</u>. But gas is <u>not</u> the <u>only</u> <u>option</u>, as you really ought to know if you've been concentrating at all over the last few pages.

When looking at the options for a <u>new power station</u>, there are <u>several factors</u> to consider:

1) How much it <u>costs</u> to set up and run, <u>how long</u> it takes to <u>build</u>, <u>how much power</u> it can generate, etc.

2) Then there are also the trickier factors like <u>damage to the environment</u> and <u>impact on local communities</u>. And because these are often <u>very contentious</u> issues, getting <u>permission</u> to build certain types of power station can be a <u>long-running</u> process, and hence <u>increase</u> the overall <u>set-up time</u>.

Steam plays a massive role in generating electricity

Steam engines were invented as long ago as the 17th century, and yet we're still using that idea to produce most of our electricity today, over 300 years later. Amazing...

Comparison of Energy Resources

There are lots of factors to consider when deciding which energy resource is the most suitable to use...

Set-up costs

Renewable resources often need bigger power stations than non-renewables for the same output. And as you'd expect, the bigger the power station, the more expensive.

Nuclear reactors and hydroelectric dams also need huge amounts of engineering to make them safe, which bumps up the cost.

Set-up time

This is affected by the size of the power station, the complexity of the engineering and also the planning issues (e.g. discussions over whether they should be allowed to build a nuclear power station on a stretch of beautiful coastline can last years).

Gas is one of the quickest to set up.

Reliability issues

All the non-renewables are reliable energy providers (until they run out).

Many of the renewable sources depend on the weather, which means they're pretty unreliable here in the UK. The exceptions are tidal power and geothermal (which don't depend on weather).

Running/fuel costs

Renewables usually have the lowest running costs, because there's no actual fuel involved.

Location issues

This is fairly common sense — a power station has to be near to the stuff it runs on.

Solar — pretty much anywhere, though the sunnier the better

Gas — pretty much anywhere there's piped gas (most of the UK)

Biomass — pretty much anywhere

Hydroelectric — hilly, rainy places with floodable valleys, e.g. the Lake District, Scottish Highlands

Wind — exposed, windy places like moors and coasts or out at sea

Oil — near the coast (oil transported by sea)

Waves — on the coast

Coal — near coal mines, e.g. Yorkshire, Wales

Nuclear — away from people (in case of disaster), near water (for cooling)

Tidal — big river estuaries where a dam can be built

Geothermal — fairly limited, only in places where hot rocks are near the Earth's surface

Environmental issues

If there's a fuel involved, there'll be waste pollution and you'll be using up resources.

If it relies on the weather, it's often got to be in an exposed place where it sticks out like a sore thumb.

Atmospheric Pollution
Coal, Oil, Gas, Biomass
(+ others, though less so)

Visual Pollution
Coal, Oil, Gas, Nuclear, Tidal, Waves, Wind, Hydroelectric, Biomass

Other Problems
Nuclear (dangerous waste, explosions, contamination), Hydroelectric (dams bursting)

Using Up Resources
Coal, Oil, Gas, Nuclear

Noise Pollution
Coal, Oil, Gas, Nuclear, Wind, Biomass

Disruption of Habitats
Hydroelectric, Tidal

Disruption of Leisure
Activities (e.g. boats)
Waves, Tidal

Of course — the biggest problem is we need too much electricity

It would be lovely if we could get rid of all the nasty polluting power stations and replace them all with clean, green fuel, just like that... but it's not quite that simple. Renewable energy has its own problems too, and probably isn't enough to power the whole country without having a wind farm in everyone's back yard.

Warm-Up and Exam Questions

Warm-up questions first, then a few exam questions to practise.
Make the most of this page by working through everything carefully — it's all useful stuff.

Warm-Up Questions

1) Give two ways in which using coal as an energy source causes problems.
2) Describe the major problems with using nuclear fuel to generate electricity.
3) Give two reasons why solar cells are not widely used to generate electricity.
4) Describe the difference between a pumped storage scheme and a hydroelectric power scheme.
5) Explain what is meant by biomass.

Exam Questions

1   Geothermal energy can be described as a renewable energy source.
   (a) What is geothermal energy?
(1 mark)
   (b) What does 'renewable energy' mean?
(1 mark)
   (c) Why is geothermal energy not used much in the UK?
(1 mark)

2   The diagram shows a pumped storage plant. Match up the labels 1 – 4 on the diagram with
     the energy transfers A, B, C and D.
   A   gravitational potential to kinetic
   B   kinetic to electrical
   C   electrical to kinetic
   D   kinetic to gravitational potential

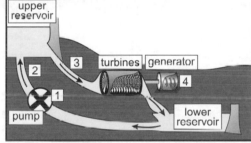

(4 marks)

3   An old coal-fired power station has an output of 2 MW (2 million watts).
     The electricity generating company plans to replace it with wind turbines which have
     a maximum output of 4000 W each.
   (a) Calculate the minimum number of wind turbines required to replace the
        old power station.
(1 mark)
   (b) Why might more wind turbines than this be needed in reality?
(1 mark)
   (c) Suggest why some people might oppose the wind farm development.
(2 marks)

4   The inhabitants of a remote island do not have the resources or expertise to build a nuclear
     power plant. They have no access to fossil fuels.
   (a) The islanders have considered using wind, solar and hydroelectric
        power to generate electricity. Suggest two other renewable energy
        resources they could use.
(2 marks)
   (b) The islanders decide that both solar and hydroelectric power could reliably
        generate enough electricity for all their needs. Suggest two other factors they
        should consider when deciding which method of electricity generation to use.
(2 marks)

Revision Summary for Physics 1a

Phew... what a relief, you've made it to the end of a nice long section. This section's been fairly straightforward though — after all, about half of it just covered the pros and cons of different renewable energy resources. But don't kid yourself, there are definitely a shedload of facts to remember here and you need to know the lot of them. The best way to check that you know it all is to work your way through these revision questions — and make sure you go back and revise anything you get wrong.

1) Describe the three ways that heat energy can be transferred.

2) The two designs of car engine shown are made from the same material. Which engine will transfer heat quicker? Explain why.

Engine A   Engine B

3) Explain why solar hot water panels have a matt black surface.

4) Describe the process that transfers heat energy through a metal rod.

5) Describe how the heat from an immersion heater is transferred throughout the water in a kettle. What is this process called?

6) What improvements could be made to a mug to keep its contents warmer for longer? Explain your improvements.

7) Name nine types of energy and give an example of each.

8) State the principle of the conservation of energy.

9) What is the useful type of energy delivered by a motor? In what form is energy wasted?

10)* What is the efficiency of a motor that converts 100 J of electrical energy into 70 J of useful kinetic energy?

11) List the energy transformations that occur in a battery-powered toy car.

12)* The following energy transformation diagram shows how energy is converted in a catapult.

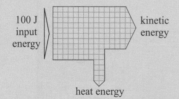

100 J input energy → kinetic energy / heat energy

a) How much energy is converted into kinetic energy?

b) How much energy is wasted?

c) What is the efficiency of the catapult?

13) Name five ways of improving energy efficiency in the home. Explain how each improvement reduces the amount of heat lost from a house.

14)* The following table gives some information about two different energy-saving light bulbs.

a) What is the payback time for light bulb A?

b) Which light bulb is more cost-effective?

c) Light bulb A is rated at 0.1 kW. If one unit of electricity costs 8p, how much will it cost if the bulb is left on for 5 hours?

	Price of bulb	Annual saving
Light bulb A	£2.50	£1.25
Light bulb B	£3.00	£2.00

15) Explain why a very high electrical voltage is used to transmit electricity in the National Grid.

16) What is meant by a non-renewable energy resource? Name four different non-renewable energy resources.

17) State two disadvantages of using fossil fuels to generate electricity.

18) Explain how electricity is generated in a gas-fired power station. Describe the useful energy transformations that occur.

19) Describe how the following renewable resources are used to generate electricity. State one advantage and one disadvantage for each resource.

a) wind   b) solar energy   c) the tide
d) waves   e) geothermal energy   f) biomass

* Answers on page 221.

Electromagnetic Waves

Electromagnetic waves are things like radio waves, microwaves and X-rays.

Electromagnetic waves carry energy but not matter

1) Electromagnetic radiation travels as electromagnetic waves (EM waves).
2) Like other waves, they transfer energy from one place to another without moving any matter (stuff).

All waves have wavelength, frequency, amplitude and speed

If you look at waves on a beach, they vary in height and in how far apart they are. Some travel faster than others, and some slow down as they get nearer the beach.

✱ 1) WAVELENGTH is the distance from one peak to the next.

✱ 2) FREQUENCY is how many complete waves there are per second (passing a certain point). It's measured in hertz (Hz). 1 Hz is 1 wave per second.

✱ 3) AMPLITUDE is just the height of the wave (from the midline to the peak).

✱ 4) The SPEED is, well, how fast it goes.

10^3 Hz = kHz,
10^6 Hz = MHz.

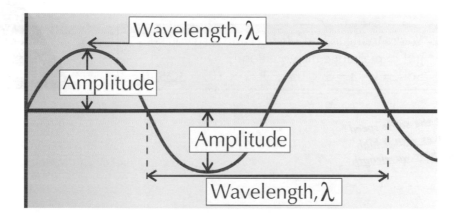

There's a continuous spectrum of EM waves

EM waves with different wavelengths (or frequencies) have different properties. We group them into seven basic types, but the different regions actually merge to form a continuous spectrum. They're shown below with increasing frequency (decreasing wavelength) from left to right.

✱

RADIO WAVES	MICRO WAVES	INFRA RED	VISIBLE LIGHT	ULTRA VIOLET	X-RAYS	GAMMA RAYS
1 m – 10^4 m	10^{-2} m (3 cm)	10^{-5} m (0.01 mm)	10^{-7} m	10^{-8} m	10^{-10} m	10^{-12} m

wavelength →

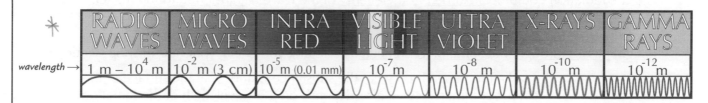

1) All the different types of electromagnetic wave travel at the same speed in a vacuum (e.g. space).
2) EM waves with higher frequencies have lower wavelengths.

Electromagnetic Waves

Wave speed = frequency × wavelength

You need to learn this equation (it's not given in the exam) and <u>practise using it</u>.

$$\text{Speed} = \text{Frequency} \times \text{Wavelength}$$
$$\text{(m/s)} \qquad \text{(Hz)} \qquad \text{(m)}$$

Or you can use the shortened version:

$$v = f\lambda$$

Wavelength (that's the Greek letter 'lambda')

Speed (v is for <u>velocity</u>)

Frequency

<u>EXAMPLE</u>: A radio wave has a frequency of 92.2×10^6 Hz. Find its wavelength. (The speed of all EM waves is 3×10^8 m/s.)

<u>ANSWER</u>: You're trying to find λ using f and v, so you've got to rearrange the equation. So $\lambda = v \div f = 3 \times 10^8 \div 9.22 \times 10^7 = \underline{3.25 \text{ m}}$.

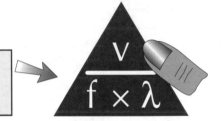

All EM waves travel at the same speed in a vacuum — so <u>waves with a high frequency must have a short wavelength</u>.

EM radiation can be *absorbed*, *reflected* or *transmitted*

1) The different <u>wavelengths</u> of EM radiation <u>interact</u> differently with <u>matter</u>. When a wave meets some matter, like air or glass, three things can happen:

- The radiation might be <u>transmitted</u> — just <u>pass through</u> the substance, as light passes through glass.
- It could be <u>reflected</u> — <u>bounce back</u>, like light reflected from a mirror.
- Or the radiation could be <u>absorbed</u> — the <u>energy</u> of the wave is <u>transferred</u> to the <u>matter</u>.

2) Two or three of these things can happen at the same time. E.g. when sunlight shines on glass a lot of the light <u>passes through</u>, but <u>some of it</u> is <u>reflected</u> — letting you check your hair in shop windows.

3) What happens to the radiation depends on <u>what the substance is</u> and what the <u>surface</u> of the substance is like — colour, shininess, etc. It also depends on the <u>wavelength</u> of the radiation.

4) When <u>EM radiation</u> is <u>absorbed</u> it can have <u>two effects</u>:

   See also pages 41–42.

   a) The <u>substance</u> absorbing it gets <u>hotter</u>.
   b) It sets up a <u>tiny alternating current</u> with the <u>same frequency</u> as the EM wave.

Uses of Waves — Radio and Microwaves

Radio waves are used mainly for communications

1) Radio waves are EM radiation with wavelengths longer than about 10 cm.

2) Long-wave radio (wavelengths of 1 – 10 km) can be transmitted from London, say, and received halfway round the world. That's because long wavelengths bend around the curved surface of the Earth. They also get around hills, into tunnels and all sorts.

3) The radio waves used for TV and FM radio transmissions have very short wavelengths (10 cm – 10 m). To get reception, you must be in direct sight of the transmitter — the signal doesn't bend around hills or travel far through buildings.

4) Short-wave radio signals (wavelengths of about 10 m – 100 m) can, like long-wave, be received at long distances from the transmitter. That's because they are reflected from the ionosphere — an electrically charged layer in the Earth's upper atmosphere. Medium wave signals (well, the shorter ones) can also reflect from the ionosphere, depending on atmospheric conditions and time of day.

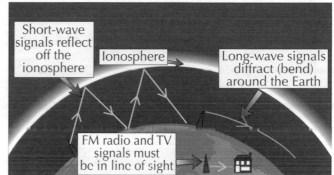

Short-wave signals reflect off the ionosphere

Ionosphere

Long-wave signals diffract (bend) around the Earth

FM radio and TV signals must be in line of sight

Microwaves are used for satellite communication

1) Communication to and from satellites (including satellite TV signals and satellite phones) uses microwaves. But you need to use microwaves which can pass easily through the Earth's watery atmosphere.

2) For satellite TV, the signal from a transmitter is transmitted into space...

3) ... where it's picked up by the satellite receiver dish orbiting thousands of kilometres above the Earth. The satellite transmits the signal back to Earth in a different direction...

microwaves

clouds and water vapour

4) ... where it's received by a satellite dish on the ground.

5) Mobile phone calls also travel as microwaves from your phone to the nearest transmitter.

6) And microwaves are used by remote-sensing satellites — to 'see' through the clouds and monitor oil spills, track the movement of icebergs, see how much rainforest has been chopped down and so on.

Funnily enough, microwaves also use microwaves
But the microwaves involved in communications are of different lengths from those used in ovens.

Uses of Waves — Optical Fibres

Total internal reflection happens above the critical angle

1) <u>Total internal reflection</u> can only happen when a wave travels <u>through a dense substance</u> like glass, water or perspex <u>towards a less dense</u> substance like air.

2) It all depends on whether the angle of incidence (i.e. the angle it hits at) is <u>bigger</u> than the <u>critical angle</u>...

If the angle of incidence (i) is:

The <u>angle of incidence</u> (i) and the <u>angle of reflection</u> (r) are always measured from the <u>normal</u> (a line at right angles to the surface).

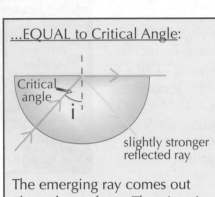

...LESS than Critical Angle:

Most of the light <u>passes out</u> but a <u>little</u> bit of it is <u>internally reflected</u>.

Angle of reflection, r, equals the <u>angle of incidence</u>, i.

...EQUAL to Critical Angle:

Critical angle

slightly stronger reflected ray

The emerging ray comes out <u>along the surface</u>. There's quite a bit of <u>internal reflection</u>.

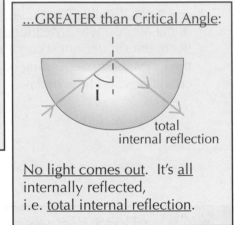

...GREATER than Critical Angle:

total internal reflection

<u>No light comes out</u>. It's <u>all</u> internally reflected, i.e. <u>total internal reflection</u>.

3) Different materials have different critical angles. The critical angle for <u>glass</u> is about 42°.

4) Optical fibres use <u>total internal reflection</u> to carry data over long distances. The data is carried as pulses of light or infrared (IR) radiation.

5) They work by bouncing <u>visible</u> or <u>infrared</u> light waves off the sides of a thin <u>inner core</u> of glass or plastic using total internal reflection. The wave enters one end of the fibre and is reflected repeatedly until it emerges at the other end.

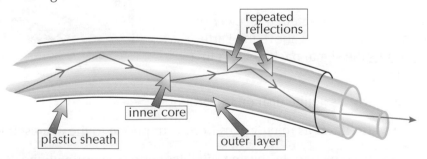

repeated reflections

inner core

plastic sheath

outer layer

6) Optical fibres <u>can be bent</u>, but <u>not sharply</u>, or the <u>angle of incidence</u> might fall <u>below</u> the critical angle.

Total internal reflection can be amazingly useful

Optical fibres are a good way to send data over long distances — the EM waves travel fast, and they can't be tapped into or suffer interference (unlike a signal that's <u>broadcast</u> from a transmitter, like radio).

Hazards of EM Radiation

Electromagnetic radiation can be dangerous.

Some types of radiation are **more harmful** than others

When EM radiation enters <u>living tissue</u> — like <u>you</u> — it's often harmless, but sometimes it creates havoc.

1) Some EM radiation mostly <u>passes through soft tissue</u> without being absorbed — e.g. radio waves.

2) Other types of radiation are absorbed and cause <u>heating</u> of the cells — e.g. microwaves.

3) Some radiations cause <u>cancerous changes</u> in living cells — e.g. UV can cause skin cancer.

4) Some types of EM radiation can actually <u>destroy cells</u> — as in 'radiation sickness' after a nuclear accident.

5) What effect radiation has depends on what <u>type</u> it is (its wavelength) and the size of <u>dose</u> you get.

Higher frequency EM radiation is usually **more dangerous**

1) As far as we know, <u>radio</u> waves are pretty harmless.

2) This is because the <u>energy</u> of any electromagnetic wave is <u>directly proportional</u> to its <u>frequency</u>.

3) <u>Visible light</u> isn't harmful unless it's really bright. People who work with powerful <u>lasers</u> (very intense light beams) need to wear eye protection.

4) <u>Infrared</u> can cause <u>burns</u> or <u>heatstroke</u> (when the body overheats) — but they're <u>easily avoidable</u> risks.

In general, waves with <u>lower frequencies</u> (like radio) are <u>less harmful</u> than <u>high frequency</u> waves like X-rays and gamma rays.

<u>Higher frequency</u> waves have <u>more energy</u>. And it's the <u>energy</u> of a wave that does the <u>damage</u>.

Microwaves — **may** or **may not** be **harmful**

1) Some wavelengths of microwaves are <u>absorbed</u> by <u>water</u> molecules and <u>heat</u> them up. If the water in question happens to be in <u>your cells</u>, you might start to <u>cook</u>.

2) Mobile phone networks use microwaves, and some people think that using your mobile a lot, or living near a <u>mast</u>, could damage your <u>health</u>. There isn't any conclusive proof either way yet.

In general, the more energy a wave has, the more damage it can do

If you can remember the electromagnetic spectrum, this page should be a doddle. Just think about the two ends of the spectrum — would you rather have some tuneful radio waves or scary gamma rays? I'd go for the radio waves any day — the dangers of the other types of radiation fit nicely in between.

Hazards of EM Radiation

Information about the dangers of too much Sun is everywhere nowadays, but getting a tan can't be that bad for you... can it?

*Ultraviolet radiation can cause **skin cancer***

1) If you spend a lot of time in the <u>sun</u>, you'll get a <u>tan</u> and maybe <u>sunburn</u> (with attractive <u>peeling</u>).

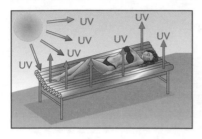

2) The more time you spend in the sun, the more chance you also have of getting <u>skin cancer</u>. This is because the Sun's rays include <u>ultraviolet radiation</u> (UV) which damages the DNA in your cells.

3) <u>Dark skin</u> gives some protection against UV rays — it <u>absorbs</u> more UV radiation, stopping it from reaching the more <u>vulnerable</u> tissues deeper in the body.

4) Everyone should protect themselves from overexposure to the Sun, but if you're pale skinned, you need to take extra care, and use a sunscreen with a higher <u>Sun Protection Factor</u> (SPF).

An <u>SPF</u> of <u>15</u> means you can spend <u>15 times as long</u> in the sun as you otherwise could <u>without burning</u> (if you keep reapplying the sunscreen).

5) The gas inside <u>fluorescent tubes</u> (often used for kitchen and office lighting) emits UV radiation. <u>Special coatings</u> are used on lamps to <u>absorb</u> the <u>UV</u> and emit <u>visible light</u> instead.

*X-rays are used in **hospitals**, but are **pretty dangerous***

1) <u>Radiographers</u> in <u>hospitals</u> take <u>X-ray photographs</u> to help doctors diagnose <u>broken bones</u> — X-rays pass <u>easily through flesh</u> but not through <u>denser material</u> like <u>bones</u> or metal.

2) X-rays can cause <u>mutations</u> which lead to <u>cancer</u>.

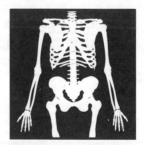

The <u>brighter bits</u> are where <u>fewer X-rays</u> get through. This is a <u>negative image</u>. The plate starts off <u>all white</u>.

3) Radiographers wear <u>lead aprons</u> and stand behind a <u>lead screen</u> or <u>leave the room</u> to <u>minimise</u> their <u>exposure</u> to X-rays.

4) The <u>patient</u> is also given <u>lead shields</u> to protect the parts of their body which are not being investigated (especially the reproductive organs — which are very susceptible to damage).

5) Pregnant women shouldn't have X-rays — the developing baby is especially vulnerable.

Staying in the sun for too long can cause cancer

There's no point being paranoid — a little bit of sunshine won't kill you (in fact it might do you good). But don't be daft... getting cancer from sunbathing for hours on end is just <u>stupid</u>.

Warm-Up and Exam Questions

You must be getting used to the routine by now — the warm-up questions get you, well, warmed up, and the exam questions give you some idea of what you'll have to cope with on the day.

Warm-Up Questions

1) What is meant by the frequency of a wave?
2) In what circumstances does total internal reflection of light occur?
3) What is an optical fibre? Why don't they work if they're bent sharply?
4) Why can it be dangerous for living cells to absorb infrared radiation?
5) How does a radiographer minimise their exposure to X-rays?

Exam Questions

1   Which of the following types of electromagnetic wave has the highest frequency?

   A   Radio waves

   B   Ultraviolet

   C   Gamma rays

   D   Microwaves

(1 mark)

2   The speed of electromagnetic waves in a vacuum is approximately 300 000 000 m/s.
   Use this figure to calculate the wavelength of a 100 MHz radio signal.

   A   3 m

   B   300 m

   C   30 000 m

   D   3 000 000 m

(1 mark)

3   Look at this displacement-time graph for a water wave.

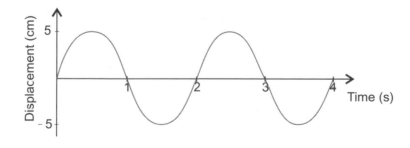

   (a)   What is the amplitude of this wave?

(1 mark)

   (b)   Calculate the frequency of the wave.

(1 mark)

   (c)   If the frequency of the wave doubles but its speed stays the same, what will happen to its wavelength?

(1 mark)

Exam Questions

4   The diagram shows a light ray entering an optical fibre.

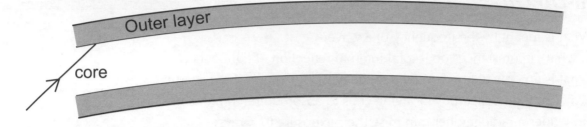

(a)   Sketch the path taken by the light ray.

(1 mark)

(b)   Explain why the light ray follows this path.

(1 mark)

5   The radiation used in mobile phone networks

   A   is definitely safe

   B   has a higher frequency than visible light

   C   may cause damage to cells

   D   is known to cause health problems

(1 mark)

6   Match the words A, B, C and D with the spaces 1-4 in the sentences.

   A   Visible light

   B   Radio

   C   Infrared

   D   Ultraviolet

   Using sunscreen will give you some protection from ...**1**... radiation emitted by the Sun.

   Grills use ...**2**... radiation to cook food.

   ...**3**... is not usually dangerous unless it's very bright e.g. lasers.

   ...**4**... waves are not known to have any ill effects on the body.

(4 marks)

7   (a)   Give one hazard and one practical use of microwave radiation

(2 marks)

   (b)   Give one way in which you can reduce your exposure to UV radiation
         from the Sun.

(1 mark)

Analogue and Digital Signals

Digital technology is gradually taking over. By 2012, you won't be able to watch TV unless you've got a digital version — that's when the Government's planning to switch off the last analogue signal.

Information is converted into signals

Information is being transmitted everywhere all the time.

1) Information, such as sounds and pictures, is converted into <u>electrical signals</u> before it's transmitted.

2) It's then sent long distances down <u>telephone wires</u> or carried on <u>EM waves</u>.

Analogue signals vary...

1) The <u>amplitude</u> and <u>frequency</u> of an analogue signal <u>vary continuously</u>. An analogue signal can take <u>any</u> value in a particular range.

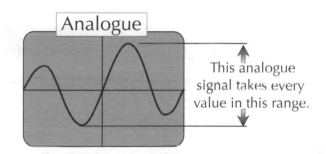

Analogue

This analogue signal takes every value in this range.

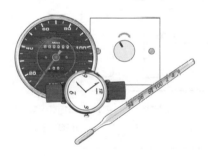

2) Dimmer switches, thermometers, speedometers and old-fashioned watches are all <u>analogue</u> devices.

...but digital's either on or off

1) Digital signals are <u>coded pulses</u> — they can only take <u>two</u> values (the two values sometimes get different names, but the key thing is that there are only <u>two</u> of them): on or off, true or false, 0 or 1...

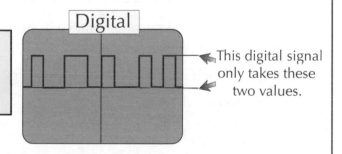

Digital

This digital signal only takes these two values.

2) On/off switches and the displays on digital clocks and meters are all <u>digital</u> devices.

Analogue and Digital Signals

It's all very well being able to transmit signals, but you need to be able to makes sense of them when you receive them too, or it's all a bit of a waste of time.

Signals have to be amplified

Both digital and analogue signals <u>weaken</u> as they travel, so they may need to be <u>amplified</u> along their route.

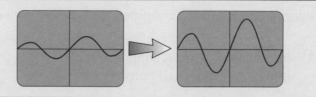

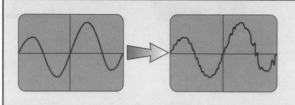

They also pick up <u>interference</u> or <u>noise</u> from <u>electrical disturbances</u> or <u>other signals</u>.

Digital signals are far better quality

1) <u>Noise</u> is less of a problem with <u>digital</u> signals.
   If you receive a noisy digital signal, it's pretty obvious what it's supposed to be.

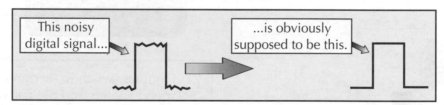

This noisy digital signal... ...is obviously supposed to be this.

2) But if you receive a noisy <u>analogue</u> signal, it's difficult to know what the <u>original</u> signal would have looked like. And if you amplify a noisy analogue signal, you amplify the noise as well.

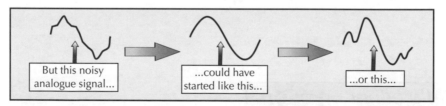

But this noisy analogue signal... ...could have started like this... ...or this...

3) This is why digital signals are much <u>higher quality</u> — the information received is the <u>same</u> as the original.

4) Digital signals are also easy to <u>process</u> using <u>computers</u>, since computers are digital devices too.

5) And another advantage of digital technology is that you can transmit <u>several signals at once</u> using just one cable or EM wave — so you can send <u>more information</u> (in a given time) than using analogue signals.

Remember: analogue varies but digital's either on or off

Digital signals are great — unless you live in a part of the country which currently has poor reception of digital broadcasts, in which case you get <u>no benefit at all</u>. This is because if you don't get spot-on reception of digital signals in your area, you won't get a grainy but watchable picture (like with analogue signals) — you'll get nothing at all.

Warm-Up and Exam Questions

Learning facts and practising exam questions is the only recipe for sure-fire success.
That's what the questions on this page are all about. All you have to do — is do them.

Warm-Up Questions

1) Describe the difference between analogue and digital signals.
2) Give an example of an analogue device.
3) Give an example of a digital device.
4) Is noise more of a problem with analogue or digital signals?

Exam Questions

1   Communication signals pick up unwanted additional signals as they travel.
    This unwanted part of the signal is called

   A   analogue
   B   amplitude
   C   digital
   D   noise

(1 mark)

2   When comparing analogue and digital signals, which of the following statements
    is **not** true?

   A   They both weaken as they travel.
   B   Both signals vary continuously.
   C   Both can be used to transmit television signals.
   D   They both experience noise.

(1 mark)

3   Rick is sick of not being able to get a clear signal on his analogue radio.
    He decides to replace it with a digital radio.

   (a)   What values can digital signals take?

(1 mark)

   (b)   Explain why both digital and analogue radio signals need to be amplified when
         they reach his radio.

(1 mark)

   (c)   Give one reason why Rick will be able to hear the songs on the radio more
         clearly with his digital radio than with his analogue radio.

(1 mark)

Radioactivity

<u>Nuclear radiation</u> is <u>different</u> from <u>EM radiation</u>. So you <u>do</u> need to read these next few pages. Sorry.

Nuclei contain protons and neutrons

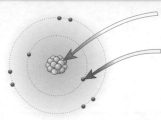

The <u>nucleus</u> contains <u>protons</u> and <u>neutrons</u>. It makes up most of the <u>mass</u> of the atom, but takes up <u>virtually no space</u> — it's <u>tiny</u>.

The <u>electrons</u> are <u>negatively charged</u> and really really <u>small</u>.

They whizz around the <u>outside</u> of the atom. Their <u>paths take up a lot of space</u>, giving the atom its <u>overall size</u> (though it's <u>mostly empty space</u>).

Isotopes are atoms with different numbers of neutrons

1) Many elements have a few different <u>isotopes</u>. Isotopes are atoms with the <u>same</u> number of <u>protons</u> but a <u>different</u> number of <u>neutrons</u>.

2) E.g. there are two common isotopes of carbon. The carbon-14 isotope has two more neutrons than 'normal' carbon (carbon-12).

3) Usually each element only has one or two <u>stable</u> <u>isotopes</u> — like carbon-12. The other isotopes tend to be <u>radioactive</u> — the nucleus is <u>unstable</u>, so it <u>decays</u> (breaks down) and emits <u>radiation</u>. Carbon-14 is an <u>unstable isotope</u> of carbon.

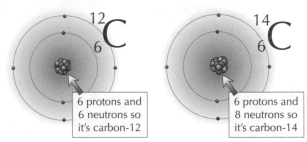

$^{12}_{6}C$

$^{14}_{6}C$

6 protons and 6 neutrons so it's carbon-12

6 protons and 8 neutrons so it's carbon-14

Radioactive decay is a random process

1) The nuclei of unstable isotopes break down at random. If you have 100 unstable nuclei, you can't say when any <u>one of them</u> is going to decay, and you can't do anything to <u>make a decay happen</u>.

2) Each nucleus just decays quite <u>spontaneously</u> in its <u>own good time</u>. It's completely unaffected by <u>physical</u> conditions like <u>temperature</u> or any sort of <u>chemical bonding</u> etc.

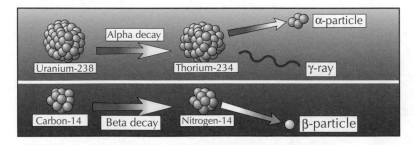

Uranium-238   Alpha decay   Thorium-234   α-particle
γ-ray
Carbon-14   Beta decay   Nitrogen-14   β-particle

3) When the nucleus <u>does</u> decay it <u>spits out</u> one or more of the three types of radiation — <u>alpha</u>, <u>beta</u> and <u>gamma</u> (see pages 49-50).

4) In the process, the <u>nucleus</u> often <u>changes</u> into a <u>new element</u>.

Protons determine the element, neutrons determine the isotope...

This isotope business can be a bit confusing at first, as you can have <u>different isotopes</u> which are all the <u>same element</u>. Remember, it's the number of <u>protons</u> which decides what <u>element</u> it is, then the number of <u>neutrons</u> decides what <u>isotope</u> of that element it is.

Radioactivity

There are three types of radiation — alpha (α), beta (β) (on this page) and gamma (γ) (on the next page). You need to remember <u>what</u> they are, how well they <u>penetrate</u> materials (including air), and their <u>ionising</u> power.

Nuclear radiation causes ionisation

1) Nuclear radiation causes <u>ionisation</u> by <u>bashing into atoms</u> and <u>knocking electrons off</u> them. Atoms (with <u>no overall charge</u>) are turned into <u>ions</u> (which are <u>charged</u>) — hence the term "<u>ionisation</u>".

2) There's a pattern: the <u>further</u> the radiation can <u>penetrate</u> before hitting an atom and getting stopped, the <u>less damage</u> it will do along the way and so the <u>less ionising</u> it is.

Alpha particles are helium nuclei

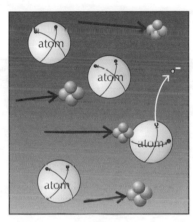

1) Alpha particles are made up of <u>2 protons and 2 neutrons</u> — they're <u>big</u>, <u>heavy</u> and <u>slow-moving</u>.

2) They therefore <u>don't penetrate</u> far into materials but are <u>stopped</u> quickly.

3) Because of their size they <u>bash into a lot of atoms</u> and <u>knock electrons off</u> them before they slow down, which creates lots of ions.

4) Because they're electrically <u>charged</u> (with a positive charge), alpha particles are <u>deflected</u> (their <u>direction changes</u>) by <u>electric</u> and <u>magnetic fields</u>.

Beta particles are electrons

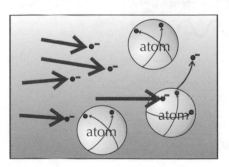

1) A beta particle is an <u>electron</u> which has been emitted from the <u>nucleus</u> of an atom when a <u>neutron</u> turns into a <u>proton</u> and an <u>electron</u>. So for every β-particle emitted, the number of <u>protons</u> in the nucleus increases by 1.

2) They move <u>quite fast</u> and they are <u>quite small</u>.

3) They <u>penetrate moderately</u> before colliding and are <u>moderately ionising</u> too.

4) Because they're <u>charged</u> (negatively), beta particles are <u>deflected</u> by electric and magnetic fields.

Learning the types of radiation is as easy as α, β, γ

The symbols for alpha, beta and gamma radiation may look a little strange — but really they're just a, b and c written using the Greek alphabet. True it might be easier to use a, b and c, but the Greek letters have been used for so long now that it'd confuse more people than it would help, sorry.

Radioactivity

Gamma radiation is quite different from alpha and beta radiation. Gamma rays are part of the electromagnetic spectrum — just like light and radio waves.

Gamma rays are very **short** wavelength **EM waves**

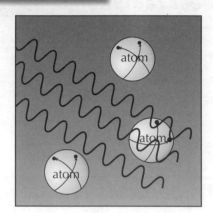

1) In a way, gamma rays are the <u>opposite of alpha particles</u>. They have <u>no mass</u> — they're just <u>energy</u> (in the form of an EM wave — see page 37).

2) They <u>penetrate a long way</u> into materials without being stopped.

3) This means they are <u>weakly ionising</u> because they tend to <u>pass through</u> rather than collide with atoms. But eventually they <u>hit something</u> and do <u>damage</u>.

4) Gamma rays have <u>no charge</u>, so they're <u>not deflected</u> by electric or magnetic fields.

You can **identify** *the* **type** *by* **what blocks it**

Make sure you know what it takes to block each of the three types of radiation:

<u>Alpha particles</u> are blocked by <u>paper</u>, <u>skin</u> or a few centimetres of <u>air</u>.

<u>Beta particles</u> are stopped by <u>thin metal</u>.

<u>Gamma rays</u> are blocked by <u>thick lead</u> or <u>very thick concrete</u>.

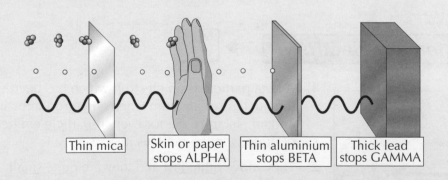

| Thin mica | Skin or paper stops ALPHA | Thin aluminium stops BETA | Thick lead stops GAMMA |

So if radiation can penetrate paper it could be beta or gamma — you'd have to test it with a metal, say, to find out which.

Remember — alpha penetrates least, gamma penetrates most

Remember: <u>alpha</u>'s big, slow and clumsy — always knocking into things. <u>Beta</u>'s lightweight and fast, and <u>gamma</u> weighs nothing and moves <u>super-fast</u>. Practise with this: if it gets through paper and is deflected by a magnetic field, it must be _____ radiation. (Answer on page 221.)

Half-Life

Half-life is a measure of the time it takes for a radioactive substance to decay.

The radioactivity of a sample always decreases over time

1) This is pretty obvious when you think about it. Each time a decay happens and alpha, beta or gamma radiation is given out, it means one more radioactive nucleus has disappeared.

2) Obviously, as the unstable nuclei all steadily disappear, the activity as a whole will decrease. So the older a sample becomes, the less radiation it will emit.

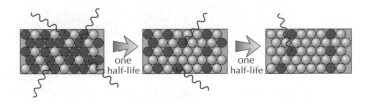

3) How quickly the activity decreases varies a lot. For some isotopes it takes just a few hours before nearly all the unstable nuclei have decayed. Others last for millions of years.

4) The problem with trying to measure this is that the activity never reaches zero, which is why we have to use the idea of half-life to measure how quickly the activity drops off.

5) Learn this important definition of half-life:

> ## HALF-LIFE is the TIME TAKEN for HALF of the NUCLEI now present to DECAY

Another useful definition of half-life is: "The time taken for the activity (or count rate) to fall by half".

6) A short half-life means the activity falls quickly, because lots of the nuclei decay quickly.

7) A long half-life means the activity falls more slowly because most of the nuclei don't decay for a long time — they just sit there, basically unstable, but kind of biding their time.

Do half-life questions step by step

A very simple example: The activity of a radioisotope is 640 cpm (counts per minute). Two hours later it has fallen to 40 cpm. Find the half-life of the sample.

You might also see radioactivity measured in becquerels (Bq). 1 Bq is 1 decay per second.

ANSWER: You must go through it in short simple steps like this:

Initial count:	(÷2)→	after one half-life:	(÷2)→	after two half-lives:	(÷2)→	after three half-lives:	(÷2)→	after four half-lives:
640		320		160		80		40

Notice the careful step-by-step method, which tells us it takes four half-lives for the activity to fall from 640 to 40. Hence two hours represents four half-lives, so the half-life is 30 minutes.

Half-Life

You can measure the <u>half-life</u> of a radioactive substance using a <u>G-M tube and counter</u>.

Measuring the half-life of a sample using a graph

1) This can <u>only be done</u> by taking <u>several readings</u> of <u>count rate</u>, usually using a <u>G-M tube and counter</u>.

2) The results can then be <u>plotted</u> as a <u>graph</u>, which will <u>always</u> be shaped like the one below.

3) The <u>half-life</u> is found from the graph, by finding the <u>time interval</u> on the <u>bottom axis</u> corresponding to a <u>halving</u> of the <u>activity</u> on the <u>vertical axis</u>.

Half-life is the time taken for the count rate to halve

1) This is how 'carbon dating' of some types of archaeological specimens works...

2) If you know the <u>half-life</u> of a particular radioactive isotope you can look at <u>how much is left</u> in your specimen now, and work out <u>how long</u> your dusty bits of bone have been around for.

3) This method is also really important in <u>geology</u> and <u>biology</u> — for working out the age of rocks (and of any <u>fossils</u> that are buried in them).

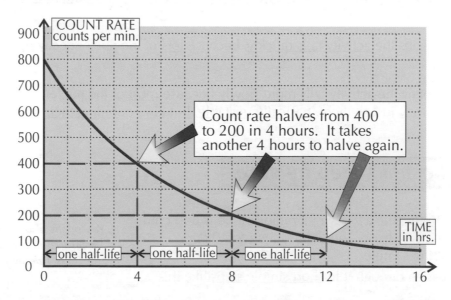

Count rate halves from 400 to 200 in 4 hours. It takes another 4 hours to halve again.

Half-lives always make curved graphs

The radioactivity of a sample always goes down over time, because every time a nucleus decays the sample gets smaller, so there are fewer nuclei left to decay. The result is that decay graphs always form nice curves like the one above. Plotting a decay graph is useful because it lets you calculate half-life.

Warm-Up and Exam Questions

There's no point in skimming through the section and glancing over the questions. Do the warm-up questions and go back over any bits you don't know. Then try the exam questions — without cheating.

Warm-Up Questions

1) Explain what isotopes are.
2) What is meant by 'radioactive decay'?
3) Name the three types of nuclear radiation.
4) Which type of nuclear radiation is also a type of electromagnetic radiation?

Exam Questions

1   The diagram shows four different materials.

thin mica   skin   aluminium   thick lead
1   2   3   4

Match up the materials 1-4 with these descriptions.

A   Stops all types of nuclear radiation.

B   Doesn't stop any types of nuclear radiation.

C   Stops alpha and beta radiation.

D   Stops only alpha radiation.

(4 marks)

2   An alpha particle is

A   a proton

B   a neutron

C   a helium nucleus

D   an electromagnetic wave

(1 mark)

3   A sample of a highly ionising radioactive gas has a half-life of two minutes.

(a)   What does 'half-life' mean?

(1 mark)

(b)   What fraction of the radioactive atoms currently present will be left after four minutes?

(1 mark)

(c)   When an atom of the gas decays, it releases an electron.
What type of nuclear radiation does this gas emit?

(1 mark)

Uses of Nuclear Radiation

Radiation's useful in all sorts of ways, but choose carefully — you need to use a source which emits the right <u>type</u> of radiation <u>and</u> has a suitable <u>half-life</u>.

You need a *long half-life* for devices that have to *last*

1) <u>Sterilising machines</u> in hospitals use <u>gamma</u> radiation to <u>kill bacteria</u> on medical instruments. They use a <u>powerful radioactive</u> source with a <u>long half-life</u>, so that it <u>lasts</u> for a <u>long time</u>.

2) Smoke detectors use a <u>weak</u> source of <u>alpha</u> radiation to <u>ionise</u> the air between two <u>electrodes</u> — making <u>charged particles</u> which carry a <u>current</u>. If there's a fire, the <u>smoke absorbs</u> the <u>radiation</u> — the <u>current stops</u> and the <u>alarm sounds</u>.

A source with a fairly <u>long half-life</u> is used, so that the detector will work for <u>years</u>. Although the source is radioactive for years, its alpha radiation is stopped by a few centimetres of air, so it's pretty safe to have it on your ceiling (and <u>much</u> better than sleeping while your house burns).

Gamma radiation is used in *industrial tracers*

If you're looking for a leak in an underground pipe, you could dig it up, or you could use <u>gamma</u> rays...

1) You <u>squirt</u> a γ-source into the pipe, let it flow along, and go along the outside with a detector.

2) Gamma radiation will penetrate through a metal pipe, but <u>some of it</u> gets absorbed — exactly how much depends on the thickness of the pipe and what it's made of.

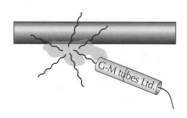

3) If there's a <u>crack</u> in the pipe, the γ–source will collect outside the pipe, and your detector will show <u>extra high</u> radioactivity at that point.

4) The isotope used <u>must</u> be a <u>gamma emitter</u>, so that the radiation can be detected even through any <u>rocks or earth</u> surrounding the pipe — alpha and beta radiation would be too <u>easily blocked</u>.

5) It should also have a <u>short half-life</u> so as not to cause a long-term <u>hazard</u> if it collects somewhere.

Choose your source carefully

To make use of radiation, you've got to match the <u>requirements of the job</u> to the <u>properties of your source</u>. A γ-source in a smoke detector wouldn't work at all — gamma radiation wouldn't ionise the air, so there'd be no current, the alarm would ring constantly, and you'd get thoroughly irradiated.

Uses of Nuclear Radiation

Medical tracers use beta or gamma radiation

Beta and gamma radiation will penetrate the skin and other body tissues.
This makes them suitable for using as <u>medical tracers</u>...

1) A source which emits β or γ radiation is <u>injected</u> into the
patient (or just <u>swallowed</u>). The radiation penetrates the
body tissues and can be <u>detected externally</u>. As the source
moves around the body, the radiographer uses a detector to
monitor its progress or to get a 'snapshot' of its distribution.

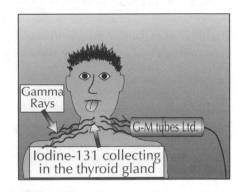

2) A computer converts the reading to an <u>on-screen display</u>
showing where the <u>radiation</u> is coming from. Doctors use
this method to check whether the organs of the body are
working as they should.

3) The radioactive source has to have a <u>short half-life</u>, so you can use
less of the radioactive source but still get a reading on your detector.

4) An <u>alpha</u> source would be <u>worse than useless</u> as a medical tracer — <u>useless</u> because it would be
stopped by the body's tissues, so you'd never detect it externally, and <u>worse</u> than useless because its
<u>strong ionising</u> power makes alpha radiation really <u>harmful</u> if it gets <u>inside</u> you (see next page).

Gamma radiation is also used to treat cancer

Radiation can <u>damage</u> living cells (see next page) and cause <u>cancer</u>. Once cancer's started, patients
are often given <u>radiotherapy</u> to <u>kill</u> the cancer cells and stop them dividing. This involves using a
<u>high</u> dose of gamma rays, carefully directed to zap the cells in the <u>tumour</u> while minimising the
dose to the rest of the body.

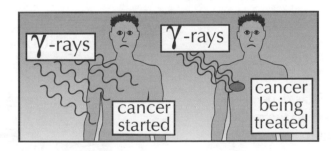

The isotope you use depends on half-life and whether it's α, β or γ

Knowing the detail is important here. For instance, swallowing an alpha source as a medical tracer
would be very foolish — alpha radiation would cause all sorts of chaos inside your body but couldn't
be detected outside, making the whole thing pointless. So learn <u>what</u> each type's used for and <u>why</u>.

Risks from Nuclear Radiation

Nuclear radiation can do nasty stuff to living cells so you have to be careful how you handle it. The effect of radiation on cells depends on the type of radiation and the size of the dose.

Radiation harms living cells

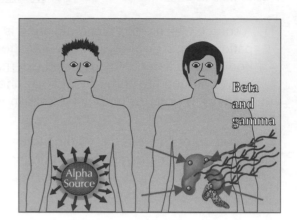

1) <u>Beta</u> and <u>gamma</u> radiation can penetrate the skin and soft tissues to reach the delicate <u>organs</u> inside the body. This makes beta and gamma sources more hazardous than alpha when outside the body.

2) Alpha radiation can't penetrate the skin, but it's a different story when it gets inside your body (by <u>swallowing</u> or <u>breathing it in</u>, say) — alpha sources do all their damage in a <u>very localised area</u>.

3) Beta and gamma sources, however, are <u>less dangerous</u> inside the body — their radiation mostly <u>passes straight out</u> without doing much.

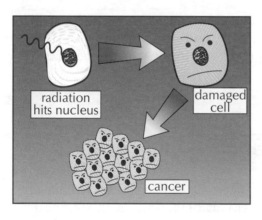

4) If radiation enters your body, it will <u>collide</u> with molecules in your cells.

5) These collisions cause <u>ionisation</u>, which <u>damages</u> or <u>destroys</u> the molecules.

6) <u>Lower</u> doses tend to cause <u>minor</u> damage without <u>killing</u> the cell. This can give rise to <u>mutant</u> cells which <u>divide uncontrollably</u> — this is <u>cancer</u>.

7) <u>Higher</u> doses tend to <u>kill cells</u> completely, causing <u>radiation sickness</u> if a large part of your body is affected at the same time.

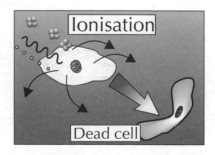

8) The <u>extent</u> of the harmful effects depends on <u>how much exposure</u> you have to the radiation, and its <u>energy</u> and <u>penetration</u>.

Nuclear radiation + living cells = cell damage, cell death or cancer

Most people could probably tell you that nuclear radiation is dangerous — what you need to know is what radiation can do to living cells and why the three types of radiation have different effects. Check out pages 49-50 if you're having trouble remembering the properties of the different radiation types.

Risks from Nuclear Radiation

You've got to be really careful with anything radioactive — no mucking about.

You should **protect yourself** in the **laboratory**...

You should always act to <u>minimise</u> your exposure to radioactive sources.

1) <u>Never</u> allow <u>skin contact</u> with a source. Always handle sources with <u>tongs</u>.

2) Keep the source at <u>arm's length</u> to keep it <u>as far</u> from the body <u>as possible</u>.

3) Keep the source <u>pointing away</u> from the body and <u>avoid looking directly at it</u>.

4) <u>Always</u> keep the source in a <u>labelled lead box</u> and put it back in <u>as soon</u> as the experiment is <u>over</u>, to keep your <u>exposure time</u> short.

...and if you **work** with **nuclear radiation**

1) Industrial nuclear workers wear <u>full protective suits</u> to prevent <u>tiny radioactive particles</u> being <u>inhaled</u> or lodging <u>on the skin</u> or <u>under fingernails</u>, etc.

2) <u>Lead-lined suits</u> and <u>lead/concrete barriers</u> and <u>thick lead screens</u> are used to prevent exposure to <u>gamma rays</u> from highly contaminated areas. (α and β radiation are stopped <u>much more easily</u>.)

3) Workers use <u>remote-controlled robot arms</u> to carry out tasks in highly radioactive areas.

Radiation's dangerous stuff — safety precautions are crucial

It's quite difficult to do research on how radiation affects humans. This is partly because it would be <u>unethical</u> to do <u>controlled experiments</u>, exposing people to huge doses of radiation just to see what happens. We rely mostly on studies of populations affected by <u>nuclear accidents</u> or nuclear <u>bombs</u>.

Warm-Up and Exam Questions

Imagine if you opened up your exam paper and all the answers were already written in for you.
Hmm, well I'm afraid that won't happen, so the only way you'll do well is through some hard work now.

Warm-Up Questions

1) How do smoke detectors work?
2) Why is nuclear radiation dangerous?
3) Give one example of a medical use of nuclear radiation.
4) Describe two precautions that should be taken when handling radioactive sources in the lab.
5) Give one way in which workers in nuclear power plants can be protected from radiation.

Exam Questions

1   Which type of nuclear radiation is the most dangerous inside the body?

   A   alpha

   B   beta

   C   gamma

   D   neutron

(1 mark)

2   Which of the following is **not** a use of gamma radiation?

   A   industrial tracers

   B   smoke detectors

   C   medical tracers

   D   sterilising machines

(1 mark)

3   Nuclear radiation has many uses within medicine.

   (a)   Give two reasons why alpha sources aren't used as medical tracers.

(2 marks)

   (b)   Why is it important that radioactive sources used in hospital sterilising machines
         have a long half-life?

(1 mark)

   (c)   Why is the dose of radiation given in radiotherapy directed only at the tumour?

(1 mark)

4   Nuclear radiation can have harmful effects on the human body.

   a)   Briefly explain how a low dose of nuclear radiation can cause cancer.

(2 marks)

   b)   Describe what can happen to the body if it receives a very high dose of
        nuclear radiation.

(1 mark)

The Origin of the Universe

Once upon a time, there was a really <u>Big Bang</u> — that's the <u>most convincing theory</u> we've got.

Light from other galaxies is red-shifted

1) When we look at <u>light from distant galaxies</u> we find that the <u>frequencies</u> are all <u>slightly lower</u> than they should be — they're <u>shifted</u> towards the <u>red end</u> of the spectrum.

2) This is called the <u>red-shift</u>. It's the same effect as the vrrroomm from a racing car — the engine sounds <u>lower-pitched</u> when the car's gone past you and is <u>moving away</u> from you. This is called the Doppler effect.

The Doppler effect

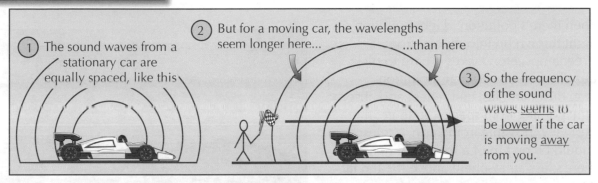

① The sound waves from a stationary car are equally spaced, like this

② But for a moving car, the wavelengths seem longer here... ...than here

③ So the frequency of the sound waves seems to be <u>lower</u> if the car is moving <u>away</u> from you.

3) <u>Measurements</u> of the red-shift suggest that <u>all the galaxies</u> are <u>moving away from us</u> very quickly — and it's the <u>same result</u> whichever direction you look in.

The further away a galaxy is, the greater the red-shift

1) <u>More distant</u> galaxies have <u>greater</u> red-shifts than nearer ones.

2) This means that more distant galaxies are <u>moving away</u> from us <u>faster</u> than nearer ones.

3) This provides evidence that the whole Universe is <u>expanding</u>.

The Big Bang theory — the universe is expanding

1) Right now, all the galaxies seem to be moving apart at great speed. But something must have <u>got them going</u>. That 'something' was probably a <u>big explosion</u> — the <u>Big Bang</u>...

2) According to this theory, all the matter and energy in the Universe must have been <u>compressed</u> into a <u>very small space</u>. Then it <u>exploded</u> and started <u>expanding</u>, and the <u>expansion</u> is still going on now.

3) The age of the Universe can be <u>estimated</u> from the <u>current rate of expansion</u>. We think the Big Bang probably happened about <u>13.7 billion years</u> ago.

4) But... it's difficult to estimate this because it's hard to tell how much the expansion has <u>slowed down</u> since the Big Bang.

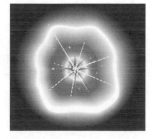

The Big Bang seems to explain most evidence

Most scientists accept the idea of the Big Bang — it's the best way to explain the evidence we have at the moment. But if new evidence turns up, the theory <u>could</u> turn out to be rubbish. After all, there wasn't anyone around 14 billion years ago, taking photos and writing things down in a little notebook.

Looking into Space

There are <u>various objects</u> in space, and they emit or reflect <u>different frequencies</u> of EM radiation. And that's what you need to detect if you want to find out what's going on 'out there'. You have two basic options — stay here on Earth, or send something into space to get a closer look.

Space telescopes have a clearer view than those on Earth

<u>Telescopes</u> help you to see distant objects clearly. But there can be problems...

1) If you're trying to detect light, Earth's <u>atmosphere</u> gets in the way — it absorbs a lot of the light coming from space before it can reach us.

2) Then there's <u>pollution</u>. <u>Light pollution</u> (light thrown up into the sky from streetlamps, etc.) makes it hard to pick out dim objects. And <u>air pollution</u> (e.g. dust particles) can reflect and absorb light coming from space. So to get the best view possible from Earth, a telescope should be on top of a mountain (where there's less atmosphere above it), and far away from any cities (e.g. on Hawaii).

MAGRATH PHOTOGRAPHY/ SCIENCE PHOTO LIBRARY

3) But to avoid the problem of the atmosphere, the thing to do is put your telescope <u>in space</u>, away from the mist and murk down here. The first space telescope (called <u>Hubble</u>) was launched by NASA in 1990. It can see objects that are about a <u>billion times fainter</u> than you can see unaided from Earth.

4) Hubble is an optical telescope (see the next page) and has a <u>mirror</u>. But because it gets a clear view into space, the mirror can be a lot <u>smaller</u> (and easier to make) than you'd need for a similar telescope on Earth.

5) It's not all plain sailing though. Getting a telescope safely into space is hard. And when things go wrong, it's difficult to get the repair men out. Hubble's first pictures were all <u>fuzzy</u>, because the mirror was the <u>wrong shape</u>. NASA had to send some astronauts up there to fix it.

6) So there are advantages to Earth-based telescopes — especially the fact that they're <u>cheaper</u> and <u>easier</u> to build and maintain.

Getting a telescope into space isn't easy

Most telescopes contain a lot of delicate, easily damaged parts. This is why it's so expensive to put them in space — they've got to be strong enough to withstand all the <u>shaking</u> on board the vehicle which takes them into orbit, but they need to be <u>lightweight</u> too.

Looking into Space

Putting a telescope in space isn't the only way to see past the atmosphere.
You can also try looking at different kinds of EM wave...

Different telescopes detect different types of EM wave

To get as full a picture of the Universe as possible, you need to detect different kinds of EM wave.

1) To see very <u>distant</u>, <u>faint</u> objects, you need a <u>very big telescope</u> or <u>lots of smaller ones</u> linked up
   — a bigger telescope 'collects' <u>more light</u> per second, making a brighter image.

2) Astronomers are usually keen to have images with good <u>resolution</u> (i.e. a lot of <u>detail</u>). The
   important thing here is how <u>big the telescope is</u> compared to the <u>wavelength</u> of the radiation.
   The <u>longer</u> the wave, the <u>bigger</u> the telescope you need to get the same level of detail.

Radio telescopes

<u>Radio telescopes</u> need to be <u>very large</u> — because radio waves are very <u>long</u>. But they're not too
badly affected by the Earth's atmosphere, and they let astronomers observe objects which are too
<u>faint</u> for optical telescopes (see below) to detect.

Optical telescopes

<u>Optical telescopes</u> detect <u>visible light</u>. They're used to look at objects close by and in
other galaxies (though they are hampered by the Earth's atmosphere).

X-ray telescopes

<u>X-ray telescopes</u> are a good way to 'see' violent, <u>high-temperature events</u> in space, like <u>exploding stars</u>.
But X-ray telescopes will <u>only</u> work <u>from space</u>, since the Earth's <u>atmosphere absorbs X-rays</u>.
They're also <u>very expensive</u>, so there aren't many about.

An X-ray image of a compact
nebula around the Vela pulsar

CHANDRA X-RAY OBSERVATORY/
NASA/ SCIENCE PHOTO LIBRARY

Warm-Up and Exam Questions

These warm-up questions are here to make sure you know the basics.
If there's anything you've forgotten, check up on the facts before you go any further.

Warm-Up Questions

1) Why are telescopes on Earth often built far away from towns and cities?
2) Describe one benefit of increasing the size of a telescope.
3) What does resolution mean in terms of the images produced by telescopes?

Exam Questions

1   Viewed from Earth, other galaxies seem to be

   A   moving away from us

   B   moving towards us

   C   contracting

   D   expanding

(1 mark)

2   (a)   How do scientists believe the Universe started?

(1 mark)

   (b)   Explain how the relationship between a galaxy's distance from Earth and its observed red shift suggests that the Universe is expanding.

(2 marks)

3   The Hubble telescope was the first optical telescope to be launched into space.

   (a)   What is the main advantage of having an optical telescope in space rather than on Earth?

(1 mark)

   (b)   Give two disadvantages of using an optical space telescope compared to an Earth-based optical telescope.

(2 marks)

4   The dish of the Arecibo radio telescope in Puerto Rico has a diameter of 305 m.

   (a)   It is not always practical to build as large telescopes as the Arecibo telescope. What alternative method is used to improve the resolution of Earth-based radio telescopes?

(1 mark)

   (b)   Explain in terms of wavelength why a radio telescope needs to be much larger than an optical telescope to achieve the same resolution.

(2 marks)

   (c)   Why would an Earth-based X-ray telescope not be useful?

(1 mark)

Revision Summary for Physics 1b

The only way that you can tell if you've learned this section is to test yourself. Try these questions, and if there's something you don't know, it means you need to go back and learn it. And don't miss any questions out — you don't get a choice about what comes up in the exam.

1) Electromagnetic waves don't carry any matter. What <u>do</u> they carry?

2) Draw a diagram to illustrate frequency, wavelength and amplitude.

3) Sketch the EM spectrum with all its details. Put the lowest frequency waves on the left.

4)* Convert to SI units (m, m/s, Hz, s): a) 500 kHz, b) 35 cm, c) 4.6 MHz, d) 4 cm/s, e) 2½ mins.

5)* Find the speed of a wave with frequency 50 kHz and wavelength 0.3 cm.

6) What happens to the energy of an EM wave when it is absorbed? What two effects can this have?

7) Describe the different ways that short and long-wave radio signals 'get around'.

8) Describe two uses of microwaves, and explain why microwaves are suitable for these uses.

9) a) Which types of EM wave are commonly used to send signals along optical fibres?
   b) Explain why sending data by optical fibre might be better than broadcasting it as a radio signal.

10)* In which of the cases A to D below would the ray of light be totally internally reflected?
    (The critical angle for glass is approximately 42°.)

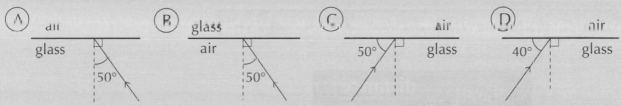

11) Which is generally more hazardous — low frequency or high frequency EM radiation?

12) Describe the main <u>known</u> dangers of microwaves, infrared, visible light, UV and X-rays.

13) Explain how X-rays can be useful in hospitals.

14) Draw diagrams illustrating analogue and digital signals. What advantages do digital signals have?

15) Sketch an atom, showing its protons, neutrons and electrons.

16) Explain what isotopes are. What does it mean when an isotope is 'unstable'?

17) Oxygen atoms contain 8 protons. What is the difference between oxygen-16 and oxygen-18?

18) Radioactive decay is a totally random process. Explain what this means.

19) Describe in detail the nature and properties of the three types of radiation: α, β and γ.

20) The data below shows the count rate for a radioactive source at various times.

Time (mins)	0	20	40	60	80	100	120
Count/minute	750	568	431	327	247	188	142

    a)* Plot a graph of this data and use it to find the half-life of the substance.
    b) The source is a γ emitter. Would it be most suitable for use in A, B or C? Explain your answer.
      A — as a medical tracer   B — in a smoke detector   C — to sterilise medical instruments

21) Explain how radiation damages the human body — a) at low doses; b) at high doses.

22) Explain what precautions you should take to protect yourself from
    a) X-rays, if you are a radiographer   b) alpha radiation, in a school laboratory
                          c) gamma rays, if you work at a nuclear reprocessing plant

23) Describe the 'Big Bang' theory for the origin of the Universe. What evidence is there for this theory?

24) How long ago do we think the Universe began?

25) How are space telescopes better than telescopes on Earth?

26) Why are space telescopes so expensive and sometimes so troublesome?

27) Describe one advantage and one disadvantage of optical, radio and X-ray telescopes.

* Answers on page 222.

Velocity and Acceleration

Speed and velocity aren't the same thing, you know. There's more to velocity than meets the eye.

Speed and velocity are both how fast you're going

Speed and velocity are both measured in <u>m/s</u> (or km/h or mph). They both simply say <u>how fast</u> you're going, but there's a <u>subtle difference</u> between them which <u>you need to know</u>:

> <u>Speed</u> is just <u>how fast</u> you're going (for example, 30 mph or 20 m/s),
> with no regard to the direction. But velocity must also have the
> direction specified, for example, 30 mph north or 20 m/s, 060°.

Seems a bit fussy I know, but they expect you to remember that distinction, so there you go.

Speed, distance and time — the formula:

$$\text{speed} = \frac{\text{distance}}{\text{time}}$$

You really ought to get <u>pretty slick</u> with this <u>very easy formula</u>.
As usual the <u>formula triangle</u> version makes it all a bit of a <u>breeze</u>:

You just need to try and think up some interesting word for
remembering the <u>order</u> of the <u>letters</u> in the triangle, s ^{d} t.
Erm... sedit, perhaps... well, you think up your own.

Example

> A cat skulks 20 m in 35 seconds. Find:
>
> a) its speed.
>
> b) how long it takes to skulk 75 m.

<u>Answer:</u>   Using the formula triangle:
a) s = d ÷ t = 20 ÷ 35 = <u>0.57 m/s</u>   b) t = d ÷ s = 75 ÷ 0.57 = 131 s = <u>2 min 11 s</u>

A lot of the time we tend to use the words 'speed' and 'velocity' interchangeably.
For example, to calculate velocity you'd just use the above formula for speed instead.

Velocity and Acceleration

I expect you were anxiously wondering where the 'acceleration' bit had got to. Don't worry, here it is...

Acceleration is how quickly you're speeding up

Acceleration is definitely not the same as velocity or speed.
Every time you read or write the word acceleration, remind yourself:

"Acceleration is completely different from velocity. Acceleration is how quickly the velocity is changing."

Velocity is a simple idea. Acceleration is altogether more subtle, which is why it's confusing.

Acceleration — the formula:

$$\text{acceleration} = \frac{\text{change in velocity}}{\text{time taken}}$$

Well, it's just another formula. Just like all the others.

Stick the three bits in a formula triangle, and hey presto:

Mind you, there are two tricky things with this one:

First there's the "Δv", which means working out the 'change in velocity' (as shown in the example below), rather than just putting a simple value for speed or velocity in.

Secondly there's the units of acceleration, which are m/s².
Not m/s, which is velocity, but m/s². Got it? No? Let's try once more: Not m/s, but m/s².

Example

A skulking cat accelerates steadily from 2 m/s to 6 m/s in 5.6 s. Find its acceleration.

Answer: Using the formula triangle:
a = Δv ÷ t = (6 − 2) ÷ 5.6 = 4 ÷ 5.6 = 0.71 m/s²

All pretty basic stuff, I'd say.

Remember — speed, velocity and acceleration are all different

Speed cameras measure the speed of motorists, using two photos taken a fraction of a second apart. Lines painted on the road help them work out how far the car travelled between the photos — and so how fast it was going. And the photos always have the car's number plate in them. Clever, eh?

D–T and V–T Graphs

Make sure you learn all these details about <u>distance-time</u> and <u>velocity-time graphs</u> really carefully. Make sure you can <u>distinguish</u> between them too.

Distance-time graphs

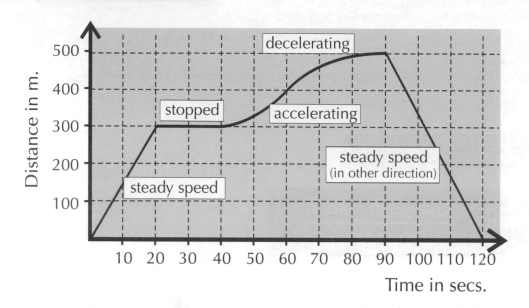

Very important notes:

1) <u>Gradient</u> = <u>speed</u>.

2) <u>Flat</u> sections are where it's <u>stopped</u>.

3) The <u>steeper</u> the graph, the <u>faster</u> it's going.

4) <u>Downhill</u> sections mean it's <u>going back</u> toward its starting point.

5) <u>Curves</u> represent <u>acceleration</u> or deceleration.

6) A <u>steepening</u> curve means it's <u>speeding up</u> (increasing gradient).

7) A <u>levelling off</u> curve means it's <u>slowing down</u> (decreasing gradient).

The *gradient* of a *distance-time* graph = the *speed*

For example, the <u>speed</u> of the <u>return</u> section of the graph is:

$$\text{Speed} = \text{gradient} = \frac{\text{vertical}}{\text{horizontal}} = \frac{500}{30} = \underline{16.7 \text{ m/s}}$$

Don't forget that you have to use the <u>scales</u> of the axes to work out the gradient.

D–T and V–T Graphs

Velocity-time graphs

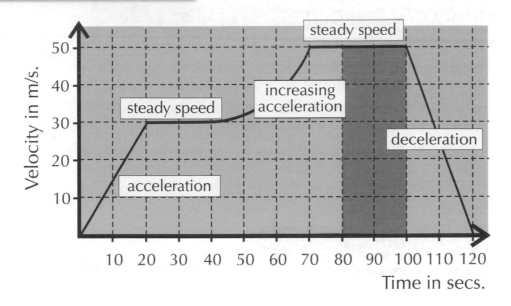

Very important notes:

1) Gradient = acceleration.

2) Flat sections represent steady speed.

3) The steeper the graph, the greater the acceleration or deceleration.

4) Uphill sections (/) are acceleration and downhill sections (\) are deceleration.

5) The area under any section of the graph (or all of it) is equal to the distance travelled in that time interval.

6) A curve means changing acceleration.

Calculating acceleration, speed and distance from a V-T graph

1) The acceleration represented by the first section of the graph is:

$$\text{Acceleration} = \text{gradient} = \frac{\text{vertical}}{\text{horizontal}} = \frac{30}{20} = 1.5 \text{ m/s}^2$$

2) The speed at any point is simply found by reading the value off the velocity axis.

3) The distance travelled in any time interval is equal to the area under the graph. For example, the distance travelled between t = 80 s and t = 100 s is equal to the shaded area which is equal to 1000 m.

Don't get the two types and what they show confused

The tricky thing about these two types of graph is that they can look pretty much the same but represent different kinds of motion. Make sure you learn all the numbered points, and whenever you're reading a motion graph, check the axis labels carefully so you know which type of graph it is.

Mass, Weight and Gravity

The only thing that stops you flying off the planet into space is gravity. You'd be <u>very lost</u> without it.

Gravity is the force of attraction between all masses

<u>Gravity</u> attracts <u>all</u> masses, but you only notice it when one of the masses is <u>really really big</u>, e.g. a planet. The <u>larger</u> the <u>mass</u> the <u>larger</u> its <u>gravitational pull</u>. So, anything near a planet or star is <u>attracted</u> to it <u>very strongly</u>. This has <u>three</u> important effects:

1) On the surface of a planet, it makes all things <u>accelerate</u> towards the <u>ground</u> (all with the <u>same</u> acceleration, g, which is about <u>10 m/s²</u> on Earth).

2) It gives everything a <u>weight</u>.

3) It keeps <u>planets</u>, <u>moons</u> and <u>satellites</u> in their <u>orbits</u>. The orbit is a <u>balance</u> between the <u>forward</u> motion of the object and the force of gravity pulling it <u>inwards</u>.

Weight and mass are not the same

To understand this you must learn all these facts about mass and weight:

1) <u>Mass</u> is just the <u>amount of 'stuff'</u> in an object. For any given object this will have the same value <u>anywhere</u> in the Universe.

2) <u>Weight</u> is caused by the <u>pull</u> of gravity. In most questions the <u>weight</u> of an object is just the <u>force</u> of gravity pulling it towards the centre of the <u>Earth</u>.

3) An object has the <u>same</u> mass whether it's on <u>Earth</u> or on the <u>Moon</u> — but its <u>weight</u> will be <u>different</u>. A 1 kg mass will <u>weigh less</u> on the moon (about 1.6 N) than it does on <u>Earth</u> (about 10 N), simply because the <u>force</u> of gravity pulling on it is <u>less</u> (because the moon has a smaller mass).

4) Weight is a <u>force</u> measured in <u>newtons</u>. It's measured using a <u>spring balance</u> or <u>newton meter</u>. <u>Mass</u> is <u>not</u> a force. It's measured in <u>kilograms</u> with a <u>mass</u> balance (an old-fashioned pair of balancing scales).

The very important formula relating mass, weight and gravity

$$\text{weight} = \text{mass} \times \text{gravitational field strength}$$

$$W = m \times g$$
(in <u>N</u>)   (in <u>kg</u>)   (in <u>N/kg</u>)

1) Remember, weight and mass are <u>not the same</u>. Mass is in <u>kg</u>, weight is in <u>newtons</u>.

2) The letter 'g' represents the <u>strength of gravity</u>, in N/kg — it's <u>different</u> for <u>different planets</u>. On Earth g ≈ 10 N/kg. On the Moon, where the gravity is weaker, g is only about 1.6 N/kg.

3) This formula is <u>hideously easy</u> to use:

<u>EXAMPLE</u>: What is the weight, in newtons, of a 5 kg mass, both on Earth and on the Moon?

<u>ANSWER</u>: 'W = m × g'. So on Earth: W = 5 × 10 = <u>50 N</u>   (The weight of the 5 kg mass is 50 N.)
On the Moon: W = 5 × 1.6 = <u>8 N</u>   (The weight of the 5 kg mass is 8 N.)

See what I mean? Hideously easy — as long as you've learnt what all the letters mean.

Warm-Up and Exam Questions

Here's another set of questions to test your knowledge. Make sure you can answer them all before you go steaming on.

Warm-Up Questions

1) A boy hops 10 m in 5 seconds. What is his speed?
2) What are the units of acceleration? and of mass? and of weight?
3) What does the gradient of a distance-time graph show?
4) A car goes from 0 to 30 m/s in 6 seconds. Calculate its acceleration.
5) Name the force that keeps the Earth orbiting around the Sun.

Exam Questions

1   A racing car is driven round a circular track of length 2400 m at a constant speed of 45 m/s.

    (a)   Explain why the car's velocity is not constant.

(1 mark)

    (b)   How long does the car take to travel once around the track?

(2 marks)

    (c)   On another lap, the speed of the car increases from 45 m/s to 59 m/s over a period of 5 seconds. What is its acceleration?

(2 marks)

2   The graph below shows the distance of a shuttle-bus from its start point plotted against time.

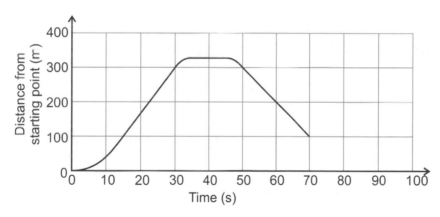

    (a)   Between 15 and 30 seconds:

        (i)   how far does the bus travel?

(1 mark)

        (ii) how fast is the bus going?

(2 marks)

    (b)   For how long does the bus stop?

(1 mark)

    (c)   Describe the bus's speed and direction between 50 and 70 seconds.

(1 mark)

    (d)   Between 70 and 100 seconds, the bus slows, coming to a standstill at 100 s to finish up where it started. Show this on the graph.

(1 mark)

Exam Questions

3 The diagram below shows the velocity of a cyclist plotted against time.

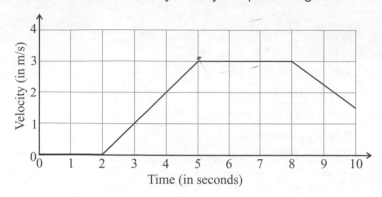

(a) Describe the motion of the cyclist between 5 and 8 seconds.

(1 mark)

(b) What is happening to the cyclist's speed between 8 and 10 seconds?

(1 mark)

(c) How far did the cyclist travel between 2 and 5 seconds.

(1 mark)

$D = \frac{S}{T} = \quad m = \frac{m/s}{s} \quad \frac{3}{3} = 1 m$

4 A spring increases in length when weights are suspended from it, as shown. When a metal ball with a mass of 0.1 kg is suspended from the spring, the spring stretches by 3 cm.

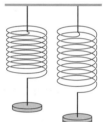

If the experiment was repeated on Mars, the spring would only be stretched by 1.1 cm.

(a) Explain why the spring would stretch less on Mars, given that the Earth's mass is 5.97×10^{24} kg and the mass of Mars is 6.42×10^{23} kg.

(3 marks)

(b) Estimate g on Mars, assuming that g on Earth is 10 m/s².

(2 marks)

5 A stone falls from the edge of a cliff. After falling for 1 second the stone has a downwards velocity of 10 m/s.

(a) What is the stone's acceleration during the first second it falls?

(1 mark)

(b) Assuming no air resistance, what is the stone's velocity after three seconds of falling?

(1 mark)

(c) The stone has a mass of 0.12 kg. What is its weight?

(1 mark)

(d) What effect would doubling the stone's mass have on its acceleration due to gravity?

(1 mark)

6 Which of the following masses exert a gravitational attraction on other masses — the Sun, the Earth, a human being, a feather, an atom?

(1 mark)

The Three Laws of Motion

Around about the time of the Great Plague in the 1660s, a chap called <u>Isaac Newton</u> worked out the <u>Three Laws of Motion</u>. At first they might seem kind of obscure or irrelevant, but to be perfectly blunt, if you can't understand these <u>three simple laws</u> then you'll never understand <u>forces and motion</u>.

First law — *balanced forces* mean *no change* in *velocity*

So long as the forces on an object are all <u>balanced</u>, then it'll just <u>stay still</u>,
or else if it's already moving it'll just carry on at the <u>same velocity</u>
— so long as the forces are all <u>balanced</u>.

1) When a train or car or bus or anything else is <u>moving</u> at a <u>constant velocity</u> then the <u>forces</u> on it must all be <u>balanced</u>.

2) Never let yourself entertain the <u>ridiculous idea</u> that things need a constant overall force to <u>keep</u> them moving — NO NO NO NO NO!

3) To keep going at a <u>steady speed</u>, there must be <u>zero resultant force</u> — and don't you forget it.

Second law — a *resultant force* means *acceleration* $F = ma$ *

If there is an <u>unbalanced force</u>, then the object
will <u>accelerate</u> in that direction.

1) An <u>unbalanced</u> force will always produce <u>acceleration</u> (or deceleration).

2) This 'acceleration' can take <u>five</u> different forms: <u>Starting</u>, <u>stopping</u>, <u>speeding up</u>, <u>slowing down</u> and <u>changing direction</u>.

3) On a force diagram, the <u>arrows</u> will be <u>unequal</u>:

<u>Don't ever say</u>: "If something's moving there must be an overall resultant force acting on it".

Not so. If there's an <u>overall</u> force it will always <u>accelerate</u>.

You get <u>steady</u> speed from <u>balanced</u> forces.

The Three Laws of Motion

Three points which should be obvious:

1) The bigger the <u>force</u>, the <u>greater</u> the <u>acceleration</u> or <u>deceleration</u>.
2) The bigger the <u>mass</u>, the <u>smaller the acceleration</u>.
3) To get a <u>big</u> mass to accelerate <u>as fast</u> as a <u>small</u> mass it needs
   a <u>bigger</u> force. Just think about pushing <u>heavy</u> trolleys and it should all seem <u>fairly obvious</u>.

The overall *unbalanced force* is often called the *resultant force*

Any <u>resultant force</u> will produce <u>acceleration</u>, and this is the <u>formula</u> for it:

$$F = ma \quad \text{or} \quad a = F \div m$$

m = mass, a = acceleration, F is always the <u>resultant force</u>.

Resultant force is really important — especially for 'F = ma'

The notion of <u>resultant force</u> is a really important one for you to get your head round.
It's not especially tricky, it's just that it seems to get <u>ignored</u>.

In most <u>real</u> situations there are at least <u>two forces</u> acting on an object along any direction.
The <u>overall</u> effect of these forces will decide the <u>motion</u> of the object — whether it will <u>accelerate</u>,
<u>decelerate</u> or stay at a <u>steady speed</u>. If the forces all point along the same direction, the 'overall effect'
is found by just <u>adding or subtracting</u> them. The overall force you get is called the <u>resultant force</u>.
And when you use the <u>formula</u> '<u>F = ma</u>', F must always be the <u>resultant force</u>.

Example

A car of mass of 1750 kg has an engine which provides a driving force of 5200 N.
At 70 mph the drag force acting on the car is 5150 N.

Find its acceleration:

a) when first setting off from rest   b) at 70 mph.

<u>Answer</u>: First draw a force diagram for both cases (no need to show the vertical forces):

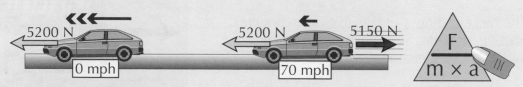

Work out the resultant force in each case, and apply 'F = ma' using the formula triangle:

a) Resultant force = 5200 N   b) Resultant force = 5200 − 5150 = 50 N
    a = F/m = 5200 ÷ 1750 = <u>3.0 m/s²</u>   a = F/m = 50 ÷ 1750 = <u>0.03 m/s²</u>

The Three Laws of Motion

The third law — *reaction forces*

> If object A <u>exerts a force</u> on object B then object B
> exerts <u>the exact opposite force</u> on object A.

1) That means if you <u>push</u> something, say a shopping trolley, the trolley will <u>push back</u> against you, <u>just as hard</u>.

2) And as soon as you <u>stop</u> pushing, <u>so does the trolley</u>. Kinda clever really.

3) So far so good. The slightly tricky thing to get your head round is this — if the forces are always equal, <u>how does anything ever go anywhere</u>? The important thing to remember is that the two forces are acting on <u>different objects</u>.

Example

Think about a pair of ice skaters:

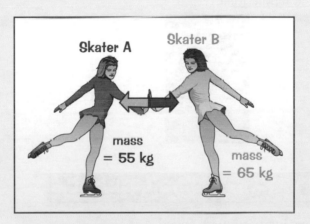

Skater A

Skater B

mass = 55 kg

mass = 65 kg

When skater A pushes on skater B (the '<u>action</u>' force), she feels an equal and opposite force from skater B's hand (the '<u>reaction</u>' force).

Both skaters feel the <u>same sized force</u>, in <u>opposite directions</u>, and so accelerate away from each other.

Skater A will be <u>accelerated</u> more than skater B, though, because she has a smaller mass — remember <u>F = ma</u>.

It's the same sort of thing when you go <u>swimming</u>. You <u>push</u> back against the <u>water</u> with your arms and legs, and the water pushes you forwards with an <u>equal-sized force</u> in the <u>opposite direction</u>.

Three laws of motion and one important task — learn them

This is like... proper Physics. It was <u>pretty fantastic</u> at the time — suddenly people understood how forces and motion worked and so they could work out the <u>orbits of planets</u> and everything. Inspired? No? Shame. Learn them anyway — you're really going to struggle in the exam if you don't.

Friction Forces

Friction is found nearly everywhere and it acts to <u>slow down</u> and <u>stop</u> moving objects. Sometimes friction is a pain, but at other times it's very helpful.

1) *Friction is always there to slow things down*

1) If an object has <u>no force</u> propelling it along it will always <u>slow down and stop</u> because of <u>friction</u> (unless you're in space where there's nothing to rub against).

2) Friction always acts in the <u>opposite</u> direction to movement.

3) To travel at a <u>steady</u> speed, the driving force needs to <u>balance</u> the frictional forces.

4) You get friction between <u>two surfaces</u> in contact, or when an object passes <u>through a fluid</u> (<u>drag</u>).

Resistance or "drag" from fluids (air or liquid)

The most important factor <u>by far</u> in <u>reducing drag</u> in fluids is keeping the shape of the object <u>streamlined</u>, like fish bodies or boat hulls or bird wings/bodies.

The <u>opposite</u> extreme is a <u>parachute</u> which is about as <u>high drag</u> as you can get — which is, of course, <u>the whole idea</u>.

2) *Drag increases as the speed increases*

Resistance from fluids always <u>increases with speed</u>.

A car has <u>much more</u> friction to <u>work against</u> when travelling at <u>70 mph</u> compared to <u>30 mph</u>. So at 70 mph the engine has to work <u>much harder</u> just to maintain a <u>steady speed</u>.

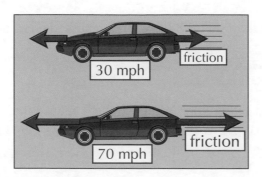

Friction's annoying when it's slowing down your boat, car or lorry...

... but it can be useful too. As well as stopping parachutists ending up as nasty messes on the floor, friction's good for <u>other stuff</u> — e.g. without it, you wouldn't be able to walk or run or skip or write.

Drag and Terminal Velocity

Free-fallers reach a *terminal speed*

When free-falling objects <u>first set off</u> they have <u>much more</u> force <u>accelerating</u> them than <u>resistance</u> slowing them down. As the <u>speed</u> increases the resistance <u>builds up</u>.

This gradually <u>reduces</u> the <u>acceleration</u> until eventually the <u>resistance force</u> is <u>equal</u> to the <u>accelerating force</u> and then it won't be able to accelerate any more.
It will have reached its maximum speed or <u>terminal speed</u>.

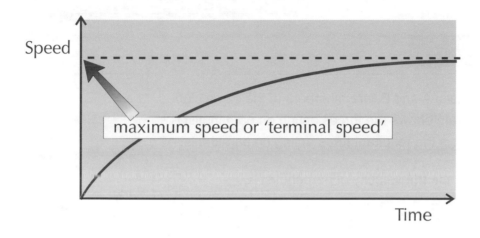

Terminal speed of *falling objects* depends on *shape* and *area*

1) The <u>accelerating force</u> acting on <u>all falling objects</u> is <u>gravity</u>, and it would make them all accelerate at the <u>same rate</u> if it wasn't for <u>air resistance</u>.

2) To prove this, on the Moon (where there's <u>no air</u>) hamsters and feathers dropped simultaneously will <u>hit the ground together</u>.

3) However, on Earth, <u>air resistance</u> causes things to fall at <u>different speeds</u>, and the <u>terminal speed</u> of any object is determined by its <u>drag</u> compared to its <u>weight</u>.

4) The drag depends on its <u>shape and area</u>.

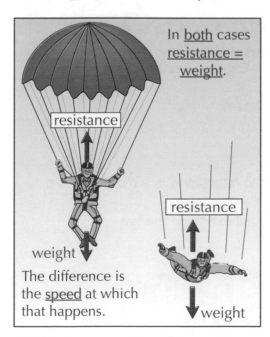

In <u>both</u> cases <u>resistance = weight</u>.

The difference is the <u>speed</u> at which that happens.

5) The best example is the <u>human skydiver</u>.

6) Without his parachute open he has quite a <u>small area</u> and a force equal to his <u>weight</u> pulling him down.

7) He reaches a <u>terminal speed</u> of about <u>120 mph</u>.

8) But with the parachute <u>open</u>, there's much more <u>air resistance</u> (at any given speed) and still only the same force pulling him down.

9) This means his <u>terminal speed</u> comes right down to about <u>15 mph</u>.

10) This is a <u>safe speed</u> to hit the ground at.

Warm-Up and Exam Questions

You're just over halfway through this section and it's time for some more questions. Wahey.

Warm-Up Questions

1) What is the resultant force on a body moving at constant velocity?
2) What happens to the acceleration of a body if the resultant force on it is doubled?
3) A rowing boat is being pulled to shore by two people with a force of 3 N each.
   A force of 1 N is resisting the movement. What is the resultant force on the boat?
4) In which direction does friction act on a body — with or against the body's motion?

Exam Questions

1 Two parachutists, A and B, are members of the same club.

   (a) The diagram shows the forces acting on parachutist A.

   900 N

   900 N

   (i) What is the resultant force acting on parachutist A?

   (1 mark)

   (ii) Describe the velocity of parachutist A.

   (1 mark)

   (b) Parachutist B is in free fall. The total mass of parachutist B and her equipment is 70 kg.

   (i) What will the force of air resistance on parachutist B be when she reaches terminal velocity? Explain your answer.

   (2 marks)

   (ii) Which parachutist, A or B, would have a higher terminal velocity? Explain your answer.

   (3 marks)

   (c) Explain why a parachutist slows down when they open their parachute.

   (1 mark)

2 Stefan weighs 600 newtons. He is accelerating upwards in a lift at 2.5 m/s².

   (a) The forces acting on Stefan are his weight and the upwards force exerted on him by the floor of the lift. Which force is greater? Explain your answer.

   (1 mark)

   (b) What is the size of the resultant force acting on Stefan?

   (2 marks)

3 Damien's cricket bat has a mass of 1.2 kg. He uses it to hit a ball with a mass of 160 g forwards with a force of 500 N.

   (a) Use Newton's third law to state the force that the ball exerts on the bat. Explain your answer.

   (2 marks)

   (b) Which is greater — the acceleration of the bat or the ball? Explain your answer.

   (2 marks)

Stopping Distances

If you <u>need to stop</u> in a <u>given distance</u>, then the <u>faster</u> you're going, the <u>bigger the braking force</u> you'll need. But real life's not quite that simple — there are loads of <u>other factors</u> too...

Many factors affect your total stopping distance

The stopping distance of a car is the distance covered in the time between the driver <u>first seeing</u> a hazard and the car coming to a <u>complete stop</u>. They're pretty keen on this for exams, so <u>learn it properly</u>. The distance it takes to stop a car is divided into the <u>thinking distance</u> and the <u>braking distance</u>.

1) Thinking distance

"The distance the car travels in the split-second between a hazard appearing and the driver applying the brakes..."

It's affected by <u>three main factors</u>:

a) How <u>fast</u> you're going — obviously. Whatever your reaction time, the <u>faster</u> you're going, the <u>further</u> you'll go.

b) How <u>dopey</u> you are — This is affected by <u>tiredness</u>, <u>drugs</u>, alcohol, <u>old age</u>, and a <u>careless</u> attitude.

c) How the <u>visibility</u> is — lashing rain and oncoming lights, etc. make <u>hazards</u> harder to spot.

> The figures below for typical stopping distances are from the Highway Code. It's frightening to see just how long it takes to stop when you're going at 70 mph.

2) Braking distance

"The distance the car travels during its deceleration while the brakes are being applied..."

It's affected by <u>four main factors</u>:

a) How <u>fast</u> you're going — The <u>faster</u> you're going, the <u>further</u> you'll go before you stop. More details on page 80.

b) How <u>heavy</u> the load is — with the <u>same</u> brakes, <u>a heavily laden</u> vehicle takes <u>longer to stop</u>. A car won't stop as quickly if it's full of people and luggage and towing a caravan.

c) The <u>brakes'</u> condition — all brakes must be checked and maintained <u>regularly</u>. Worn or faulty brakes will let you down <u>catastrophically</u> just when you need them the <u>most</u>, i.e. in an <u>emergency</u>.

d) How good the <u>grip</u> is — this depends on <u>three things</u>:
• <u>road surface</u>, • <u>weather</u> conditions, • <u>tyres</u>.

So even at <u>30 mph</u>, you should drive no closer than <u>6 or 7 car lengths</u> away from the car in front — just in case. This is one reason why <u>speed limits</u> are so important, and some <u>residential areas</u> are now <u>20 mph zones</u>.

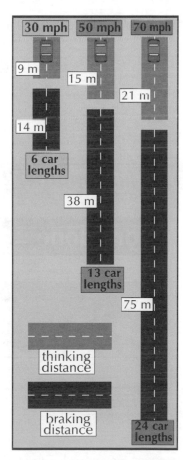

Stop right there — and learn this page...

Leaves and oil spills on roads are <u>serious hazards</u> because they're <u>unexpected</u>. <u>Wet</u> or <u>icy roads</u> are always more <u>slippy</u> than dry roads, but often you only realise this when you try to <u>brake</u> hard. Tyres should have a minimum <u>tread depth</u> of <u>1.6 mm</u> — essential for getting rid of the <u>water</u> in wet conditions. Without <u>tread</u>, a tyre will simply <u>ride</u> on a <u>layer of water</u> and skid <u>very easily</u>.

78

Work Done

Work (like a lot of things) means something slightly different in Physics than it does in everyday life.

Doing **work** involves **transferring energy**

When a force moves an object, ENERGY IS TRANSFERRED and WORK IS DONE.

That statement sounds far more complicated than it needs to. Try this:

1) Whenever something moves, something else is providing some sort of 'effort' to move it.
2) The thing putting the effort in needs a supply of energy (like fuel or food or electricity, etc.).
3) It then does 'work' by moving the object — and one way or another it transfers the energy it receives (as fuel) into other forms.
4) Whether this energy is transferred 'usefully' (e.g. by lifting a load) or is 'wasted' (e.g. lost as heat through friction), you can still say that 'work is done'. Just like Batman and Bruce Wayne, 'work done' and 'energy transferred' are indeed 'one and the same'.   (And they're both given in joules.)

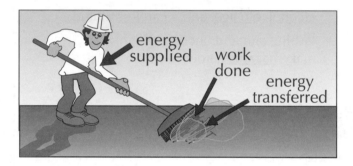

It's just **another trivial formula**:

work done = force × distance

Whether the force is friction or weight or tension in a rope, it's always the same. To find how much energy has been transferred (in J), just multiply the force in N by the distance moved in m.

Example

Some naughty kids drag an old tractor tyre 5 m over rough ground.
They pull with a total force of 340 N. Find the energy transferred.

Answer: W = F × d = 340 × 5 = 1700 J.

PHYSICS 2(i) — FORCES IN MOTION

Kinetic and Potential Energy

<u>Kinetic energy</u> is the energy something has when it is moving. Think about it — if you bump into something <u>heavy</u> that's rushing downhill at <u>top speed</u>, it will do a lot more damage than if you bump into something <u>light</u> that's just <u>sitting there</u>.

Kinetic energy is energy of movement

Anything that's <u>moving</u> has <u>kinetic energy</u>.
There's a slightly <u>tricky formula</u> for it, so you have to concentrate a little bit <u>harder</u> for this one.
But hey, that's life — it can be tough sometimes:

$$\text{kinetic energy} = \tfrac{1}{2} \times \text{mass} \times \text{speed}^2$$

Example

A car with a mass of 2450 kg is travelling at 38 m/s.
Calculate its kinetic energy.

<u>Answer:</u>   It's easy. You just plug the numbers into the formula.
Watch the 'v^2' though...
K.E. $= \tfrac{1}{2}mv^2$
$= \tfrac{1}{2} \times 2450 \times 38^2$
$= \underline{1\ 768\ 900\ J}$ (<u>joules</u> because it's <u>energy</u>)

38 m/s

2450 kg

Remember, the <u>kinetic energy</u> of something depends both on <u>mass</u> and <u>speed</u>.
The <u>more it weighs</u> and the <u>faster it's going</u>, the <u>bigger</u> its kinetic energy will be.

small mass, not fast
low kinetic energy

big fast
lorries Ltd

big mass, very fast
high kinetic energy

Kinetic and Potential Energy

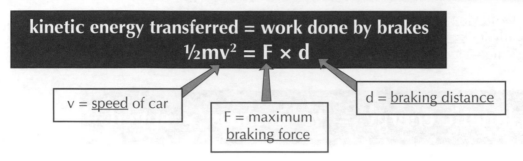

Stopping distances *increase alarmingly* with *extra speed*
— mainly because of the *v²* bit in *K.E. = ½mv²*

To stop a car, the <u>kinetic energy</u>, ½mv², has to be <u>converted to heat energy</u> at the <u>brakes and tyres</u>:

> **kinetic energy transferred = work done by brakes**
> **½mv² = F × d**

v = <u>speed</u> of car

F = maximum <u>braking force</u>

d = <u>braking distance</u>

<u>Learn this really well</u>:

1) If you <u>double the speed</u>, you double the value of v, but the v² means that the <u>kinetic energy</u> is actually increased by a factor of <u>four</u>.

2) However, 'F' is always the <u>maximum possible</u> braking force which <u>can't</u> be increased, so <u>d</u> must also increase by a factor of <u>four</u> to make the equation <u>balance</u>.

3) So, if you go <u>twice as fast</u>, the <u>braking distance</u> 'd' must increase by a <u>factor of four</u> to dissipate the extra <u>kinetic energy</u>.

Energy can be *stored* as *potential energy*

Elastic potential energy

Things like springs and elastic bands are <u>elastic</u> — if you stretch them then let go, they go back to their original shape. <u>Elastic potential energy</u> is the energy <u>stored</u> when work is done on an elastic object to <u>change its shape</u>.

This is released as kinetic energy (and a bit of heat) when the object springs back into shape.

Gravitational potential energy

Gravitational potential energy (PE) is the energy <u>stored in an object</u> when you raise it to a height <u>against</u> gravity.

You can think of PE as a way of <u>storing kinetic energy</u>. You have to <u>move</u> something to increase its gravitational potential energy, and that energy is only released when the object <u>falls</u> (movement again).

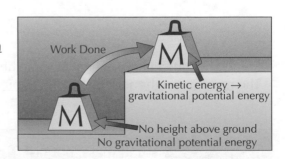

Work Done

Kinetic energy → gravitational potential energy

No height above ground
No gravitational potential energy

K.E. and P.E. are closely linked in falling objects

This page explains why braking distance goes up so much with speed. Bet you've been dying to find that out — and now you know. What you probably <u>don't</u> know yet, though, is that rather lovely formula at the top of the last page. I mean, it's got more than three letters in it — how special is that?

Momentum and Collisions

A <u>large</u> rugby player running very <u>fast</u> is going to be a lot harder to stop than a scrawny one out for a Sunday afternoon stroll — that's <u>momentum</u> for you.

Momentum = mass × velocity

1) The <u>greater</u> the <u>mass</u> of an object and the <u>greater</u> its <u>velocity</u>, the <u>more momentum</u> the object has.

2) Momentum is a <u>vector</u> quantity — it has size <u>and</u> direction (like <u>velocity</u>, rather than speed).

Momentum (kg m/s) = mass (kg) × velocity (m/s)

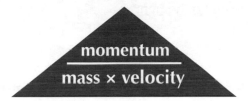

$$\frac{\text{momentum}}{\text{mass} \times \text{velocity}}$$

Momentum before = momentum after

<u>Momentum is conserved</u> when no external forces act, i.e. the total momentum <u>after</u> is the <u>same</u> as it was <u>before</u>.

Example 1:

Two skaters approach each other, collide and move off together as shown. At what velocity do they move after the collision?

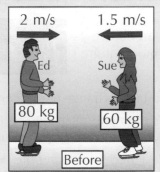

2 m/s   1.5 m/s   velocity (v) = ?

Ed   Sue

80 kg   60 kg   (80+60) kg

Before   After

1) Choose which direction is <u>positive</u>.
   I'll say '<u>positive</u>' means '<u>to the right</u>'.

2) Total momentum <u>before</u> collision

   = momentum of Ed + momentum of Sue

   = (80 × 2) + [60 × (–1.5)] = <u>70 kg m/s</u>

3) Total momentum <u>after</u> collision

   = momentum of Ed and Sue together

   = <u>140 × v</u>

4) So 140 × v = 70,

   i.e. <u>v = 0.5 m/s to the right</u>

Momentum and Collisions

You know what they say — when it comes to <u>momentum</u>, one example is never enough.

Example 2:

A gun fires a bullet as shown. At what speed does the gun move backwards?

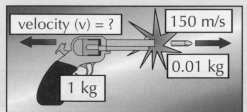

1) Choose which direction is <u>positive</u>.

   Again, I reckon 'positive' means '<u>to the right</u>'.

2) <u>Total momentum before</u> firing

   = <u>0 kg m/s</u>

3) <u>Total momentum after</u> firing

   = momentum of bullet + momentum of gun

   = (0.01 × 150) + (1 × v)

   = <u>1.5 + v</u>

4) So 1.5 + v = 0, i.e. v = −1.5 m/s

   So the gun moves backwards at <u>1.5 m/s</u>.

   This is the gun's <u>recoil</u>.

Forces *cause* changes *in* momentum

1) When a <u>force</u> acts on an object, it causes a <u>change</u> in momentum:

$$\text{Force acting (N)} = \frac{\text{change in momentum (kg m/s)}}{\text{time taken for change to happen (s)}}$$

2) A <u>larger</u> force means a <u>faster</u> change of momentum (and so a greater <u>acceleration</u>).

3) Likewise, if someone's momentum changes <u>very quickly</u> (like in a <u>car crash</u>), the <u>forces</u> on the body will be very <u>large</u>, and more likely to cause <u>injury</u>.

4) This is why cars are designed to slow people down over a <u>longer time</u> when they have a crash — the longer it takes for a change in <u>momentum</u>, the <u>smaller</u> the <u>force</u>.

| <u>CRUMPLE ZONES</u> crumple on impact, <u>increasing the time</u> taken for the car to stop. | <u>SEAT BELTS</u> stretch slightly, <u>increasing the time</u> taken for the wearer to stop. This <u>reduces the forces</u> acting on the chest. | <u>AIR BAGS</u> also slow you down more <u>gradually</u>. |

Momentum is a pretty fundamental bit of Physics — learn it well

Momentum is always <u>conserved</u> in collisions and explosions when there are no external forces acting. The bit at the bottom of the page is just another way of writing Newton's 2nd law of motion. Learn it.

Warm-Up and Exam Questions

It's very nearly the end of this section. But don't shed a tear — try these questions instead.

Warm-Up Questions

1) What is meant by 'thinking distance' as part of the total stopping distance of a car?
2) What must be added to thinking distance to find the total stopping distance of a car?
3) Why can 'work done' be measured in the same units as energy?
4) What is gravitational potential energy?
5) If the speed of a car triples, what happens to its kinetic energy?
6) Give the equation for momentum.
7) Name two safety features that increase the time taken for the car driver to stop in a collision.

Exam Questions

1   The graph below shows how thinking distance and stopping distance vary with speed.

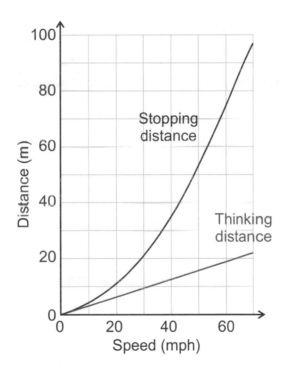

(a) Use the graph to determine the following distances for a car travelling at 40 mph.

(i)   Thinking distance

(ii) Total stopping distance

(iii) Braking distance

(3 marks)

(b) Which is greater at 50 miles per hour, thinking distance or braking distance?

(1 mark)

(c) Is stopping distance proportional to speed? How can this be seen from the graph?

(2 marks)

Exam Questions

2   Two ice hockey players are skating towards the puck. Player A has a mass of 100 kg and is travelling right at 6 m/s. Player B has a mass of 80 kg and is travelling left at 9 m/s.
(a)   Calculate the momentum of:
(i)   Player A
(1 mark)

(ii)   Player B
(1 mark)

(b)   The two players collide and become joined together.
(i)   What is the speed of the two joined players just after the collision?
(2 marks)

(ii)   Which direction do they move in?
(1 mark)

3   A train with a mass of 40 000 kg is driven 700 m while accelerating at 1.05 m/s².

(a)   Calculate the driving force acting on the train. Ignore any friction.
(2 marks)

(b)   Find the work done by the driving force.
(1 mark)

(c)   The train reaches a constant speed at which its kinetic energy is 29 400 000 J.
It then decelerates with a braking force of 29 400 N.
Calculate its braking distance.
(2 marks)

(d)   How would the braking distance change if the train was only going half as fast when it began to decelerate?
(1 mark)

(e)   What form of energy is the train's kinetic energy transformed into when the brakes are applied?
(1 mark)

4   A car with a mass of 2750 kg is travelling at 12 m/s.
(a)   Calculate its kinetic energy.
(2 marks)

(b)   A van with a mass of 3120 kg is travelling at the same speed.
Which has more kinetic energy?
(1 mark)

(c)   How would the kinetic energy of the car change if its speed was doubled?
(1 mark)

(d)   The car accelerates and reaches a constant speed at which its kinetic energy is 550 000 J. The car then brakes and comes to rest in 25 m.
Calculate its braking force.
(2 marks)

Revision Summary for Physics 2(i)

Yay   revision summary! I <u>know</u> these are your favourite bits of the book, all those jolly questions. There are lots of formulas and laws and picky little details to learn in this section. So, practise these questions till you can do them all standing on one leg with your arms behind your back whilst being tickled on the nose with a purple ostrich feather. Or something.

1)   What's the difference between speed and velocity? Give an example of each.

2)*   Write down the formula for working out speed. Find the speed of a partly chewed mouse which hobbles 3.2 m in 35 s. Find how far he would get in 25 minutes.

3)*   A speed camera is set up in a 30 mph (13.4 m/s) zone. It takes two photographs 0.5 s apart. A car travels 6.3 m between the two photographs. Was the car breaking the speed limit?

4)   What is acceleration? What are its units?

5)*   Write down the formula for acceleration. What's the acceleration of a soggy pea, flicked from rest to a speed of 14 m/s in 0.4 s?

6)   Sketch a typical distance-time graph and point out all the important parts of it.

7)   Explain how to calculate velocity from a distance-time graph.

8)   Sketch a typical velocity-time graph and point out all the important parts of it.

9)   Explain how to find speed, distance and acceleration from a velocity-time graph.

10)   What is gravity? List three effects gravity produces.

11)   Explain the difference between mass and weight. What units are they measured in?

12)   What's the formula for weight? Illustrate it with a worked example of your own.

13)   Write down Newton's first law of motion. Illustrate it with a diagram.

14)   Write down Newton's second law of motion. Illustrate it with a diagram. What's the formula for it?

15)*   A force of 30 N pushes on a trolley of mass 4 kg. What will be its acceleration?

16)*   What's the mass of a cat which accelerates at 9.8 m/s^2 when acted on by a force of 56 N?

17)   Explain what "resultant force" is. Illustrate with a diagram.

18)*   A skydiver has a mass of 75 kg. At 80 mph, the drag force on the skydiver is 650 N. Find the acceleration of the skydiver at 80 mph (take g = 10 N/kg).

19)   Write down Newton's third law of motion. Illustrate it with a diagram.

20)   Describe how friction in fluids is affected by speed.

21)   What is "terminal velocity"?

22)   What are the two main factors affecting the terminal velocity of a falling object?

23)   What are the two different parts of the overall stopping distance of a car?

24)   List two factors that affect each of the two sections of stopping distance.

25)*   What's the formula for work done? A crazy dog drags a big branch 12 m over the next-door neighbour's front lawn, pulling with a force of 535 N. How much work was done?

26)*   Write down the formula for kinetic energy. Find the KE of a 78 kg sheep moving at 23 m/s.

27)   Explain why the stopping distance of a car increases so much with speed.

28)   What are elastic potential energy and gravitational potential energy?

29)*   Write down the formula for momentum. Find the momentum of a 78 kg sheep falling at 15 m/s.

30)   If the total momentum of a system before a collision is zero, what is the total momentum of the system after the collision?

31)*   A gymnast (mass 50 kg) jumps off a beam and hits the floor at a speed of 7 m/s. She bends her knees and stops moving in 0.5 s. What is the average force acting on her?

32)   Explain how air bags, seat belts and crumple zones reduce the risk of serious injury in a car crash.

* Answers on page 224.

Static Electricity

Static electricity is all about charges which are <u>not</u> free to move. This causes them to build up in one place and it often ends with a <u>spark</u> or a <u>shock</u> when they do finally move.

Build-up of *static* is caused by *friction*

1) When two <u>insulating</u> materials are <u>rubbed</u> together, electrons will be <u>scraped off</u> one of them and <u>dumped</u> onto the other.

2) This will leave a <u>positive</u> static charge on one and a <u>negative</u> static charge on the other.

3) <u>Which way</u> the electrons are transferred depends on the <u>two materials</u> involved.

4) The classic examples are <u>polythene</u> and <u>acetate</u> rods being rubbed with a <u>cloth duster</u>, as shown in the diagrams below.

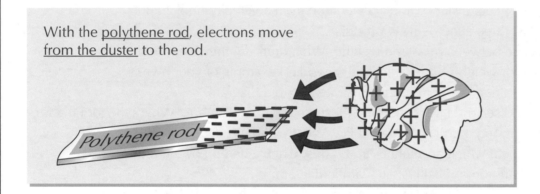

With the <u>polythene rod</u>, electrons move <u>from the duster</u> to the rod.

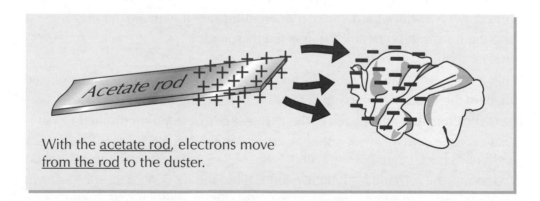

With the <u>acetate rod</u>, electrons move <u>from the rod</u> to the duster.

5) Electrically charged objects <u>attract</u> small objects placed near them. (Try this: rub a balloon with a cloth, then put the balloon near some bits of paper and watch them jump.)

Static electricity is caused by electrons being transferred

Static electricity's great fun. You must have tried it — rubbing a balloon against your jumper and trying to get it to stick to the ceiling. It really works... well, sometimes. <u>Bad hair days</u> are caused by static too — it builds up on your hair, so your strands of hair repel each other. Which is nice...

Static Electricity

Only electrons move — *never the positive charges*

1) <u>Watch out for this in exams</u> — both positive and negative electrostatic charges are only ever produced by the movement of the <u>negative electrons</u>. The positive charges <u>definitely do not move</u>.

2) A <u>positive</u> static charge is always caused by <u>electrons moving away</u> elsewhere and taking their negative charges with them, as shown on the last page.

3) A charged conductor can be <u>discharged safely</u> by connecting it to earth with a <u>metal strap</u>.

4) The electrons flow <u>down</u> the strap to the ground if the charge is <u>negative</u> and flow <u>up</u> the strap from the ground if the charge is <u>positive</u>.

5) The <u>flow</u> of <u>electrical charge</u> is called <u>electric current</u> (see page 91).

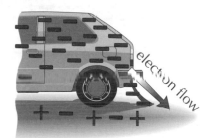 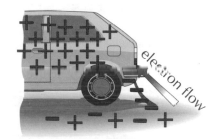

Like *charges repel,* opposite *charges attract*

This is easy and, I'd have thought, <u>kind of obvious</u>.

Two things with <u>opposite</u> electric charges are <u>attracted</u> to each other. Two things with the <u>same</u> electric charge will <u>repel</u> each other.

These forces get <u>weaker</u> the <u>further apart</u> the two things are.

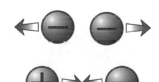

As charge *builds up, so does the* voltage *— causing* sparks

1) The greater the <u>charge</u> on an <u>isolated</u> object, the greater the <u>voltage</u> between it and the earth.

2) If the voltage gets <u>big enough</u> there's a <u>spark</u> which <u>jumps</u> across the gap.

3) High voltage cables can be <u>dangerous</u> for this reason. Big sparks have been known to <u>leap</u> from <u>overhead cables</u> to earth. But not often.

Static Electricity

They like asking you to give <u>quite detailed examples</u> in exams. Make sure you <u>learn all these details</u>.

*Static electricity is **annoying** more often than it is dangerous*

Clothing clings and crackles

When <u>synthetic clothes</u> are <u>dragged</u> over each other (like in a <u>tumble drier</u>) or over your <u>head</u>, electrons get scraped off, leaving <u>static charges</u> on both parts. That leads to the inevitable — <u>attraction</u> (they stick together and cling to you) and little <u>sparks</u> or <u>shocks</u> as the charges <u>rearrange themselves</u>.

*Static electricity can be **dangerous**:*

1) A lot of charge can build up on clothes

1) A lot of <u>static charge</u> can build up on clothes made out of <u>synthetic materials</u> if they rub against other synthetic fabrics — like when wriggling about on a <u>car seat</u>.

2) Eventually, this <u>charge</u> can become <u>large enough</u> to make a <u>spark</u> — which is really bad news if it happens near any <u>inflammable gases</u> or <u>fuel fumes</u>... KABOOM!

2) Lightning

Raindrops and ice <u>bump together</u> inside storm clouds, knocking off electrons and leaving the top of the cloud positively charged and the bottom of the cloud <u>negative</u>. This creates a <u>huge voltage</u> and a <u>big spark</u>.

Earth

So it's not just bad hair days and fun with balloons then

<u>Lightning</u> always chooses the <u>easiest path</u> between the sky and the ground — even if that means going through tall buildings, trees or you. That's why it's never a good idea to fly a kite in a thunderstorm...

Uses of Static Electricity

Static electricity isn't always a nuisance. It's actually got loads of <u>applications</u>.
Read on for some examples...

1) Dust precipitators — cleaning up emissions

<u>Smoke</u> is made up of <u>tiny particles</u> which can be removed with a <u>precipitator</u>.
There are several different designs of precipitator — here's a very simple one:

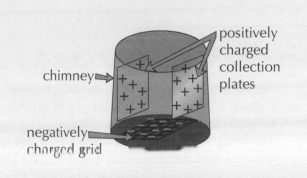

1) As smoke particles reach the bottom of the chimney, they meet a <u>wire grid</u> with a high <u>negative charge</u>, which charges the particles negatively.

2) The charged smoke particles are <u>attracted</u> to <u>positively</u> charged <u>metal plates</u>. The smoke particles <u>stick together</u> to form larger particles.

3) When they're heavy enough, the particles fall or are <u>knocked off</u> the plates. They fall to the bottom of the chimney and are removed.

4) The gases coming out of the chimney contain <u>very few smoke particles</u>.

Labels: chimney, positively charged collection plates, negatively charged grid

2) Photocopiers — er... copying stuff

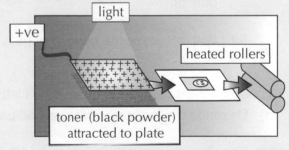

1) The <u>image plate</u> is positively charged. An image of what you're copying is projected onto this image plate.

2) Whiter bits of the thing you're copying make <u>light</u> fall on the plate and the charge <u>leaks away</u> in those places.

3) The charged bits attract negatively charged <u>black powder</u>, which is transferred onto positively charged paper.

4) The paper is <u>heated</u> so the powder sticks.

5) Voilà, a photocopy of your piece of paper (or whatever else you've shoved in there).

6) Laserjet printers work in a similar way. Instead of an image plate, the printer has a rotating <u>image drum</u>. And the light comes from a <u>controlled laser beam</u>.

Labels: light, +ve, heated rollers, toner (black powder) attracted to plate

---

Dust precipitators are important for the environment

Most power stations (see page 33) that burn <u>fossil fuels</u> have dust precipitators in their chimneys.
Removing smoke particles means that the amount of pollution they give out is greatly <u>reduced</u>.

Warm-up and Exam Questions

By this point you'll probably have worked out that static electricity isn't the most exciting of topics. Don't worry — there's just these few questions before you get on to much more interesting stuff.

Warm-Up Questions

1) What are the two types of electric charge?
2) Do similar charges attract or repel one another?
3) Suggest how a charged conductor might be safely discharged.
4) Describe a situation where static electricity can be dangerous.
5) What particles move when an electrically charged object is brought near another object?

Exam Questions

1   Jane hangs an uncharged balloon from a thread. She brings a negatively charged polythene rod towards the balloon. The diagram on the right shows how the positive and negative charges in the balloon rearrange themselves when she does this.

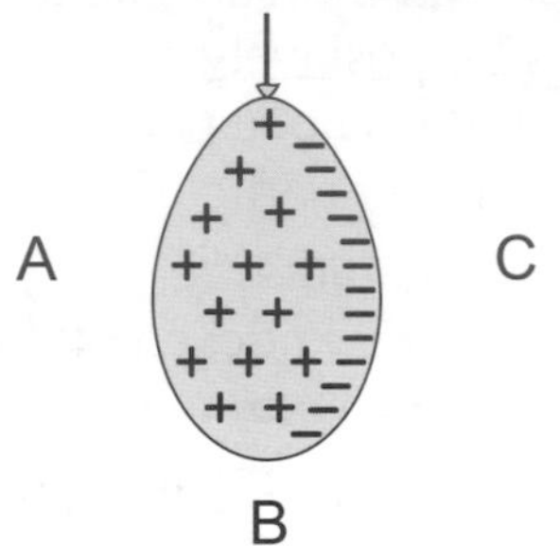

(a)   In which of the positions labelled A, B and C on the diagram did Jane hold the polythene rod? Explain your answer.

(2 marks)

(b)   Why are the positive charges still spread evenly over the balloon?

(1 mark)

(c)   Jane brings the rod closer to the balloon. Why does the balloon swing towards it?

(2 marks)

(d)   Jane keeps the rod close to the balloon, then touches the negatively charged side of the balloon with her finger.

(i)   Describe what happens to the negative charges when she touches the balloon.

(1 mark)

(ii)   Will this leave the balloon negatively charged, positively charged or neutral?

(1 mark)

2   A positive static charge builds up on a cloth when it is used to wipe a surface.
(a)   Describe the movement of charged particles that gives the cloth its charge.

(1 mark)

(b)   The cloth's charge makes it more effective at dusting. Why?

(1 mark)

3   Lightning is one of the dangerous effects of static electricity.
(a)   What causes the build-up of static electricity before lightning occurs?

(1 mark)

(b)   Describe the distribution of charge within a cloud before a lightning strike.

(1 mark)

(c)   A lightning rod is a metal spike fixed to the top of a tall building and connected to Earth by a conducting wire. Explain how lightning rods can protect a building.

(2 marks)

Circuits — the Basics

You can use a <u>test circuit</u> to work out the <u>resistance</u> of just about anything. But first, the basics...

1) <u>Current</u> (I, measured in A) is the <u>flow</u> of electrons round the circuit, which only happens if there's a <u>voltage</u>.

2) <u>Voltage</u> (in V) is the <u>driving force</u> that pushes the current round.

3) <u>Resistance</u> (in Ω) is anything in the circuit which <u>slows the flow down</u>.

4) <u>There's a balance</u>: the <u>voltage</u> tries to <u>push</u> the current round the circuit, and the <u>resistance opposes</u> it — the <u>relative sizes</u> of voltage and resistance decide <u>how big</u> the current will be:

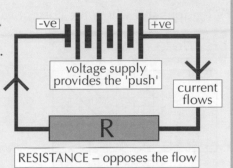

- If you <u>increase the voltage</u>, <u>more current</u> will flow.
- If you <u>increase the resistance</u>, <u>less current</u> will flow. (*or more voltage is needed for the same current*).

The standard *test circuit*

This is without doubt the most totally bog-standard circuit the world has ever known. So learn it.

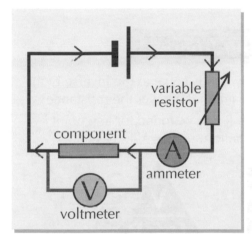

The *ammeter*

1) Measures the <u>current</u> flowing through the component.
2) Must be placed <u>in series</u> (see pages 94-95).
3) Can be put <u>anywhere</u> in series in the <u>main circuit</u>, but <u>never</u> in parallel like the voltmeter.

The *voltmeter*

1) Measures the <u>voltage</u> across the component.
2) Must be placed <u>in parallel</u> (see pages 96-97) around the <u>component</u> under test (<u>not</u> the variable resistor or battery).
3) The <u>proper</u> name for '<u>voltage</u>' is '<u>potential difference</u>' (P.D.).

Five important points

1) This <u>very basic</u> circuit is used for testing <u>components</u>, and for getting <u>V-I graphs</u> for them (see next page).

2) The <u>component</u>, the <u>ammeter</u> and the <u>variable resistor</u> are all in <u>series</u>, which means they can be put in <u>any order</u> in the main circuit. The <u>voltmeter</u>, on the other hand, can only be placed <u>in parallel</u> around the <u>component under test</u>, as shown.

3) As you <u>vary</u> the <u>variable resistor</u> it alters the <u>current</u> flowing through the circuit.

4) This allows you to take several <u>pairs of readings</u> from the <u>ammeter</u> and <u>voltmeter</u>.

5) You can then <u>plot</u> these values for <u>current</u> and <u>voltage</u> on a <u>V-I graph</u>.

The current is always shown flowing from positive to negative

The funny thing is — the <u>electrons</u> in circuits actually move from <u>–ve to +ve</u>... but scientists always think of <u>current</u> as flowing from <u>+ve to –ve</u>. Basically it's just because that's how the <u>early physicists</u> thought of it (before they found out about the electrons), and now it's become <u>convention</u>.

Resistance and V = I × R

Three hideously important voltage-current graphs

V-I graphs show how the current varies as you change the voltage. Learn these three really well:

Different resistors	Filament lamp	Diode

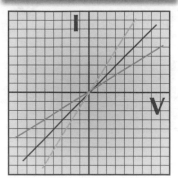
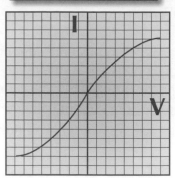
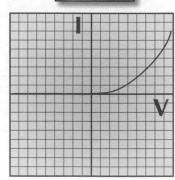

The current through a <u>resistor</u> (at constant temperature) is <u>proportional to voltage</u>.

<u>Different resistors</u> have different <u>resistances</u>, hence the different <u>slopes</u>.

As the <u>temperature</u> of the filament <u>increases</u>, the <u>resistance increases</u>, hence the <u>curve</u>.

Current will only flow through a diode <u>in one direction</u>, as shown.

Calculating resistance: R = V ÷ I, (or R = "1/gradient")

For the <u>straight-line graphs</u> the resistance of the component is <u>steady</u> and is equal to the <u>inverse</u> of the <u>gradient</u> of the line, or "<u>1/gradient</u>". In other words, the <u>steeper</u> the graph the <u>lower</u> the resistance.

If the graph <u>curves</u>, it means the resistance is <u>changing</u>. In that case R can be found for any point by taking the <u>pair of values</u> (V, I) from the graph and sticking them in the formula <u>R = V/I</u>. Easy.

$$\text{Resistance} = \frac{\text{Potential Difference}}{\text{Current}}$$

Calculating resistance — an example

<u>EXAMPLE</u>. Voltmeter V reads 6 V and resistor R is 4 Ω. What is the current through Ammeter A?

<u>ANSWER</u>. Use the formula V = I × R.
We need to find I, so the version we need is
I = V/R.
The answer is then: 6/4 which is <u>1.5 A</u>.

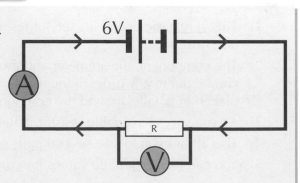

You have to be able to interpret V-I graphs for your exam

Remember — the <u>steeper</u> the <u>slope</u>, the <u>lower</u> the <u>resistance</u>. And you need to know that equation inside out, back to front and upside down too — it's really useful and important.

Circuit Symbols and Devices

Circuit symbols *you should* **know**:

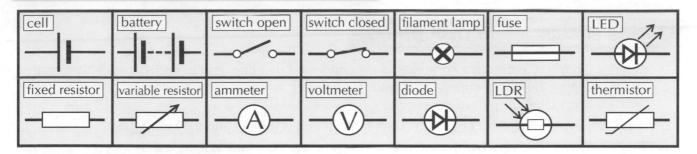

| cell | battery | switch open | switch closed | filament lamp | fuse | LED |
| fixed resistor | variable resistor | ammeter | voltmeter | diode | LDR | thermistor |

1) *Variable resistor*

1) A <u>resistor</u> whose resistance can be <u>changed</u> by twiddling a knob or something.
2) The old-fashioned ones are huge coils of <u>wire</u> with a <u>slider</u> on them.
3) They're great for <u>altering</u> the current flowing through a circuit.
   Turn the resistance <u>up</u>, the current drops Turn the resistance <u>down</u>, the current goes up

2) *"Semiconductor diode" or just "diode"*

A special device made from <u>semiconductor</u> material such as <u>silicon</u>.

It lets current flow freely through it in <u>one direction</u>, but <u>not</u> in the other (i.e. there's a very high resistance in the <u>reverse</u> direction).

This turns out to be real useful in various <u>electronic circuits</u>.

3) *Light-Dependent Resistor or "LDR" to you*

1) In <u>bright light</u>, the resistance <u>falls</u>.
2) In <u>darkness</u>, the resistance is <u>highest</u>.
3) This makes it a useful device for various <u>electronic circuits</u>, e.g. <u>automatic night lights</u>, <u>burglar detectors</u>.

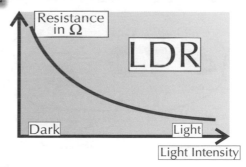

4) *Thermistor (temperature-dependent resistor)*

1) In <u>hot</u> conditions, the resistance <u>drops</u>.
2) In <u>cool</u> conditions, the resistance goes <u>up</u>.
3) Thermistors make useful <u>temperature detectors</u>, e.g. <u>car engine</u> temperature sensors and electronic <u>thermostats</u>.

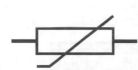

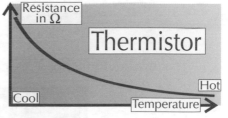

Know what each of the circuit symbols represents

You have to learn those circuit symbols so you can read circuit diagrams in the exam. It's not too bad remembering how LDRs and thermistors behave — <u>low</u> light/heat means <u>high</u> resistance.

Series Circuits

You need to be able to tell the difference between series and parallel circuits <u>just by looking at them</u>. You also need to know the <u>rules</u> about what happens with both types. Read on.

Series circuits — all or nothing

1) In <u>series circuits</u>, the different components are connected <u>in a line</u>, <u>end to end</u>, between the positive and negative of the power supply. (Except for <u>voltmeters</u>, which are always connected <u>in parallel</u>, but they don't count as part of the circuit.)

2) If you remove or disconnect <u>one</u> component, the circuit is <u>broken</u> and they all <u>stop</u>.

3) This is generally <u>not very handy</u>, and in practice <u>very few things</u> are connected in series.

*1) Potential difference is **shared***:

In series circuits the <u>total P.D.</u> of the <u>supply</u> is <u>shared</u> between the various <u>components</u>. So the <u>voltages</u> round a series circuit <u>always add up</u> to equal the <u>source voltage</u>:

$$V = V_1 + V_2 + V_3$$

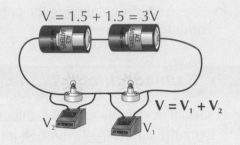

$V = 1.5 + 1.5 = 3V$

$V = V_1 + V_2$

V_2 V_1

*2) Current is the **same** everywhere*:

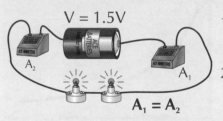

$V = 1.5V$

A_2 A_1

$A_1 = A_2$

1) In series circuits the <u>same current</u> flows through <u>all parts</u> of the circuit, i.e.: $$A_1 = A_2$$

2) The <u>size</u> of the current is determined by the <u>total P.D.</u> of the cells and the <u>total resistance</u> of the circuit, i.e. $I = V/R$

*3) Resistance **adds up***:

1) In series circuits the <u>total resistance</u> is just the <u>sum</u> of all the resistances: $$R = R_1 + R_2 + R_3$$

2) The <u>bigger</u> the <u>resistance</u> of a component, the bigger its <u>share</u> of the <u>total P.D.</u>

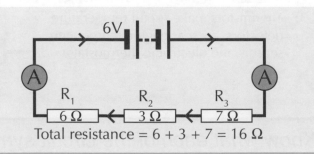

6V

A   A

R_1 R_2 R_3

6 Ω   3 Ω   7 Ω

Total resistance = 6 + 3 + 7 = 16 Ω

Series Circuits

4) Cell voltages *add up*:

1) There is a bigger potential difference when more cells are in series, provided the cells are all <u>connected</u> the <u>same way</u>.

2) For example, when two batteries of voltage 1.5 V are <u>connected in series</u> they supply 3 V <u>between them</u>.

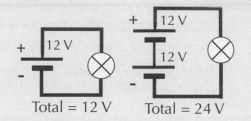

Total = 12 V   Total = 24 V

Example of a *series circuit*

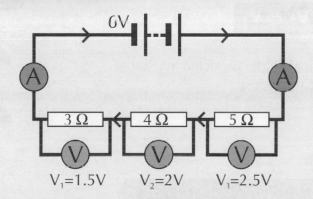

$V_1 = 1.5$V $V_2 = 2$V $V_3 = 2.5$V

<u>Voltages</u> add to equal the <u>source voltage</u>: $1.5 + 2 + 2.5 = 6$ V

<u>Total resistance</u> is the sum of the resistances in the circuit: $3 + 4 + 5 = 12$ ohms

<u>Current</u> flowing through all parts of the circuit $= V/R = 6/12 = 0.5$ A

(If an extra cell was added of voltage 3 V then the voltage across each resistor would increase.)

Christmas *fairy lights* are often wired in *series*

<u>Christmas fairy lights</u> are about the <u>only</u> real-life example of things connected in <u>series</u>, and we all know what a <u>pain</u> they are when the <u>whole lot go out</u> just because <u>one</u> of the bulbs is slightly dicky. The only <u>advantage</u> is that the bulbs can be <u>very small</u> because the total 230 V is <u>shared out</u> between them, so each bulb only has a <u>small</u> voltage across it.

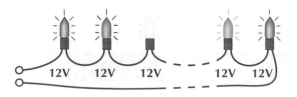

12V   12V   12V   12V   12V

Series circuits aren't used very much in the real world

A lot of fairy lights are actually done on a parallel circuit these days — they have an adapter that brings the voltage down, so the lights can still be diddy but it doesn't matter if one of them blows.

Parallel Circuits

Parallel circuits are much more sensible than series circuits and so are much more common in real life.

Parallel circuits — *independence* and *isolation*

1) In parallel circuits, each component is separately connected to the +ve and –ve of the supply.

2) If you remove or disconnect one of them, it will hardly affect the others at all.

3) This is obviously how most things must be connected, for example in cars and in household electrics. You have to be able to switch everything on and off separately.

1) P.D. is the **same** across all components:

1) In parallel circuits all components get the full source P.D., so the voltage is the same across all components:

$$V_1 = V_2 = V_3$$

2) This means that identical bulbs connected in parallel will all be at the same brightness.

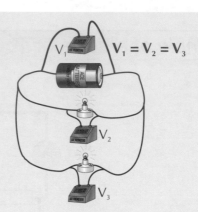

$V_1 = V_2 = V_3$

2) Current is **shared** between branches:

1) In parallel circuits the total current flowing around the circuit is equal to the total of all the currents in the separate branches. $A = A_1 + A_2 + A_3$

2) In a parallel circuit, there are junctions where the current either splits or rejoins. The total current going into a junction has to equal the total current leaving it.

3) If two identical components are connected in parallel, the same current flows through each one.

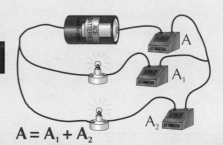

$A = A_1 + A_2$

3) Resistance is *tricky*:

1) The current through each component depends on its resistance. The lower the resistance, the bigger the current that'll flow through it.

2) The total resistance of the circuit is tricky to work out, but it's always less than that of the branch with the smallest resistance.

Parallel Circuits

Voltmeters and ammeters are exceptions to the rule:

1) Ammeters and voltmeters are <u>exceptions</u> to the series and parallel rules.
2) Ammeters are <u>always</u> connected in <u>series</u> even in a parallel circuit.
3) Voltmeters are <u>always</u> connected in <u>parallel with a component</u> even in a series circuit.

Example of a parallel circuit

1) The <u>voltage</u> across each resistor in the circuit is the same as the <u>supply voltage</u>. Each voltmeter will read 6 V.
2) The current through each resistor will be <u>different</u> because they have different values of <u>resistance</u>.
3) The current through the battery is the same as the <u>sum</u> of the other currents in the branches.
   i.e. $A_1 = A_2 + A_3 + A_4 \Rightarrow A_1 = 1.5 + 3 + 1 = 5.5$ A
4) The <u>total resistance</u> in the whole circuit is <u>less</u> than the <u>lowest branch</u>, i.e. lower than 2 Ω.
5) The <u>biggest current</u> flows through the <u>middle branch</u> because that branch has the <u>lowest resistance</u>.

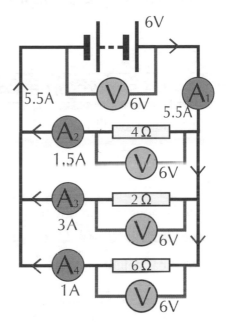

Everything electrical in a car is connected in parallel

<u>Parallel connection</u> is <u>essential</u> in a car to give these <u>two features</u>:

1) Everything can be <u>turned on and off separately</u>.
2) Everything always gets the <u>full voltage</u> from the battery.

The only <u>slight effect</u> is that when you turn <u>lots of things on</u> the lights may go <u>dim</u> because the battery can't provide <u>full voltage</u> under <u>heavy load</u>. This is normally a <u>very slight</u> effect. You can spot the same thing at home when you turn a kettle on, if you watch very carefully.

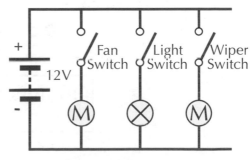

Ⓜ *is the symbol for a motor.*

All the electrics in your house will be wired in parallel circuits

Parallel circuits might look a bit scarier than series ones, but they're much more useful — and you don't have to learn as many equations for them. Remember: each branch has the <u>same voltage</u> across it, and the overall resistance is lower than that of the least resistant branch.

AC Electricity

There are two different kinds of electricity supply, AC (alternating current) and DC (direct current).

Mains supply is **AC**, battery supply is **DC**

1) The UK mains is an AC supply (alternating current), which means the current is constantly changing direction (at a frequency of 50 Hz).

2) By contrast, cells and batteries supply direct current (DC). This just means that the current keeps flowing in the same direction.

AC can be shown on an **oscilloscope** screen

1) A cathode ray oscilloscope (CRO) is basically a snazzy voltmeter.

2) If you plug an AC supply into an oscilloscope, you get a 'trace' on the screen that shows how the voltage of the supply changes with time.

3) The trace goes up and down in a regular pattern — some of the time it's positive and some of the time it's negative.

4) The vertical height of the trace at any point shows the input voltage at that point.

5) There are dials on the front of the oscilloscope called the TIMEBASE and the GAIN. You can use these to set the scales of the horizontal and vertical axes of the display.

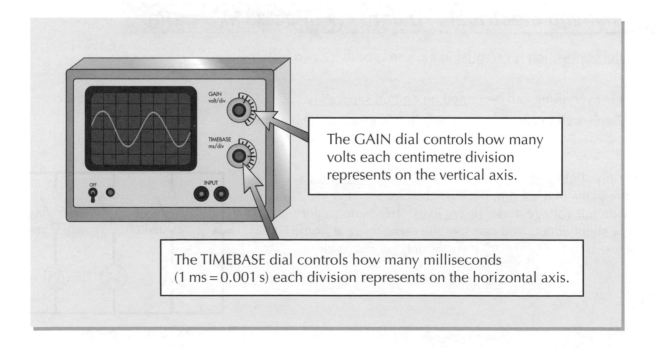

The GAIN dial controls how many volts each centimetre division represents on the vertical axis.

The TIMEBASE dial controls how many milliseconds (1 ms = 0.001 s) each division represents on the horizontal axis.

AC Electricity

Learn how to *read* an *oscilloscope trace*

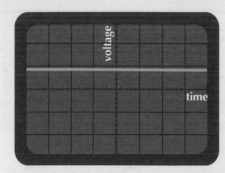 A <u>DC source</u> is always at the <u>same voltage</u>, so you get a <u>straight line</u>.

An <u>AC source</u> gives a <u>regularly repeating wave</u>. From that, you can work out the <u>period</u> and the <u>frequency</u> of the supply.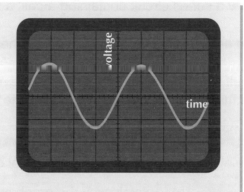

You work out the <u>frequency</u> using:

$$\text{frequency (Hz)} = \frac{1}{\text{time period (s)}}$$

Example:

The trace shown comes from an oscilloscope with the timebase set to 5 ms/div. Find:
a) the time period b) the frequency of the AC supply.

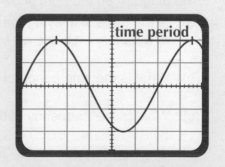

Answer:
a) To find the time period, measure the horizontal distance between two peaks.
    The time period of the signal is 6 divisions. Multiply by the timebase:
    Time period = 5 ms × 6 = 0.005 s × 6 = <u>0.03 s</u>
b) Using the frequency formula: Frequency = 1/0.03 = <u>33 Hz</u>

Be prepared to use traces like these to do calculations

AC's a bit harder to get your head round than DC, but it's got its advantages — especially for mains power. With AC, you can use a <u>transformer</u> to change the voltage and current, which can give more efficient transfer of electricity through the National Grid. Transformers don't work with DC currents.

Warm-Up and Exam Questions

Phew — circuits aren't the easiest thing in the world, are they? Make sure you've understood them though, by trying these questions. If you get stuck, just go back and reread the relevant page.

Warm-Up Questions

1) What are the units of resistance?
2) If the resistance of a circuit is increased, what happens to the current?
3) Draw the symbol for a light-emitting diode (LED).
4) What is the frequency of UK mains electricity supply?
5) What is the time period of a wave with a frequency of 100 Hz?

Exam Questions

1   (a)   (i)   Draw a series circuit containing a cell, a filament lamp and an ammeter.

(3 marks)

(ii)   Add arrows to your diagram showing the direction of conventional current.

(1 mark)

(b)   In a circuit like the one you have drawn, the resistance of the filament lamp is 5 Ω and the ammeter reads 0.3 A. Calculate the potential difference across the cell.

(1 mark)

2   The graph below shows current against potential difference (P.D.) for a diode.

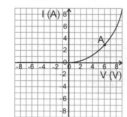

(a)   Explain why the graph shows zero current for negative P.D.s?

(1 mark)

(b)   What is the resistance of the diode at the point marked A?

(2 marks)

3   The diagram on the right shows a trace on a CRO.

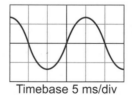

Timebase 5 ms/div

(a)   Is the trace displaying the output from the mains or a battery? Give a reason for your answer.

(1 mark)

(b)   What is the time period of the wave?

(1 mark)

(c)   What is the frequency of the wave?

(1 mark)

(d)   What will happen to the CRO trace if the voltage of the supply is reduced?

(1 mark)

4   A parallel circuit is connected as shown. Complete the readings on the voltmeters and ammeters on the diagram.

(5 marks)

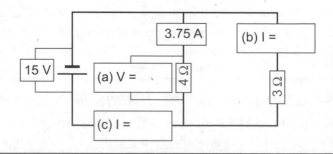

Plugs and Cables

It's important to know how to correctly <u>wire a plug</u> and to be able to spot any <u>mistakes</u> — plugs that aren't wired correctly are a <u>dangerous</u> thing.

Hazards in the *home* — *eliminate* them before they *eliminate you*

A likely <u>exam question</u> will show you a picture of domestic bliss but with various <u>electrical hazards</u> in the picture such as kids shoving their fingers into sockets and stuff like that, and they'll ask you to <u>list all the hazards</u>. This should be mostly <u>common sense</u>, but it won't half help if you already know some of the likely hazards, so learn these 9 examples:

1) <u>Long cables</u>.
2) <u>Frayed cables</u>.
3) <u>Cables</u> in contact with something <u>hot</u> or <u>wet</u>.
4) <u>Water near sockets</u>.
5) <u>Shoving</u> things into sockets.
6) <u>Damaged plugs</u>.
7) Too many plugs into one socket.
8) Lighting sockets <u>without bulbs in</u>.
9) Appliances without their <u>covers</u> on e.g. a computer with its case open.

Plugs and *cables* — learn the *safety features*

Get the wiring right:

1) The <u>right coloured wire</u> to each pin, and <u>firmly</u> screwed in.
2) <u>No bare wires</u> showing inside the plug.
3) <u>Cable grip</u> tightly fastened over the cable <u>outer layer</u>.

Plug features:

1) The <u>metal parts</u> are made of copper or brass because these are <u>very good conductors</u>.
2) The case, cable grip and cable insulation are all made of <u>plastic</u> or <u>rubber</u> because these are really good <u>insulators</u> and are <u>flexible</u> too.
3) This all keeps the electricity flowing <u>where it should</u>.

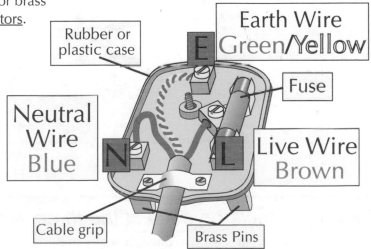

Rubber or plastic case

Earth Wire
Green/Yellow

Fuse

Neutral Wire Blue

Live Wire Brown

Cable grip

Brass Pins

Plugs and Cables

Plug wiring *errors*

They're pretty keen on these diagrams in the exam so make sure you know them.

The diagram on the previous page shows <u>how to wire a plug properly</u>. Shown below are examples of <u>how not to wire a plug</u>. A badly wired plug is really dangerous so <u>learn these diagrams</u>.

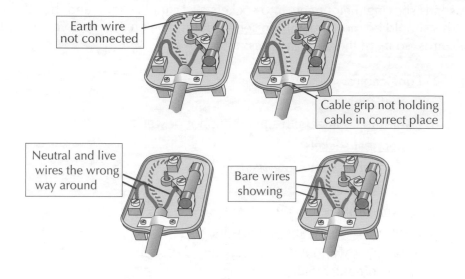

Earth wire not connected

Cable grip not holding cable in correct place

Neutral and live wires the wrong way around

Bare wires showing

Mains **cables** *have* **three** *separate wires*

1) The brown <u>LIVE WIRE</u> in a mains supply alternates between a <u>HIGH +VE AND –VE VOLTAGE</u>.

2) The blue <u>NEUTRAL WIRE</u> is always at <u>0V</u>. Electricity normally flows in and out through the live and neutral wires only.

3) The green and yellow <u>EARTH WIRE</u> is just for safety, and works together with a fuse to prevent fire and shocks.

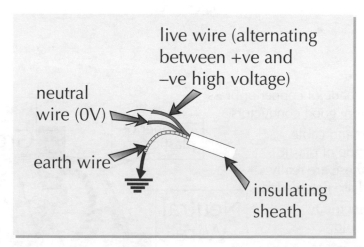

live wire (alternating between +ve and –ve high voltage)

neutral wire (0V)

earth wire

insulating sheath

Know your facts on each of the three wires

Learning the stuff on the last two pages is really important, and not just for your exam — one shock from the mains can kill you (okay, lecture over). Make sure you know how to wire a plug properly, and trickier, can spot when one's wired badly.

Fuses and Earthing

Fuses prevent electric shocks

1) To prevent <u>surges of current</u> in electrical circuits and danger of electric shocks, a fuse is normally placed in the circuit. [You can sometimes use a <u>circuit breaker</u> (a resettable fuse) instead, which works slightly differently.]

2) If the current in the circuit <u>gets too big</u> (bigger than the fuse rating), the fuse wire <u>heats up</u> and <u>melts</u>, breaking the circuit and preventing any electric shocks.

3) <u>Fuses</u> should be <u>rated</u> as near as possible but just <u>higher</u> than the normal <u>operating current</u> (see page 105).

4) The fuse should always be the <u>same value</u> as the manufacturer recommends.

Earthing prevents fires and shocks

The <u>EARTH WIRE</u> and <u>fuse</u> work together like this:

1) The earth pin is <u>connected</u> to the case via the <u>earth wire</u> (the <u>yellow</u> and <u>green</u> wire).

2) If a <u>fault</u> develops in which the <u>live</u> somehow touches the <u>metal case</u>, then because the case is <u>earthed</u>, a <u>big current</u> flows in through the <u>live</u>, through the <u>case</u> and out down the <u>earth wire</u>.

3) This <u>surge</u> in current <u>blows the fuse</u>, which <u>cuts off</u> the <u>live supply</u>. This prevents electric shocks from the case.

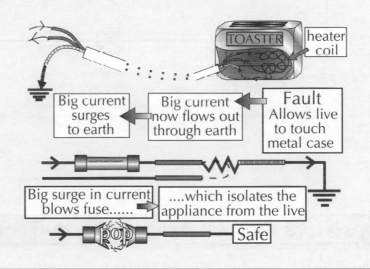

All appliances with <u>metal cases</u> must be "<u>earthed</u>" to avoid the danger of <u>electric shock</u>. "Earthing" just means attaching the metal case to the <u>earth wire</u> in the cable.

Fuses — you'll find them in exams and kettles

Sometimes, you can use a <u>Residual Current Circuit Breaker</u> (RCCB) instead of a fuse and an earth wire. RCCBs work a bit differently. Normally, <u>exactly</u> the same current flows through the live and neutral wires, but if somebody touches the live wire a huge current flows through them to earth. That leaves the neutral wire carrying <u>less current</u> than the live wire. The circuit breaker instantly detects this difference in current and cuts off the power. RCCBs can be <u>reset</u> at the flick of a switch, so they're much more convenient than fuses that have to be replaced each time they melt. Clever, eh?

Energy and Power in Circuits

You can look at <u>electrical circuits</u> in <u>two ways</u>. The first is in terms of a voltage <u>pushing the current</u> round and the resistances opposing the flow, as on page 91. The <u>other way</u> of looking at circuits is in terms of <u>energy transfer</u>. Learn them <u>both</u> and be ready to tackle questions about <u>either</u>.

Energy is transferred from cells and other sources

Anything which <u>supplies electricity</u> is also supplying <u>energy</u>.

So cells, batteries, generators, etc. all <u>transfer energy</u> to components in the circuit:

| <u>Motion</u>: motors | <u>Light</u>: light bulbs | <u>Heat</u>: Hairdryers/kettles | <u>Sound</u>: speakers |

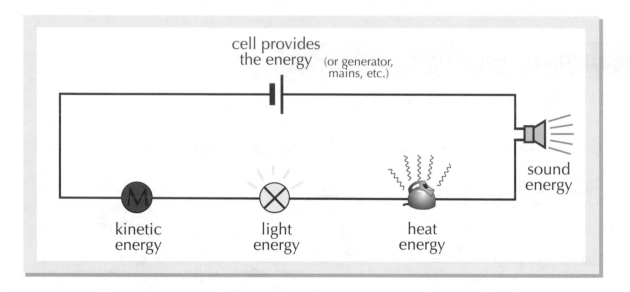

cell provides the energy (or generator, mains, etc.)

kinetic energy   light energy   heat energy   sound energy

All resistors produce heat when a current flows through them

1) Whenever a <u>current</u> flows through anything with <u>electrical resistance</u> (which is pretty well everything) then <u>electrical energy</u> is converted into <u>heat energy</u>.

2) The <u>more current</u> that flows, the more heat is produced.

3) A <u>bigger voltage</u> means more heating because it pushes more current through.

4) You can <u>measure</u> the amount of heat produced by putting a resistor in a known amount of water, or inside a solid block, and measuring the increase in temperature.

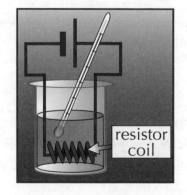

resistor coil

Energy and Power in Circuits

<u>Power ratings</u> tell you how much energy a device transfers per second.

Power ratings of appliances

A light bulb converts <u>electrical energy</u> into <u>light</u> and has a power rating of 100 watts (W), which means it transfers <u>100 joules/second</u>.

A kettle converts <u>electrical energy</u> into <u>heat</u> and has a power rating of 2.5 kW, transferring <u>2500 joules/second</u>.

The total energy transferred by an appliance depends on <u>how long</u> it is on for and on its <u>power rating</u>. The formula for energy transferred is:

$$\text{ENERGY} = \text{POWER} \times \text{TIME} \quad (E = P \times t)$$

<u>For example</u>, if the kettle above is left on for <u>five minutes</u>, the energy transferred by the kettle in this time is:

$300 \times 2500 = 750\,000\,J = \underline{750\,kJ}.$ (5 minutes = 300 seconds)

Electrical power and fuse ratings

1) The formula for <u>electrical power</u> is:

$$\text{POWER} = \text{VOLTAGE} \times \text{CURRENT} \quad (P = V \times I)$$

2) Most electrical goods show their <u>power rating</u> and <u>voltage rating</u>. To work out the <u>fuse</u> needed, you need to work out the <u>current</u> that the item will normally use:

Example:

A hairdryer is rated at 230 V, 1 kW. Find the fuse needed.

<u>Answer:</u> $I = P/V = 1000/230 = 4.3\,A.$
Normally, the fuse should be rated just a bit higher than the normal current, so a 5 amp fuse is ideal for this one.

Don't just pick the nearest fuse value — a lower one is no good

In the UK, you can usually get fuses rated at 3 A, 5 A or 13 A, and that's about it. You should bear that in mind when you're working out fuse ratings. If you find you need a 10.73 A fuse — tough.

Charge, Voltage and Energy

Total charge *through a circuit depends on* current *and* time

1) Current is the <u>flow of electrical charge</u> (in coulombs, C) around a circuit.

2) When a <u>current</u> (I) flows past a point in a circuit for a <u>time</u> (t) then the <u>charge</u> (Q) that has passed is given by:

> **total charge (C) = current (A) × time (s)**

3) <u>More charge</u> passes around the circuit when a <u>bigger current</u> flows.

Example:

> A battery charger passes a current of 2.5 A through a cell for a period of 4 hours. How much charge does the charger transfer to the cell in total?

> <u>Answer:</u> Q = I × t = 2.5 × (4 × 60 × 60) = 36 000 C (36 kC).

Voltage *is the* energy *transferred per* charge passed

1) When an electrical <u>charge</u> (Q) goes through a <u>change</u> in voltage (V), then <u>energy</u> (E) is <u>transferred</u>.

2) Energy is <u>supplied</u> to the charge at the <u>power source</u> to 'raise' it through a voltage.

3) The charge <u>gives up</u> this energy when it '<u>falls</u>' through any <u>voltage drop</u> in <u>components</u> elsewhere in the circuit. The formula is really simple:

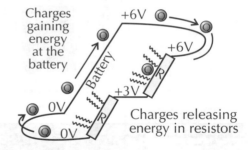

> **energy transformed = charge × potential difference**

4) The <u>bigger</u> the <u>change</u> in voltage (or P.D.), the <u>more energy</u> is transferred for a <u>given amount of charge</u> passing through the circuit.

5) That means that a battery with a <u>bigger voltage</u> will supply <u>more energy</u> to the circuit for every <u>coulomb</u> of charge which flows round it, because the charge is raised up '<u>higher</u>' at the start (see above diagram) — and as the diagram shows, <u>more energy</u> will be <u>dissipated</u> in the circuit too.

Example:

> A motor is attached to a 3 V battery. If a current of 0.8 A flows through the motor for 3 minutes:
> a) Calculate the total charge passed.
> b) Calculate the energy transformed by the motor.
> c) Explain why the kinetic energy output of the motor will be less than your answer to b).

> <u>Answer:</u> a) Using the formula above, Q = I × t = 0.8 × (3 × 60) = <u>144 C</u>.
> b) Use E = Q × V = 144 × 3 = <u>432 J</u>.
> c) The motor won't be 100% efficient. Some energy will be transformed into <u>sound and heat</u>.

Warm-Up and Exam Questions

You're well over half way through this section now. Check you can do the straightforward stuff with this warm-up, then have a go at the exam questions below.

Warm-Up Questions

1) Which of the live, neutral or earth wires is always at 0 volts?
2) Why is the case of a plug usually made out of plastic?
3) What energy transformation occurs when electric current flows through a resistor?
4) What is the name for the rate at which electrical charge flows round a circuit?
5) What is the equation linking Q, V and E?

Exam Questions

1   (a)   What colour are each of the following wires in an electric plug?

      (i)   live

      (ii)   neutral

      (iii) earth

(3 marks)

   (b)   Which two wires usually carry the same current?

(1 mark)

   (c)   What type of safety device contains a wire that is designed to melt when the current passing through it goes above a certain value?

(1 mark)

2   A domestic appliance has a plug containing live, neutral and earth wires and a fuse, all correctly wired to the household circuit.

   (a)   Describe the current that flows in each of the wires in the following situations:

      (i)   normal operation

      (ii)   the instant after the live wire has come into contact with the metal cover

      (iii) after the fuse has blown

(3 marks)

   (b)   If there were no earth wire or fuse present and a person touched the live wire, what path would the current take?

(1 mark)

3   A current of 0.5 A passes through a torch bulb. The torch is powered by a 3 V battery.

   (a)   What is the power of the torch?

(2 marks)

   (b)   If the torch is on for half an hour, how much charge has passed through the battery?

(2 marks)

   (c)   How much electrical energy does the bulb transfer in half an hour?

(2 marks)

Atomic Structure

Ernest Rutherford didn't just pick the nuclear model of the atom out of thin air. It all started with a Greek fella called Democritus in the 5th Century BC. He thought that <u>all matter</u>, whatever it was, was made up of <u>identical</u> lumps called "atomos". And that's about as far as the theory got until the 1800s...

Rutherford scattering and the demise of the plum pudding

1) In 1804 <u>John Dalton</u> agreed with Democritus that matter was made up of <u>tiny spheres</u> ("atoms") that couldn't be broken up, but he reckoned that <u>each element</u> was made up of a <u>different type</u> of "atom".

2) Nearly 100 years later, J J Thomson discovered that <u>electrons</u> could be <u>removed</u> from atoms. So Dalton's theory wasn't quite right (atoms could be broken up). Thomson suggested that atoms were <u>spheres of positive charge</u> with tiny negative electrons <u>stuck in them</u> like plums in a <u>plum pudding</u>.

3) That "plum pudding" theory didn't last very long though. In 1909 <u>Ernest Rutherford</u> and his merry men tried firing <u>alpha particles</u> at <u>thin gold foil</u>. Most of them just went <u>straight through</u>, but the odd one came <u>straight back</u> at them, which was frankly a bit of a <u>shocker</u> for Ernie and his pals.

4) Being a pretty clued-up guy, Rutherford realised this meant that <u>most of the mass</u> of the atom was concentrated at the <u>centre</u> in a <u>tiny nucleus</u>, with a <u>positive charge</u>.

5) And that most of an atom is just <u>empty space</u>, which is also a bit of a <u>shocker</u> when you think about it.

Rutherford came up with the nuclear model of the atom

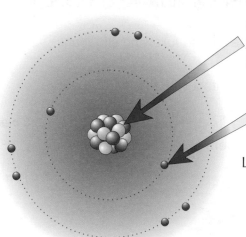

The <u>nucleus</u> is <u>tiny</u> but it makes up most of the <u>mass</u> of the atom. It contains <u>protons</u> (which are <u>positively charged</u>) and <u>neutrons</u> (which are <u>neutral</u>) — which gives it an overall positive charge.

The rest of the atom is mostly <u>empty space</u>. The <u>negative electrons</u> whizz round the outside of the nucleus really fast. They give the atom its <u>overall size</u>.

Learn the relative charges and masses of each particle:

PARTICLE	MASS	CHARGE
Proton	1	+1
Neutron	1	0
Electron	$\frac{1}{2000}$	-1

Now would be a good time to read up on isotopes (see page 48).

The nuclear model is just one way of thinking about the atom

It works really well for explaining a lot of Chemistry, but it's certainly not the whole story. Other bits of science are explained using <u>different</u> models of the atom. The beauty of it though is that no one model is <u>more right</u> than the others.

Radioactive Decay Processes

When nuclei decay by alpha or beta emission, they change from one element to a different one.

Alpha particles are helium nuclei

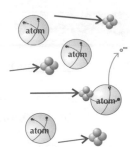

1) They are relatively <u>big</u> and <u>heavy</u> and <u>slow moving</u>.
2) They therefore <u>don't</u> penetrate very far into materials but are <u>stopped quickly</u>.
3) Because of their size they are <u>strongly</u> ionising, which just means they <u>bash into</u> a lot of atoms and <u>knock electrons off</u> them before they slow down, which creates lots of ions — hence the term "<u>ionising</u>".

Alpha emission:

A typical <u>alpha emission</u>:

An <u>α-particle</u> is simply a <u>helium nucleus</u>, mass 4 and charge of +2, made up of 2 protons and 2 neutrons.

Beta particles are electrons

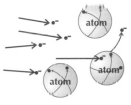

1) These are <u>in between</u> alpha and gamma in terms of their <u>properties</u>.
2) They move <u>quite</u> fast and they are <u>quite</u> small (they're electrons).
3) They penetrate <u>moderately</u> before colliding and are <u>moderately ionising</u> too.
4) For every <u>β-particle</u> emitted, a <u>neutron</u> turns to a <u>proton</u> in the nucleus.

Beta emission:

A typical <u>beta emission</u>:

A <u>β-particle</u> is simply an <u>electron</u>, with virtually no mass and a charge of –1.

Gamma rays are very short wavelength EM waves

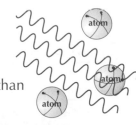

1) They are the <u>opposite</u> of alpha particles in a way.
2) They <u>penetrate a long way</u> into materials without being stopped.
3) This means they are <u>weakly</u> ionising because they tend to <u>pass through</u> rather than colliding with atoms. Eventually they <u>hit something</u> and do <u>damage</u>.

Gamma emission:

A typical combined <u>α and γ emission</u>:

A <u>γ-ray</u> is a <u>photon</u> with no mass and no charge.

After an <u>alpha or beta emission</u> the nucleus sometimes has <u>extra energy to get rid of</u>. It does this by emitting a <u>gamma ray</u>. Gamma emission <u>never changes</u> the <u>proton or mass numbers</u> of the nucleus.

Alpha and beta emissions are particles, gamma emissions are rays

Learn all the details about the three different types of radiation — alpha, beta and gamma. When a nucleus decays by <u>alpha</u> emission, its <u>atomic number</u> goes down by <u>two</u> and its <u>mass number</u> goes down by <u>four</u>. <u>Beta</u> emission increases the atomic number by <u>one</u> (the mass number <u>doesn't change</u>).

Background Radiation

* We're constantly exposed to <u>very low levels</u> of radiation — and all without us noticing.

Background radiation comes from *many sources*

<u>Background radiation</u> comes from:

* 1)   Radioactivity of naturally occurring <u>unstable isotopes</u> which are <u>all around us</u> —
in the <u>air</u>, in <u>food</u>, in <u>building materials</u> and in the <u>rocks</u> under our feet.

* 2)   Radiation from <u>space</u>, which is known as <u>cosmic rays</u>. These come mostly from the <u>Sun</u>.
Luckily, the Earth's <u>atmosphere protects</u> us from much of this radiation. The Earth's <u>magnetic field</u>
also deflects cosmic rays away from Earth.

* 3)   Radiation due to <u>human activity</u>, e.g. <u>fallout</u> from <u>nuclear explosions</u> or <u>dumped nuclear waste</u>.
But this represents a <u>tiny</u> proportion of the total background radiation.

The <u>relative proportions</u> of background radiation are:

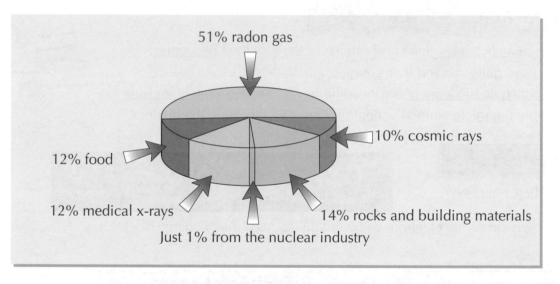

51% radon gas

12% food

10% cosmic rays

12% medical x-rays

Just 1% from the nuclear industry

14% rocks and building materials

The level of **background radiation** *depends on* **where you are**

1)   At <u>high altitudes</u> (e.g. in <u>jet planes</u>) it <u>increases</u> because of more
exposure to <u>cosmic rays</u>. That means commercial pilots have an
increased risk of getting some types of cancer.

2)   <u>Underground in mines</u>, etc. it increases because of the <u>rocks</u> all around.

3)   Certain <u>underground rocks</u> (e.g. granite) can cause higher levels at the
<u>surface</u>, especially if they release <u>radioactive radon gas</u>, which tends to
get <u>trapped inside people's houses</u>.

Background radiation is everywhere

Background radiation was first discovered <u>accidentally</u>. Scientists were trying to work out which
materials were radioactive, and couldn't understand why their reader still showed radioactivity when
there was <u>no material</u> being tested. They realised it must be natural background radiation.

Background Radiation

Radon gas accounts for over half of the <u>background radiation</u> on Earth.

Exposure to **radon gas** causes **lung cancer**

1) Studies have shown that exposure to <u>high doses</u> of radon gas can cause <u>lung cancer</u> — and the <u>greater</u> the radon concentration, the <u>higher the risk</u>.

2) Some medical professionals reckon that about <u>1 in 20</u> deaths from <u>lung cancer</u> (about 2000 per year) are caused by radon exposure.

3) Evidence suggests that the risk of developing lung cancer from radon is <u>much greater</u> for <u>smokers</u> compared to nonsmokers.

4) The scientific community is a bit divided on the effects of <u>lower doses</u>, and there's still a lot of debate over what the highest safe(ish) concentration is.

Radon gas concentration varies depends on **rock type**

The <u>radon concentration</u> in people's houses <u>varies widely</u> across the UK, depending on what type of <u>rock</u> the house is built on.

Level of radiation from rocks

Ventilation systems reduce radon concentration

1) <u>New houses</u> in areas where high levels of radon gas might occur must be designed with good <u>ventilation systems</u>. These reduce the concentration of radon in the living space.

2) In <u>existing houses</u>, the Government recommends that ventilation systems are put in wherever the radon concentration is higher than a certain level.

Radon gas is the largest source of background radiation

Radon gas is the subject of <u>scientific debate</u> — no one knows quite how much is too much. It's tricky to study because you can't accurately measure how much a person has been exposed to over their life. The best thing you can do is <u>not smoke</u>, as it <u>increases</u> the risk of developing radon-induced cancer.

Nuclear Fission

Nuclear fission is a type of <u>reaction</u> used in nuclear reactors to <u>release</u> huge amounts of useful energy.

Nuclear fission — the splitting up of big atomic nuclei

<u>Nuclear power stations</u> and <u>nuclear submarines</u> are both powered by <u>nuclear reactors</u>.

In a nuclear reactor, a controlled <u>chain reaction</u> takes place in which atomic nuclei <u>split up</u> and <u>release energy</u> in the form of <u>heat</u>. This heat is then simply used to <u>heat water</u> to drive a <u>steam turbine</u>. So nuclear reactors are really just <u>glorified steam engines</u>!

The "<u>fuel</u>" that's split is usually either <u>uranium-235</u> or <u>plutonium-239</u> (or both).

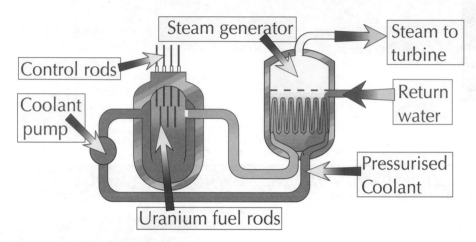

The chain reactions:

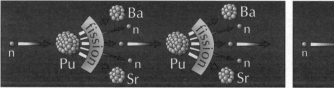 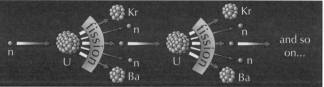

1) If a <u>slow-moving neutron</u> gets absorbed by a uranium or plutonium nucleus, the nucleus can <u>split</u>.

2) Each time a <u>uranium</u> or <u>plutonium</u> nucleus <u>splits up</u>, it spits out <u>two or three neutrons</u>, one of which might hit <u>another</u> nucleus, causing it to <u>split</u> also, and thus keeping the <u>chain reaction</u> going.

3) When a large atom splits in two it will form <u>two new lighter elements</u>. These new nuclei are usually <u>radioactive</u> because they have the "<u>wrong</u>" number of neutrons in them. This is the <u>big problem</u> with nuclear power — it produces <u>huge</u> amounts of <u>radioactive material</u> which is very <u>difficult</u> and <u>expensive</u> to dispose of safely.

4) Each nucleus <u>splitting</u> (called a <u>fission</u>) gives out <u>a lot of energy</u> — a lot more energy than you get with a <u>chemical</u> bond between two atoms. Make sure you remember that. <u>Nuclear processes</u> release <u>much more energy</u> than chemical processes do. That's why <u>nuclear bombs</u> are <u>so much</u> more powerful than ordinary bombs (which rely on <u>chemical</u> reactions).

Nuclear power releases a lot of energy, but it has its downsides

Nothing to it really, chuck in some sluggish neutrons, split some atoms, get some heat, make some steam, turn a turbine, drive a generator and ta da — some <u>electricity</u>. But the big problem is how to dispose of <u>waste</u> — the products left over are generally radioactive, so they can't just be thrown away.

Nuclear Fusion

The main problem with nuclear fission is that there's lots of radioactive mess to clean up afterwards. This is why scientists have been looking into producing energy the same way stars do — through <u>fusion</u>.

Nuclear fusion — the *joining* of small atomic nuclei

1) <u>Nuclear fusion</u> is just the <u>opposite</u> of fission — two <u>light nuclei</u> (e.g. hydrogen) can <u>combine</u> to create a larger nucleus.

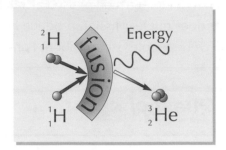

2) Fusion releases <u>a lot</u> of energy (more than fission for a given mass of fuel). So people are trying to develop <u>fusion reactors</u> to make <u>electricity</u>.

3) Fusion <u>doesn't</u> leave behind a lot of radioactive <u>waste</u> and there's <u>plenty</u> of hydrogen about for <u>fuel</u>

4) The <u>big problem</u> is that fusion only happens at <u>really high temperatures</u> — over <u>10 000 000 °C</u>.

5) <u>No material</u> can stand that kind of temperature without being <u>vaporised</u>, so fusion reactors are really difficult to build. You have to contain the hot hydrogen in a <u>magnetic field</u> instead of in a physical container.

6) There are a few <u>experimental</u> reactors around, but none of them are generating electricity yet. At the moment it takes <u>more</u> power to get up to the right temperature than the reactor can produce.

Cold fusion — *hoax* or *energy of the future*?

1) Cold fusion is <u>nuclear fusion</u> which occurs at around <u>room temperature</u>.

2) In 1989 two scientists, <u>Stanley Pons</u> and <u>Martin Fleischmann</u>, claimed to have released energy from cold fusion using a simple experiment.

3) This caused a lot of <u>excitement</u> — cold fusion would make it possible to generate lots of electricity, easily and cheaply.

4) Many scientists were <u>sceptical</u>, and the results have never been repeated reliably enough to be accepted by the scientific community.

5) Not all scientists have given up though — there's still a lot of research into cold fusion, so you never know...

And as usual, some people see only the potential for a great big bomb

At about the same time as research started on fusion reactors, physicists were working on a <u>fusion bomb</u>. These 'hydrogen bombs' are incredibly powerful — they can release a few thousand times more energy than the nuclear bombs that destroyed Hiroshima and Nagasaki at the end of World War II.

Warm-Up and Exam Questions

The end of another section — they just go far too quickly. Make sure you've understood it all by doing these questions (and the revision summary on the next page) before you whizz on to the next section.

Warm-Up Questions

1) Give one source of background radiation.
2) Name two elements often used as nuclear fuel.
3) What does nuclear fission produce in addition to energy? Why is this a problem?
4) Why were people excited about Pons and Fleischmann's cold fusion experiment?

Exam Questions

1 (a) What relative charge do the following particles have?
    (i)   electron
    (ii) proton
    (iii) neutron

(3 marks)

  (b) What two types of particle does the nucleus of an atom contain?

(2 marks)

  (c) What happens to the atomic number of a nucleus when a beta particle is emitted?

(1 mark)

  (d) What happens to the mass number of a nucleus after alpha emission?

(1 mark)

2 Nuclear reactors often use uranium-235.

  (a) Explain how uranium-235 is split in a nuclear reactor.

(3 marks)

  (b) How is the heat energy released by nuclear fission used to generate electricity?

(2 marks)

3 The table shows some information about various elements and isotopes.

Element/isotope	Deuterium	Hydrogen	Krypton	Plutonium	Thorium	Tin
Relative mass	2	1	84	239	232	119

  (a) Which two substances in the table would be most likely to be used in a fusion reaction?

(2 marks)

  (b) Explain why scientists are interested in developing fusion power.

(2 marks)

  (c) Why is fusion not used to generate electricity at present?

(1 mark)

Revision Summary for Physics 2(ii)

There's some pretty heavy physics in this section. But just take it one page at a time and it's not so bad. When you think you know it all, try these questions and see how you're getting on. If there are any you can't do, look back at the right bit of the section, learn it, then come back here and try again.

1) What causes the build-up of static electricity? Which particles move when static builds up?

2) Give one example each of static electricity being: a) a nuisance, b) dangerous.

3) Give two examples of how static electricity can be helpful. Write all the details.

4) Explain what current, voltage and resistance are in an electric circuit.

5) Sketch typical voltage-current graphs for: a) a resistor, b) a filament lamp, c) a diode. Explain the shape of each graph.

6)* Calculate the resistance of a wire if the voltage across it is 12 V and the current through it is 2.5 A.

7) Describe how the resistance of an LDR varies with light intensity. Give an application of an LDR.

8)* Find each unknown voltage, current or resistance in this circuit.

9) Why are parallel circuits often more useful than series ones?

10)* An oscilloscope is plugged into the mains (50 Hz). Sketch what you would expect to see on the screen if the timebase is set to 2 ms/div.

11) Sketch a properly wired three pin plug.

12) Explain fully how a fuse and earth wire work together.

13)* Find the appropriate fuse (3 A, 5 A or 13 A) for these appliances:
a) a toaster rated at 230 V, 1100 W   b) an electric heater rated at 230 V, 2000 W

14)* Calculate the energy transformed by a torch using a 6 V battery when 530 C of charge pass through.

15) Describe the "plum pudding" model of the atom.

16) Describe Rutherford's scattering experiment with a diagram. What were the results of the experiment, and what did Rutherford conclude from it?

17) Draw a table stating the relative mass and charge of the three basic subatomic particles.

18)* Write down the number of protons, neutrons and electrons in an atom of $^{230}_{90}$Th.

19) Describe in detail the nature and properties of the three types of radiation: α, β and γ.

20)* Write down the nuclear equation for the alpha decay of: a) $^{234}_{92}$U, b) $^{230}_{90}$Th and c) $^{226}_{88}$Ra.
(You may need the periodic table below.)

21)* Write down the nuclear equation for the combined beta and gamma decay of:
a) $^{234}_{90}$Th, b) $^{234}_{91}$Pa and c) $^{14}_{6}$C.
(You may need the periodic table on the right.)

22) List three places where the level of background radiation is increased and explain why.

23) Draw a diagram to illustrate the fission of uranium-235 or plutonium-239 and explain how the chain reaction works.

24) What is nuclear fusion? Why is it difficult to construct a working fusion reactor?

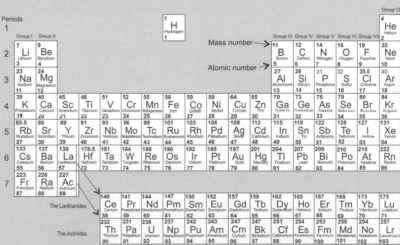

* Answers on p226.

Physics 2(ii) — Electricity and the Atom

Turning Forces and Centre of Mass

Turning forces — full of spanners and levers. You should have a good idea about calculating moments, pivots and centre of mass by the time you've finished these pages.

A *moment* is the *turning effect* of a force

MOMENT (Nm) = FORCE (N) × perpendicular DISTANCE (m)
(between line of action and pivot)

1) The force on the spanner causes a turning effect or moment on the nut. A larger force would mean a larger moment.

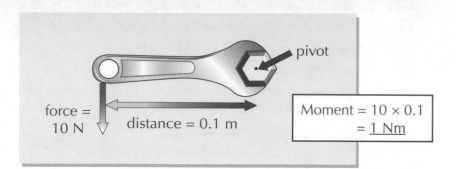

force = 10 N   distance = 0.1 m   pivot

Moment = 10 × 0.1
= 1 Nm

2) Using a longer spanner, the same force can exert a larger moment because the distance from the pivot is greater.

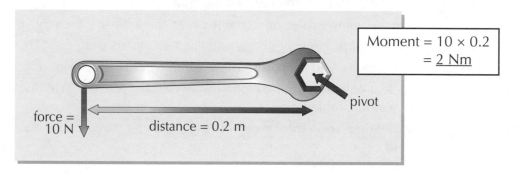

Moment = 10 × 0.2
= 2 Nm

force = 10 N   distance = 0.2 m   pivot

3) To get the maximum moment (or turning effect) you need to push at right angles (perpendicular) to the spanner.

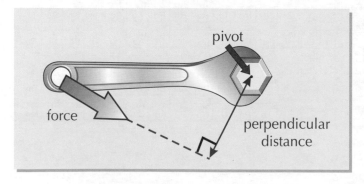

pivot

force

perpendicular distance

4) Pushing at any other angle means a smaller moment because the perpendicular distance between the line of action and the pivot is smaller.

Turning Forces and Centre of Mass

The centre of mass hangs *directly below* the *point of suspension*

✲ 1) You can think of the <u>centre of mass</u> of an object as the point where its <u>whole</u> mass is concentrated.

2) A freely suspended object will <u>swing</u> until its centre of mass is <u>vertically below</u> the <u>point of suspension</u>.

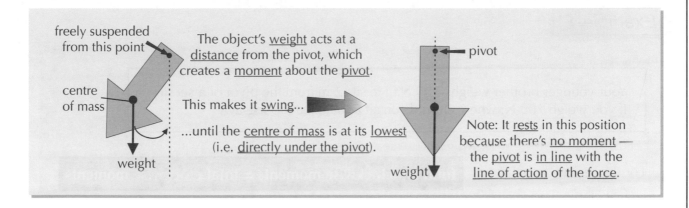

3) This means you can find the <u>centre of mass</u> of any flat shape like this:

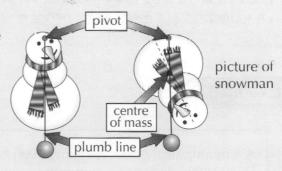

   a) Suspend the shape and a <u>plumb line</u> from the same point, and wait until they <u>stop moving</u>.

   b) <u>Draw</u> a line along the plumb line.

   c) Do the same thing again, but suspend the shape from a <u>different</u> pivot point.

   d) The centre of mass is where your two lines <u>cross</u>.

4) But you don't need to go to all that trouble for <u>simple</u> shapes. You can quickly guess where the centre of mass is by looking for <u>lines of symmetry</u>.

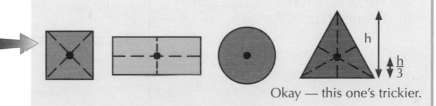

Okay — this one's trickier.

Take your time with turning forces and centre of mass

Think of the extra force you need to open a door by pushing it <u>near the hinge</u> compared to <u>at the handle</u> — the <u>distance from the pivot</u> is <u>less</u>, so you need <u>more force</u> to get the <u>same moment</u>. For the centre of mass, try and get <u>loads of practice</u> finding it for different shapes, until you're sure.

Balanced Moments and Stability

Once you can calculate moments, you can work out if a <u>seesaw is balanced</u>. Useful thing, Physics.

A question of *balance* — are the *moments equal*?

If the <u>anticlockwise moments</u> are equal to the <u>clockwise moments</u>, the object <u>won't turn</u>.

Example 1

> Your younger brother weighs 300 N. He sits 2 m from the pivot of a seesaw.
> If you weigh 700 N, where should you sit to balance the seesaw?

For the seesaw to <u>balance</u>: **total anticlockwise moments = total clockwise moments**

anticlockwise moment = clockwise moment
$$300 \times 2 = 700 \times y$$
$$y = \underline{0.86 \text{ m}}$$

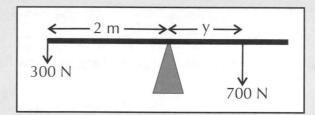

Ignore the weight of the seesaw — its centre of mass is on the pivot, so it doesn't have a turning effect.

Example 2

> A 6 m long steel girder weighing 1000 N rests horizontally on a pole 1 m from one end.
> What is the tension in a supporting cable attached vertically to the other end?

The '<u>tension in the cable</u>' bit makes it sound harder than it actually is.
But the girder's <u>weight</u> is <u>balanced</u> by the tension <u>force</u> in the cable, so...

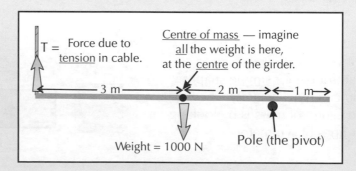

anticlockwise moment   =   clockwise moment
(due to weight)   (due to tension in cable)
$$1000 \times 2 = T \times 5$$
$$2000 = 5T$$
and so $\underline{T = 400 \text{ N}}$

Balanced Moments and Stability

And if the moments aren't equal...

If the total anticlockwise moments do not equal the total clockwise moments, there will be a resultant moment

...so the object will <u>turn</u>.

Low and wide objects are most stable

<u>Unstable</u> objects tip over easily, and <u>stable</u> objects don't. The position of the <u>centre of mass</u> is all-important in determining whether an object is stable or not.

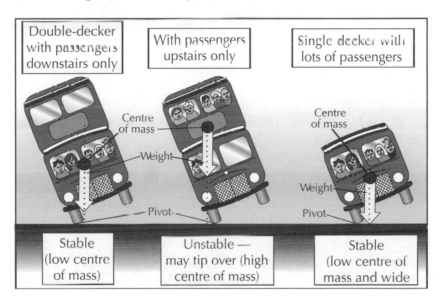

1) The most <u>stable</u> objects have a <u>wide base</u> and a <u>low centre of mass</u>.

2) An object will begin to <u>tip over</u> if its centre of mass moves <u>beyond</u> the edge of its base.

3) Again it's because of <u>moments</u> — if the weight <u>doesn't</u> act <u>in line</u> with the <u>pivot</u>, it'll cause a <u>resultant moment</u>.

4) This will either right the object or tip it over.

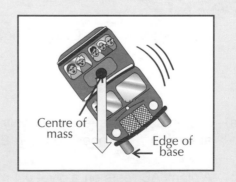

You can often tell just by looking what will tip easily and what won't

If you've got two <u>equal and opposite moments</u>, you've got <u>equilibrium</u>, and your thing-on-a-pivot will stay still. Remember that and you won't go far wrong (as long as you calculate the moments properly). <u>Learn</u> the factors that make an object hard to tip over — a <u>low centre of mass</u> and a <u>wide base</u>.

Warm-Up and Exam Questions

You know the drill — some warm-up questions to make sure you're awake, then some proper exam style questions to make sure you really know your stuff. Don't forget to check up on any tricky bits.

Warm-Up Questions

1) How do you calculate the moment of a force around a pivot?
2) What unit is used to describe the moment of a force?
3) What is meant by the centre of mass of an object?
4) What happens to an object if the clockwise and anticlockwise moments on it are not equal?
5) Why will an object begin to tip over if its centre of mass moves beyond the edge of its base?

Exam Questions

1 Bolts are often secured using an Allen key, as shown in the diagram. One end of the Allen key is put into the bolt and the other is turned to tighten the bolt.

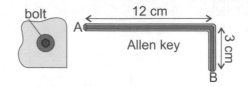

(a) Calculate the moment on the bolt when:

(i) End A of the Allen key is put into the bolt and a force of 15 N is applied to end B.

(2 marks)

(ii) End B of the Allen key is put into the bolt and a force of 15 N is applied to end A.

(2 marks)

(b) Which end of the Allen key (A or B) should be put into the bolt to make it easier to tighten the bolt? Give a reason for your answer.

(2 marks)

2 Maurice has made a window decoration, as shown in the diagram.
He wants to attach a string to it so that it hangs with the M the right way up.

(a) Maurice's dad says he should find the decoration's centre of mass. How would this help Maurice know where to place the string?

(1 mark)

(b) Describe how Maurice could find the decoration's centre of mass.

(4 marks)

3 (a) Robert says, "A seesaw will only balance if the masses on either side of the pivot are equal." Is Robert correct? Explain your answer.

(2 marks)

(b) A plank AB rests on a pivot 0.4 m from end A. End B is supported by a cord so that the plank is horizontal. The plank is 2.8 m long and weighs 50 N.

(i) Draw a diagram of the plank showing the pivot and the forces acting on the plank.

(3 marks)

(ii) Calculate the tension in the cord.

(2 marks)

Circular Motion

Circular motion — *velocity* is *constantly changing*

1) Velocity is both the speed and direction of an object.
2) If an object is travelling in a circle it is <u>constantly changing direction</u>, which means it's <u>accelerating</u>.
3) This means there <u>must</u> be a <u>force</u> acting on it.
4) This force acts towards the centre of the circle.
5) The force that keeps something moving in a circle is called a <u>centripetal force</u>.

Pronounced sen-tree-pee-tal

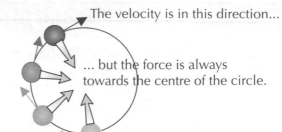

The velocity is in this direction...

... but the force is always towards the centre of the circle.

Tension, *friction* or *gravity* can provide a centripetal force

In the exam, you can be asked to say <u>which force</u> is actually providing the centripetal force in a given situation. It can be <u>tension</u>, or <u>friction</u>, or even <u>gravity</u> (see next page). Have a look at these examples:

<u>A car going round a bend</u>:
1) Imagine the bend is part of a <u>circle</u> — the centripetal force is towards the <u>centre</u>.
2) The force is from <u>friction</u> between the car's tyres and the road.

friction

tension

<u>A bucket whirling round on a rope</u>:
The centripetal force comes from <u>tension in the rope</u>. Break the rope, and the bucket flies off at a tangent.

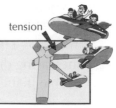

tension

<u>A spinning fairground ride</u>:
The centripetal force comes from <u>tension</u> in the <u>spokes of the ride</u>.

Centripetal force depends on *mass*, *speed* and *radius*

1) The <u>faster</u> an object's moving, the <u>bigger</u> the centripetal force has to be to keep it moving in a <u>circle</u>.
2) And the <u>heavier</u> the object, the <u>bigger</u> the centripetal force has to be to keep it moving in a <u>circle</u>.
3) You also need a <u>larger force</u> to keep something moving in a <u>small circle</u> — it has 'more turning' to do.

Example

Two cars are driving at the same speed around the same circular track. One has a mass of 900 kg, the other has a mass of 1200 kg. Which car has the larger centripetal force?

The <u>three things</u> that mean you need a <u>bigger centripetal force</u> are:
<u>more speed</u>, <u>more mass</u>, <u>smaller radius</u> of circle.

In this example, the speed and radius of circle are the same — the <u>only difference</u> is the <u>masses</u> of the cars. So you don't need to calculate anything — you can confidently say:

The <u>1200 kg car</u> (the heavier one) must have the <u>larger centripetal force</u>.

Gravity and Planetary Orbits

Gravity is not just important for keeping us all stuck to the ground — it's also the force that keeps the Moon and satellites orbiting round the Earth, and planets orbiting round stars...

Gravity is the centripetal force that keeps planets in orbit

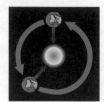

1) Gravity is the force of attraction between masses — the larger the masses the greater the force of gravity between them (you're strongly attracted to a big mass like the Earth, but not to a small mass like a toaster).

2) This gravitational force can act as the centripetal force that keeps one object moving in a circular path (orbit) round another. An orbit is possible when there's a balance between the forward motion of the object and the gravitational force pulling it inwards. (If there wasn't a balance, the smaller object would either get pulled inwards or fly off at a tangent.)

3) Planets always orbit around stars. E.g. the Earth orbits around the Sun, and the centripetal force needed is provided by the gravitational attraction between the Earth and the Sun. (And likewise all the other planets in the Solar System of course.)

4) These orbits are all slightly elliptical (elongated circles) with the Sun at one focus of the ellipse.

5) The further the planet is from the Sun, the longer its orbit takes (see below).

Gravity decreases quickly as you get further away

1) With very large masses like stars and planets, gravity is very big and is felt a long way out.

2) The closer you get to a star or a planet, the stronger the force of attraction.

3) To counteract the stronger gravity, planets nearer the Sun move faster, covering their orbit quicker.

4) Comets are also held in orbit by gravity, as are moons and satellites and space stations.

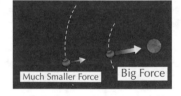

5) The size of the force of gravity decreases very quickly with increasing distance. E.g. if you double the distance of an object from a planet, the size of the force on it will be four times less.

In practice that means...

1) A long way out from the Sun, where Uranus orbits, the Sun's gravitational effect is weaker than here on Earth. So Uranus has a bigger orbit, travels slower and takes longer to complete its orbit than Earth.

2) Likewise, further in towards the Sun, its gravitational effect is stronger. Mercury is nearer the Sun than Earth, so it has a smaller orbit, travels faster and takes less time to complete its orbit than Earth.

Example:

Look at the following table of data. Is Planet X closer to or further away from the Sun than Earth?

Planet	Orbital period (earth days)	Distance from Sun (km)
Mercury	88	57 910 000
Earth	365	149 600 000
Mars	687	227 940 000
Uranus	30685	2 870 990 000
Planet X	4333	not given

Planet X has a longer orbital period than Earth. A longer orbital period means a slower orbit speed and a bigger orbit, i.e. a bigger distance from the Sun.

(Even without knowing the theory, you could probably work that out from the table — so remember that if you're stuck in the exam.)

Satellites

A <u>satellite</u> is any object that <u>orbits</u> around a <u>larger object</u> in space. There are natural satellites, like <u>moons</u>, but these pages just look at the artificial ones that we put there ourselves.

Satellites are set up by humans for many different purposes

You need to know a few examples of what satellites are used for:

1) Monitoring <u>weather</u> and climate.

2) <u>Communications</u>, e.g. phone and TV.

3) <u>Space research</u>, such as the Hubble Telescope.

4) <u>Spying</u>

5) <u>Navigation</u>, e.g. the Global Positioning System (GPS).

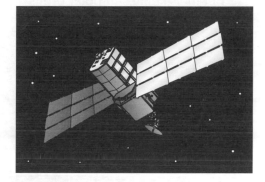

Communications satellites stay over the same point on Earth

1) Communications satellites are put into <u>quite a high orbit</u> over the <u>equator.</u>

2) This orbit takes <u>exactly 24 hours</u> to complete.

3) This means that the satellites stay above the <u>same point</u> on the Earth's surface, because the Earth <u>rotates below them</u>.

4) So this type of satellite is called a <u>geostationary</u> satellite (geo (= Earth)–stationary) or sometimes a <u>geosynchronous</u> satellite.

5) They're <u>ideal</u> for <u>telephone</u> and <u>TV</u> because they're always in the <u>same place</u> and can <u>transfer signals</u> from one side of the Earth to the other in a <u>fraction of a second</u>.

6) There's room for about <u>400</u> geostationary satellites around the Earth — any more than that and the signals will begin to <u>interfere</u>.

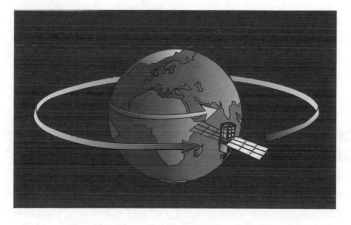

Satellites

Low polar orbit satellites are for *weather* and *spying*

1) In a <u>low polar orbit</u>, the satellite sweeps over <u>both poles</u> whilst the Earth <u>rotates beneath it</u>.
2) The time taken for each full orbit is just <u>a few hours</u>.
3) Each time the satellite comes round it can <u>scan</u> the next bit of the globe.
4) This allows the <u>whole surface</u> of the planet to be <u>monitored</u> each day.
5) Geostationary satellites are <u>too high</u> to take good weather or spying photos, but the satellites in <u>polar orbits</u> are <u>nice and low</u>.

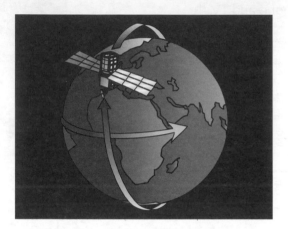

Example

The table gives data about two satellites.

<u>Q1</u>: Which satellite would be more useful for transmitting TV signals? Why?

<u>Q2</u>: Which satellite would be more useful for monitoring Earth's weather? Why?

	Orbital period (in Earth days)	Distance from Earth (km)	Position
Satellite A	0.07	800	Pole to pole
Satellite B	1	35 800	Around equator

<u>Satellite B</u> would be more useful for transmitting TV signals. This satellite is in a high orbit around the equator which takes exactly one day — so it's in a <u>geostationary</u> orbit.

<u>Satellite A</u> would be more useful for monitoring Earth's weather. This satellite is in a fast, low orbit. It sweeps over both poles (i.e. a polar orbit) as the Earth rotates, scanning the whole Earth.

Know the two main kinds of orbit used by satellites

There are other kinds of satellite as well, e.g. GPS (Global Positioning System) satellites, which are in a different kind of orbit altogether. They work by transmitting their position and the time. These signals are received by GPS devices, e.g. in cars, and once 4 signals have been received, the device can work out its exact location. It's all clever stuff. And you don't need to learn it, which is even better.

Warm-Up and Exam Questions

Another page of questions for your enjoyment. Make sure you can do them all properly...

Warm-Up Questions

1) What's the general name for a force that keeps an object moving in a circle?
2) What force keeps satellites in orbit around the Earth?
3) What shape are the planets' orbits around the Sun?
4) Suggest two uses for satellites.

Exam Questions

1   A car is being driven round a circular track at constant speed.
   (a) Name two forces acting on the car.

(1 mark)

   (b) Are all the forces acting on the car balanced or unbalanced?
Give a reason for your answer.

(2 marks)

2   Levi is writing a report on different types of satellite. He is researching two satellites, A and B. Satellite A transmits television signals while B is used to monitor the weather.

   (a) What type of orbit does satellite A use?

(1 mark)

   (b) How long does satellite A take to complete one orbit?

(1 mark)

   (c) Satellite B is able to take pictures of the whole surface of the Earth in one day without changing its orbit.
     (i)   Describe how this is possible.

(2 marks)

     (ii) Which satellite is closer to the Earth, A or B? Give a reason for your answer.

(1 mark)

3   The Earth is, on average, 1.39 times further from the Sun than Venus.

   (a) Which planet, Earth or Venus, travels faster? Explain your answer.

(2 marks)

   (b) Which planet, Earth or Venus, experiences a stronger gravitational force from the sun.

(1 mark)

Images

This next bit is all about <u>how light behaves</u> when it hits a lens or mirror. Be prepared for lots of diagrams on the next few pages.

A *real* image is *actually there* — a *virtual* image is *not*

1) A <u>real image</u> is where the <u>light from an object</u> comes together to form an <u>image on a 'screen'</u> — like the image formed on an eye's <u>retina</u> (the 'screen' at the back of an <u>eye</u>).

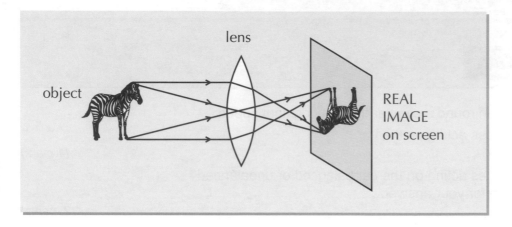

2) A <u>virtual image</u> is when the rays are diverging, so the light from the object <u>appears</u> to be coming from a completely <u>different place</u>.

3) When you look in a <u>mirror</u> you see a <u>virtual image</u> of your face — because the <u>object</u> (your face) <u>appears</u> to be <u>behind the mirror</u>.

4) You can get a virtual image when looking at an object through a <u>magnifying lens</u> — the virtual image looks <u>bigger</u> and <u>further away</u> than the object <u>actually</u> is.

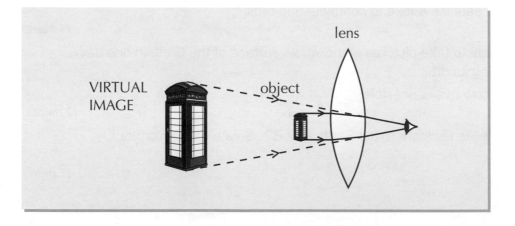

To describe an image properly, you need to say <u>three things</u>:

> 1) <u>How big it is</u> compared to the object
>
> 2) Whether it's <u>upright or inverted</u> (upside down)
>
> 3) Whether it's <u>real or virtual</u>.

Images

Reflection of light lets you see things

1) <u>Reflection of light</u> is what allows us to <u>see</u> objects. Light bounces off them into our eyes.

2) When light reflects off an <u>uneven surface</u> such as a <u>piece of paper</u>, the light reflects off <u>at all different angles</u> and you get a <u>diffuse reflection</u>.

3) When light reflects from an <u>even surface</u> (something <u>smooth and shiny</u> like a <u>mirror</u>) then it's all reflected at the <u>same angle</u> and you get a <u>clear reflection</u>.

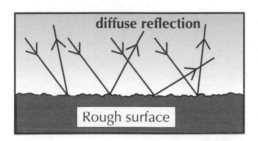

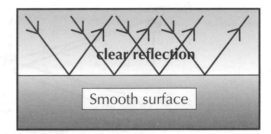

4) But don't forget, the <u>LAW OF REFLECTION</u> applies to <u>every reflected ray</u>:

angle of <u>incidence</u> = angle of <u>reflection</u>

Note that these two angles are <u>ALWAYS</u> defined between the ray itself and the <u>dotted NORMAL</u>. <u>Don't ever</u> label them as the angle between the ray and the <u>surface</u>.

The <u>normal</u> is an imaginary line that's at right angles to the surface (at the point where the light hits the surface).

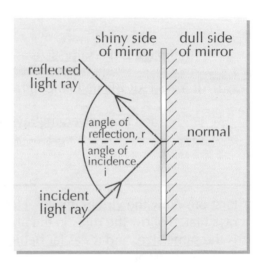

Light bends as it changes speed

1) <u>Refraction</u> of light is when the waves <u>change direction</u> as they <u>enter a different medium</u>.

2) This is caused <u>entirely</u> by the <u>change in speed</u> of the waves.

3) That's what makes ponds <u>look shallower</u> than they are — light reflects off the <u>bottom</u> and <u>speeds up</u> when it <u>leaves the water</u>, making the bottom look like it's <u>nearer</u> than it is:

See page 133 for more on refraction.

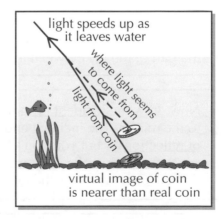

Take your time — this stuff about images can seem really odd at first

Make sure you've learnt this little lot well enough to answer typical exam questions like these:
"<u>Explain why you can see a piece of paper.</u>"   "<u>What is diffuse reflection?</u>"
"<u>What is a clear reflection?</u>"   "<u>Why do light rays bend as they leave a pond?</u>"

Mirrors

The examiners do like to see a nice diagram, so get your rulers out.

Draw a **ray diagram** for an **image** in a **plane mirror**

You need to be able to <u>reproduce</u> this entire diagram of <u>how an image is formed</u> in a <u>PLANE MIRROR</u>.

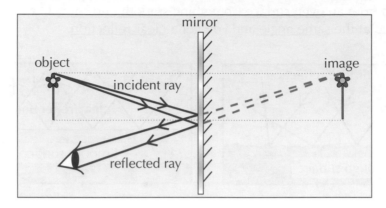

Learn these <u>three important points</u>:

    1)   The <u>image</u> is the <u>same size</u> as the <u>object</u>.

    2)   It is <u>AS FAR BEHIND</u> the mirror as the object is <u>in front</u>.

    3)   It's formed from <u>diverging rays</u>, which means it's a <u>virtual image</u>.

1)   First off, draw the <u>virtual image</u>. <u>Don't</u> try to draw the rays first. Follow the rules in the above box — the image is the <u>same size</u>, and it's <u>as far behind</u> the mirror as the object is in <u>front</u>.

2)   Next, draw a <u>reflected ray</u> going from the top of the virtual image to the top of the eye. Draw a <u>bold line</u> for the part of the ray between the mirror and eye, and a <u>dotted line</u> for the part of the ray between the mirror and the virtual image.

3)   Now draw the <u>incident ray</u> going from the top of the object to the mirror. The incident and reflected rays follow the <u>law of reflection</u> — but you <u>don't</u> actually have to measure any angles. Just draw the ray from the <u>object</u> to the <u>point</u> where the reflected ray <u>meets the mirror</u>.

4)   Now you have an <u>incident ray</u> and <u>reflected ray</u> for the <u>top</u> of the image. Do <u>steps 2 and 3 again</u> for the <u>bottom</u> of the <u>eye</u> — a reflected ray going from the image to the bottom of the eye, then an incident ray from the object to the mirror.

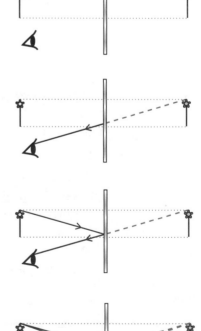

Mirrors

Curved mirrors are a little more complicated

Concave mirrors are shiny on the inside of the curve and convex mirrors are shiny on the outside.
Light shining on a concave mirror converges, and light shining on a convex mirror diverges.

1) Uniformly curved mirrors are like a round portion of a sphere. The centre of the sphere is the centre of curvature, C.

2) The centre of the mirror's surface is called the vertex.

3) Halfway between the centre of curvature and the vertex is the focal point, F.

4) The centre of curvature, vertex and focal point all lie on a line down the middle of the mirror called the axis.

5) Rays parallel to the axis of a concave mirror reflect and meet at the focal point.

6) The centre of curvature and focal point are in front of a concave mirror and behind a convex mirror.

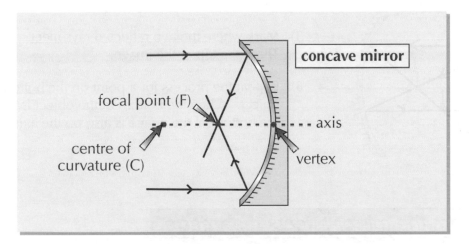

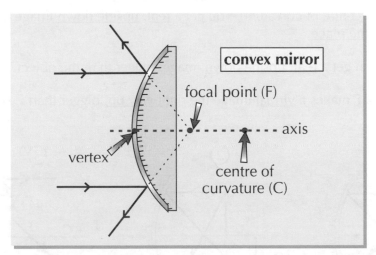

You must be able to label F, C and the vertex on a curved mirror

Reflection in a plane (flat) mirror isn't too hard to learn. Go through the method step by step — doing it "image first" instead of "rays first" gives you a nice neat diagram, even if it seems weird to do it that way round. Learn all the facts about curved mirrors — it'll make the next pages a load easier.

Mirrors

You could also get asked to draw a <u>ray diagram</u> of reflection in a curved mirror. Pay attention, it's tricky.

Draw a **ray diagram** for an **image** in a **concave mirror**

1) An incident ray <u>parallel to the axis</u> will pass through the <u>focal point</u> when it's reflected.
2) An incident ray passing <u>through the focal point</u> will be <u>parallel to the axis</u> when it's reflected.

1) Pick a point on the <u>top</u> of the object. Draw a ray going from the object to the mirror <u>parallel</u> to the axis of the mirror.

2) Draw another line going from the top of the <u>object to the mirror</u>, passing through the <u>focal point</u> on the way.

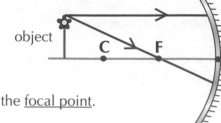

3) The incident ray that's <u>parallel</u> to the axis is <u>reflected</u> through the <u>focal point</u>. Draw a <u>reflected ray</u> passing through the focal point.

4) The incident ray that passes through the <u>focal point</u> is reflected <u>parallel</u> to the axis. Draw a reflected ray passing parallel to the axis.

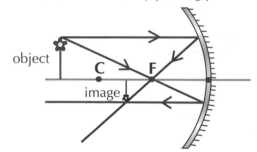

5) Mark where the two reflected rays <u>meet</u>. That's the <u>top of the image</u>.

6) Repeat the process for a point on the <u>bottom</u> of the object. When the bottom of the object is on the <u>axis</u>, the bottom of the image is <u>also</u> on the axis.

Distance from the mirror affects the **image**

1) With an object <u>at C</u> (centre of curvature), you get a <u>real</u>, <u>upside down</u> image the <u>same size</u> as the object, in the <u>same place</u>.

2) <u>Between C and F</u>, you get a <u>real</u>, <u>upside down</u> image, bigger than the object and <u>behind</u> it.

3) An object <u>in front of F</u> makes a <u>virtual</u> image the <u>right way up</u>, bigger than F, <u>behind the mirror</u>.

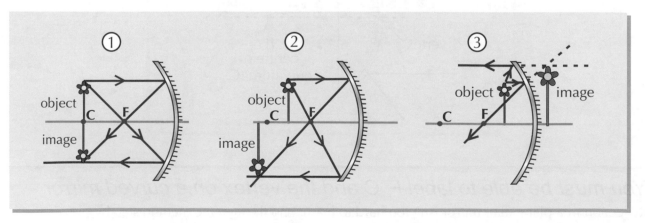

Mirrors

Draw a *ray diagram* for an *image* in a *convex mirror*

1) An incident ray <u>parallel</u> to the <u>axis</u> will reflect so that the reflected ray seems to come from the <u>focal point</u>.

2) An incident ray that can be extended to pass through the <u>focal point</u> will be <u>parallel</u> to the <u>axis</u> when it's reflected.

Always extend the lines far enough behind the mirror to be sure they pass through the focal point if they need to.

1) Pick a point on the <u>top</u> of the object. Draw a ray going from the object to the mirror <u>parallel</u> to the axis of the mirror. Make it a <u>bold line</u> when it's in front of the mirror, and a <u>dotted line</u> behind.

2) Draw another line going from the top of the <u>object to the mirror</u>, passing through the <u>focal point</u> on the other side. Make it <u>dotted</u> when it's <u>behind</u> the mirror.

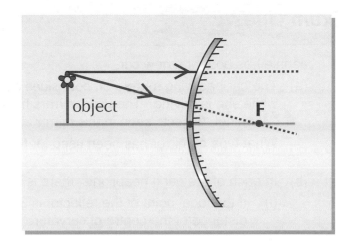

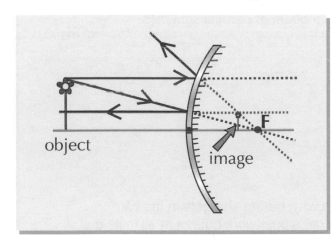

3) The incident ray that's <u>parallel</u> to the axis is <u>reflected</u> as if it starts at the <u>focal point</u>. Make sure the reflected ray <u>meets the incident ray</u> at the mirror surface.

4) The incident ray that passes through the <u>focal point</u> is reflected <u>parallel</u> to the axis. Make sure the reflected ray <u>meets the incident ray</u> at the mirror surface.

5) Mark where these two reflected rays meet behind the mirror. That's the <u>top of the image</u>.

6) Repeat the process for a point on the <u>bottom of the object</u>.

The *image* is always *smaller*

1) The image in a convex mirror is always <u>virtual</u>, <u>upright</u>, <u>smaller than the object</u> and <u>behind the mirror</u>, <u>closer than F</u>. The <u>further away</u> the <u>object</u> is from the mirror, the <u>smaller</u> the <u>image</u>.

2) You can <u>see a wide area</u> in a convex mirror, which is why they put them on dodgy road corners.

Warm-Up and Exam Questions

Time for some questions — if you think this section's firmly in your head, then have a go at these...

Warm-Up Questions

1) What is the difference between a real image and a virtual image?
2) What three things do you need to say to fully describe an image?
3) State the relationship between the angles of incidence and reflection for a reflected ray.
4) Draw a diagram of a convex mirror, showing its focal point, centre of curvature, axis and vertex.

Exam Questions

1   Jennie has bought a new car.

(a)   The car has wing mirrors on both sides so that Jennie can see what's behind her while she is driving. The wing mirrors have the following notice on them: "Warning! Objects seen in this mirror are larger than they appear."

What type of mirror has been used for the wing mirrors?

(1 mark)

(b)   In each of the car's headlights, there is a concave reflector behind the bulb.

(i)   If the focal point of the reflector is 3 cm in front of the vertex, what is the distance of the centre of curvature from the vertex?

(1 mark)

(ii)   The bulb is positioned at the focal point of the reflector. Complete the ray diagram below to show how this gives a beam of parallel light rays.

(3 marks)

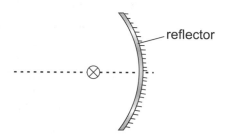

(c)   Use your knowledge of reflection to explain why, before she gets in the car, Jennie can see her reflection clearly in the car's paintwork but not at all in its dull plastic bumper.

(2 marks)

2   Gregor has dropped his mobile phone in the garden pond. When he reaches in to get it, he is surprised to find that the pond is deeper than it looks. Explain why this is, and name the phenomenon that causes this effect.

(3 marks)

3   A pencil is placed in front of a convex mirror.
Complete the ray diagram to the right to show how
the image of the pencil is formed. The black dot
on the diagram is the focal point.

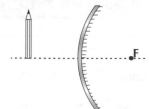

(4 marks)

Lenses

Lenses are usually made of <u>glass or plastic</u>. All lenses change the <u>direction of light rays</u> by <u>refraction</u>.

Light is **refracted** when it **enters** and **leaves glass prisms**

You can't fail to remember the '<u>ray of light through a rectangular glass block</u>' trick:

1) The ray <u>bends towards the normal</u> as it enters the <u>denser medium</u>, and <u>away</u> from the normal as it <u>emerges</u> into the <u>less dense</u> medium.

   Try to <u>visualise</u> the shape of the <u>wiggle</u> in the diagram — that can be easier than remembering the rule in words.

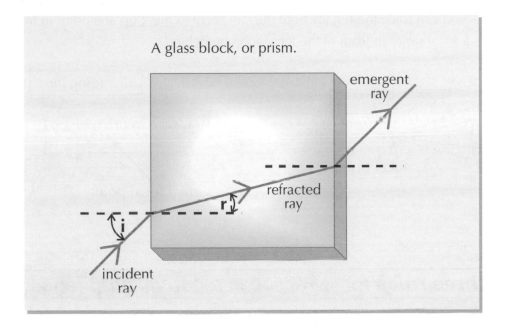

2) Note that <u>different wavelengths</u> of light refract by <u>different amounts</u>. So <u>white light</u> disperses into <u>different colours</u> as it <u>enters a prism</u>. A <u>rectangular</u> prism has parallel boundaries, so the rays bend one way as they enter, and then bend back again by the same amount as they leave — so <u>white light emerges</u>.

   But with a <u>triangular</u> prism, the boundaries aren't parallel, which means the <u>different wavelengths</u> don't recombine and you get a nice <u>rainbow effect</u>.

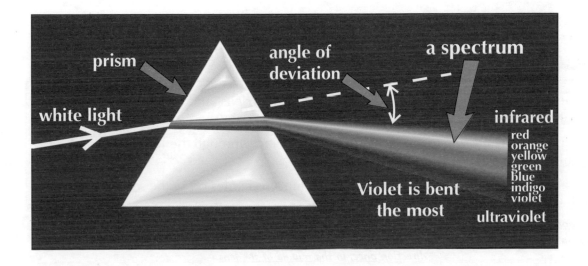

Lenses

Different lenses produce different kinds of image

There are two main types of lens — converging and diverging. They have different shapes and have opposite effects on light rays.

1) A converging lens is convex — it bulges outwards. It causes parallel rays of light to converge (move together) to a focus.

2) A diverging lens is concave — it caves inwards. It causes parallel rays of light to diverge (spread out).

3) The axis of a lens is a line passing through the middle of the lens.

4) The focal point of a converging lens is where rays hitting the lens parallel to the axis all meet.

5) The focal point of a diverging lens is the point where rays hitting the lens parallel to the axis appear to come from — you can trace them back until they all seem to meet up at a point in front of the lens.

6) Each lens has a focal point in front of the lens, and one behind.

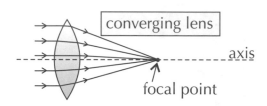

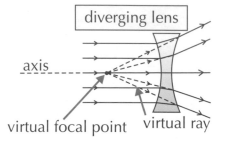

There are three rules for refraction in a converging lens...

1) An incident ray parallel to the axis refracts through the lens and passes through the focal point on the other side.

2) An incident ray passing through the focal point refracts through the lens and travels parallel to the axis.

3) An incident ray passing through the centre of the lens carries on in the same direction.

See next page for more on this.

...and three rules for refraction in a diverging lens

1) An incident ray parallel to the axis refracts through the lens, and travels in line with the focal point (so it appears to have come from the focal point).

2) An incident ray passing towards the focal point refracts through the lens and travels parallel to the axis.

3) An incident ray passing through the centre of the lens carries on in the same direction.

See page 136 for more on this.

The good thing about these rules is that they allow you to draw ray diagrams without bending the rays as they go into the lens and as they leave the lens. You can draw the diagrams as if each ray only changes direction once, in the middle of the lens.

Converging Lenses

You may have to draw a ray diagram of <u>refraction through a lens</u>. Follow the instructions very carefully...

Draw a **ray diagram** for an **image** through a **converging lens**

1) Pick a point on the <u>top</u> of the object. Draw a ray going from this point to the lens <u>parallel</u> to the axis of the lens.

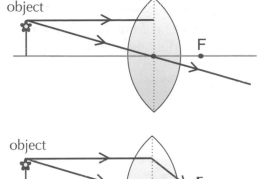

2) Draw another ray from the top of the object going right through the <u>middle</u> of the lens.

3) The incident ray that's <u>parallel</u> to the axis is <u>refracted</u> through the <u>focal point</u>. Draw a <u>refracted ray</u> passing through the <u>focal point</u>.

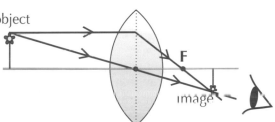

4) The ray passing through the <u>middle</u> of the lens doesn't bend.

5) Mark where the rays <u>meet</u>. That's the <u>top of the image</u>.

6) Repeat the process for a point on the bottom of the object. When the bottom of the object is on the <u>axis</u>, the bottom of the image is <u>also</u> on the axis.

If you <u>really</u> want to draw a <u>third incident ray</u> passing through the <u>focal point</u> on the way to the lens, you can (refract it so that it goes <u>parallel to the axis</u>). In the <u>exam</u>, you only need to draw <u>two rays</u>, so no need to bother with three.

Distance from the lens affects the **image**

1) An object <u>at 2F</u> will produce a <u>real</u>, <u>upside down</u> image the <u>same size</u> as the object and <u>at 2F</u>.

2) <u>Between F and 2F</u> it'll make a <u>real</u>, <u>upside down</u> image <u>bigger</u> than the object and <u>beyond 2F</u>.

3) An object <u>nearer than F</u> will make a <u>virtual</u> image the <u>right way up</u>, <u>bigger</u> than the object, on the <u>same side</u> of the lens.

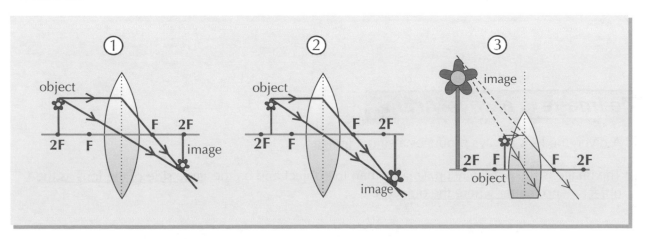

Diverging Lenses

Draw a *ray diagram* for an *image* through a *diverging lens*

1) Pick a point on the <u>top</u> of the object. Draw a ray going from the object to the lens <u>parallel</u> to the axis of the lens.

2) Draw another ray from the top of the object going right through the <u>middle</u> of the lens.

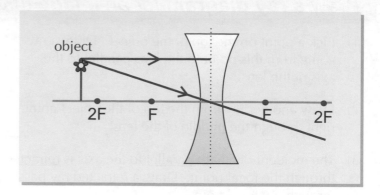

3) The incident ray that's <u>parallel</u> to the axis is <u>refracted</u> so it appears to have come from the <u>focal point</u>. Draw a <u>ray</u> from the focal point. Make it <u>dotted</u> before it reaches the lens.

4) The ray passing through the <u>middle</u> of the lens doesn't bend.

5) Mark where the refracted rays <u>meet</u>. That's the top of the image.

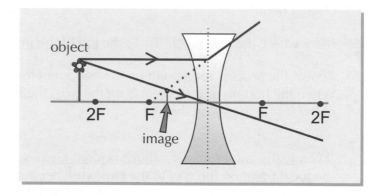

6) Repeat the process for a point on the bottom of the object. When the bottom of the object is on the <u>axis</u>, the bottom of the image is <u>also</u> on the axis.

Again, if you <u>really</u> want to draw a <u>third incident ray</u> in the direction of the <u>focal point</u> on the far side of the lens, you can. Remember to refract it so that it goes <u>parallel to the axis</u>. In the <u>exam</u>, you only need to draw <u>two rays</u>. Choose whichever two are easiest to draw — don't try to draw a ray that won't actually pass through the lens.

The *image* is always *virtual*

1) A diverging lens always produces a <u>virtual image</u>.

2) The image is the <u>right way up</u>, <u>smaller</u> than the object and on the <u>same side of the lens as the object</u> — <u>no matter where the object is</u>.

Uses — Magnification and Cameras

Converging lenses are used in magnifying glasses and in cameras.

Magnifying glasses use **convex lenses**

Magnifying glasses work by creating a magnified virtual image.

1) The object being magnified must be closer to the lens than the focal length (or you get a different kind of image — see diagrams on page 135).

2) The image produced is a virtual image. The light rays don't actually come from the place where the image appears to be.

3) Remember, 'you can't project a virtual image onto a screen' — that's a useful phrase to use in the exam if they ask you about virtual images.

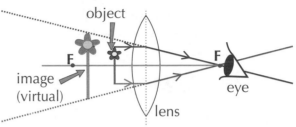

Learn the **magnification formula**

You can use the magnification formula to find the magnification produced by a lens or a mirror at a given distance:

$$\text{magnification} = \frac{\text{image height}}{\text{object height}}$$

Example

A coin with diameter 14 mm is placed a certain distance behind a magnifying lens. The virtual image produced has a diameter of 35 mm. What is the magnification of the lens at this distance?

Answer: magnification = 35 ÷ 14 = 2.5

In the exam you might have to draw a ray diagram to show where an image would be, and then measure the image so that you can work out the magnification of the lens or mirror. Another reason to draw those ray diagrams carefully...

Taking a **photo** forms an **image** on the **film**

When you take a photograph of a flower, light from the object (flower) travels to the camera and is refracted by the lens, forming an image on the film.

1) The image on the film is a real image because light rays actually meet there.

2) The image is smaller than the object, because the object's further away than the focal length of the lens.

3) The image is inverted — upside down.

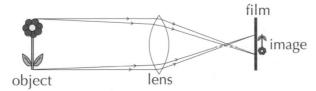

4) The same thing happens in our eye — a real, inverted image forms on the retina. Our very clever brains flip the image so that we see it the right way up.

Warm-Up and Exam Questions

Lots of questions on lenses here. Go on, answer them, you know you want to...

Warm-Up Questions

1) Name the two main types of lens.
2) Of the two types of lens, which bulges outwards at the centre and which curves inwards?
3) Of the two types of lens, which always creates a virtual image and which can create both real and virtual images?
4) What is meant by the focal point of a diverging lens?
5) State the magnification formula.
6) Give two uses for a convex lens.

Exam Questions

1 (a) Using this diagram of a triangular prism, explain what is meant by dispersion, and why it happens.

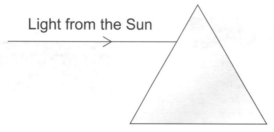

Light from the Sun

(4 marks)

(b) Why doesn't the dispersion effect occur with a rectangular glass block?

(1 mark)

2 (a) Edward is trying to start a campfire by focussing sunlight through his spectacle lens onto the firewood. The lens is concave. Explain why he cannot focus the sunlight onto the wood using this lens.

(2 marks)

(b) Edward finds a slug and uses a magnifying glass to look at it.

(i) Complete the ray diagram below to show how the image of the slug is formed.

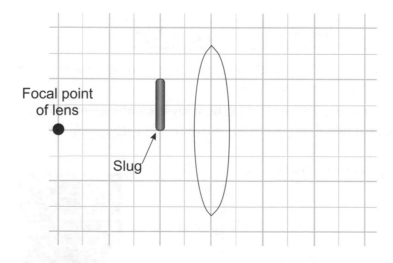

Focal point of lens

Slug

(3 marks)

(ii) What is the magnification of the lens for the slug at this distance?

(1 mark)

Sound Waves

We hear sounds when vibrations reach our eardrums. You'll need to know how <u>sound waves</u> work.

Sound travels as a wave

1) <u>Sound waves</u> are caused by <u>vibrating objects</u>. These mechanical vibrations are passed through the surrounding medium as a series of compressions. They're <u>longitudinal waves</u>.

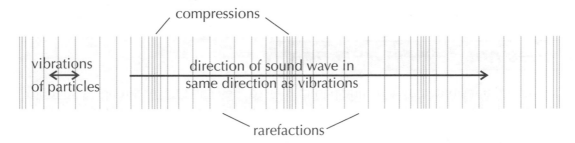

2) Sometimes the sound will eventually reach someone's <u>eardrum</u>, at which point the person might <u>hear it</u> (if it's loud enough and in the right frequency range — see next page).

3) Because sound waves are caused by vibrating particles, the <u>denser</u> the medium, the <u>faster</u> sound travels through it, generally speaking anyway. Sound generally travels <u>faster in solids</u> than in liquids, and faster in liquids than in gases.

Don't get confused by CRO displays (see next pages), which show a <u>transverse</u> wave (like a water wave) when displaying sounds. The real sound wave is <u>longitudinal</u> — the display shows a transverse wave just so you can see what's going on.

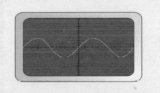

Sound waves can reflect and refract

1) Sound waves will be <u>reflected</u> by <u>hard flat surfaces</u>. Things like <u>carpets</u> and <u>curtains</u> act as <u>absorbing surfaces</u> which will <u>absorb</u> sounds rather than reflect them.

2) This is very noticeable in an <u>empty room</u>. A big empty room sounds <u>completely different</u> once you've put carpet and curtains in and a bit of furniture, because these things absorb the sound quickly and stop it <u>echoing</u> around the room.

3) <u>Sound waves</u> will also refract (change direction) as they enter <u>different media</u>. As they enter <u>denser</u> material, they <u>speed up</u>. (However, since sound waves are always <u>spreading out so much</u>, the change in direction is <u>hard to spot</u> under normal circumstances.)

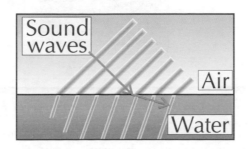

Sound Waves

We *hear* sounds in the range *20 – 20 000 Hz*

1) The <u>frequency</u> of a wave (in Hertz, Hz) is the <u>number of waves</u> in 1 second.

2) The <u>human ear</u> is capable of hearing sounds with frequencies between <u>20 Hz</u> and <u>20 000 Hz</u>. (Although in practice some people can't hear some of the higher frequency sounds.)

Sound does *not* travel in a *vacuum*

1) Sound waves are transmitted by vibrating particles — so they <u>can't travel</u> through a <u>vacuum</u>. (No particles, you see.)

2) This is <u>nicely demonstrated</u> by the jolly old <u>bell jar experiment</u>.

3) As the <u>air is sucked out</u> by the <u>vacuum pump</u>, the sound gets <u>quieter and quieter</u>.

4) The bell has to be <u>mounted</u> on something like <u>foam</u> to stop the sound from it travelling through the solid surface and making the base vibrate, because you'd hear that instead.

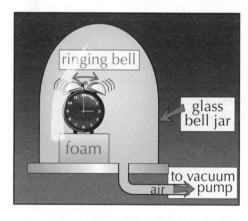

Loudness increases with *amplitude*

All sounds have <u>pitch</u> (see next page) and <u>loudness</u>. Pitch and loudness can both be measured.

1) The <u>greater the amplitude</u> of a wave, the <u>more energy</u> it carries.

2) With <u>sound</u> this means it'll be <u>louder</u>.

3) <u>Bigger amplitude</u> means a <u>louder sound</u>.

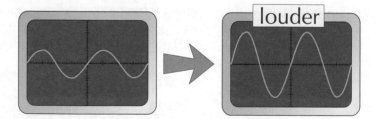

So — does a falling tree make a sound if no one hears it?...

So, we're off 'Light' and onto 'Sound' now. The thing to do here is to simply learn the facts. There's a simple equation that says <u>the more you learn now</u>, the <u>more marks you'll get</u> in the exam. A lot of questions just test whether you've learned the facts. Easy marks, really.

Sound Waves

The **higher** the **frequency**, the higher the **pitch**

1) <u>High frequency</u> sound waves sound <u>high pitched</u> (like a <u>squeaking mouse</u>).
2) <u>Low frequency</u> sound waves sound <u>low pitched</u> (like a <u>mooing cow</u>).
3) <u>Frequency</u> is the number of <u>complete vibrations</u> each second.
4) Common <u>units</u> are <u>kHz</u> (1000 Hz) and <u>MHz</u> (1 000 000 Hz).
5) <u>High frequency</u> (or high pitch) also means <u>shorter wavelength</u> (see page 38).
6) These <u>CRO traces</u> are <u>very important</u>, so make sure you know them:

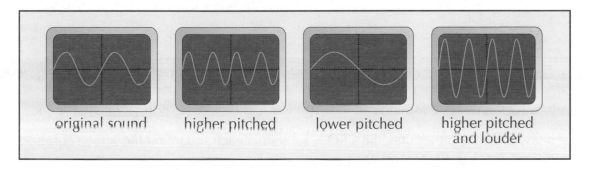

original sound   higher pitched   lower pitched   higher pitched and louder

The **quality** of a **note** depends on the **waveform**

On a CRO trace, a clear, pure sound produces a smooth, rounded waveform called a <u>sine wave</u>.

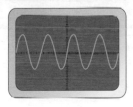

sine wave — clear, pure sound

Other kinds of sounds produce different CRO traces, for example:

1) Buzzy, brassy sounds have a <u>sawtooth waveform</u>, either with sloping 'ups' and vertical 'downs' or vertical 'ups' and sloping 'downs'.
2) A waveform of <u>rectangular peaks and troughs</u> makes a thin, <u>reedy</u> sound, a bit like an oboe.
3) A <u>square wave</u> has peaks the same length as the troughs. It makes a <u>hollow</u> sound.
4) <u>Triangle waves</u> are similar to sine waves, but they make a weaker, more <u>mellow</u> sound.

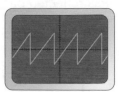 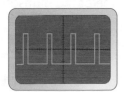 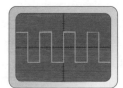 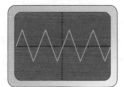

sawtooth wave — buzzy, brassy sound   pulse wave — thin, reedy sound   square wave — hollow sound   triangle wave — weak and mellow

Waves have loudness, pitch and quality

The <u>important</u> things to remember here are what makes sounds <u>higher and lower pitched</u> and what makes sounds <u>louder and softer</u>. Once that's under your belt, have a think about the different shapes you get for different sounds. You don't need to learn all the shapes, just be aware there are differences.

Ultrasound

There's sound, and then there's <u>ultrasound</u>.

Ultrasound is sound with a higher frequency than we can hear

1) Electrical devices can be made which produce <u>electrical oscillations</u> of <u>any frequency</u>.

2) These can easily be converted into <u>mechanical vibrations</u> to produce <u>sound</u> waves <u>beyond the range of human hearing</u> (i.e. frequencies above 20 kHz).

3) This is called <u>ultrasound</u> and it has loads of uses (see pages 144-145).

You can use CRO traces to compare amplitudes and frequencies

On the screen, CRO traces of ultrasound can look just like CRO traces for <u>normal pitched</u> sounds.

For showing high frequency ultrasound, the CRO is set so that <u>each square</u> on the screen corresponds to a <u>very short time</u>, e.g. <u>1 μs</u> (0.000 001 s).

This lets you see each peak and trough:

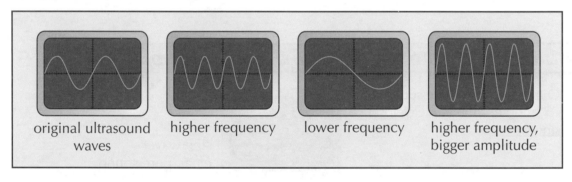

| original ultrasound waves | higher frequency | lower frequency | higher frequency, bigger amplitude |

Ultrasound waves get partially reflected at a boundary

1) When a wave passes from one medium into another, <u>some</u> of the wave is <u>reflected</u> off the boundary between the two media, and some is transmitted (and refracted). This is <u>partial reflection</u>.

2) What this means is that you can point a pulse of ultrasound at an object, and wherever there are <u>boundaries</u> between one substance and another, some of the ultrasound gets <u>reflected back</u>.

3) The time it takes for the reflections to reach a <u>detector</u> can be used to measure <u>how far away</u> the boundary is.

4) This is how <u>ultrasound imaging</u> works — see next pages.

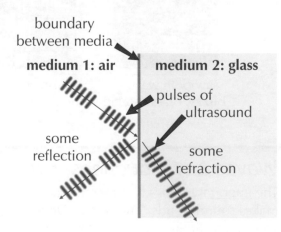

boundary between media

medium 1: air | medium 2: glass

pulses of ultrasound

some reflection

some refraction

Ultrasound

You can use *oscilloscope traces* to find boundaries

1) The CRO trace below shows an ultrasound pulse reflecting off <u>two separate boundaries</u>.

2) Given the 'seconds per division' setting of the CRO, you can work out the <u>time</u> between the pulses by measuring on the screen.

3) Given the <u>speed of sound</u> in the medium, you can work out the <u>distance</u> between the boundaries, using <u>d = v × t</u>.

4) They <u>might</u> give you the <u>frequency</u> and <u>wavelength</u> of the ultrasound and leave <u>you</u> to work out the speed using <u>v = frequency × wavelength</u> (see page 38).

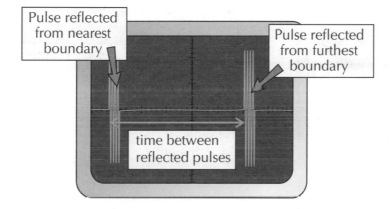

Example

> A pulse of ultrasound is beamed into a person's abdomen. The first boundary it reflects off is between fat and muscle. The second boundary is between muscle and a body cavity. A CRO trace shows that the time between the reflected pulses is 10 µs. The frequency of ultrasound used is 30 kHz, and the wavelength is 5 cm. Calculate the distance between the fat/muscle boundary and the muscle/cavity boundary, to give you the thickness of the muscle layer.

<u>Answer:</u> First work out the <u>speed</u> of the ultrasound using v = fλ. (Convert to Hz and m first.)
v = 30 000 Hz × 0.05 m. v = 1500 m/s.

Next you find the distance using d = v × t. BUT, the reflected pulses have travelled <u>there and back</u>, so the distance you calculate will be <u>twice the distance between boundaries</u>.

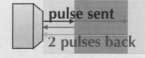

So: d = v × t = 1500 × (1 × 10^{-5}) = 0.015 m. So the distance between boundaries (i.e. thickness of muscle layer) = 0.015 ÷ 2 = 0.0075 m = <u>7.5 mm</u>.

With reflections you always get a factor of 2

Slightly trickier couple of pages there. Get the facts straight first — learn what <u>ultrasound</u> is, and what <u>partial reflection</u> is. Then cover the answer and make sure you can do the example question.

Ultrasound

Ultrasound has loads of exciting uses, including <u>cleaning</u>, <u>quality control</u>, <u>prenatal scans</u> and, erm, <u>bats</u>.

Ultrasound vibrations are used in industrial **cleaning**

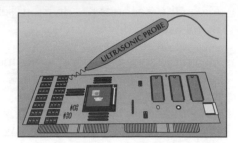

1) Ultrasound can be used to <u>clean delicate mechanisms</u> without them having to be dismantled.

2) Ultrasound waves can be directed onto <u>very precise areas</u>, and they're <u>extremely effective</u> at removing dirt and other deposits which form on delicate equipment.

3) The <u>high frequency vibrations</u> of ultrasound make the <u>components</u> of a piece of equipment vibrate at a high frequency. The <u>dirt</u> on the equipment vibrates too.

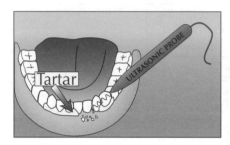

4) This vibration <u>breaks up dirt and crud</u> into very small particles, which simply fall off the equipment.

5) Alternatives to ultrasound would either <u>damage</u> the equipment (potentially), or require it to be <u>dismantled</u> before cleaning.

6) The same technique is also used by <u>dentists</u> sometimes, to clean <u>teeth</u>.

Ultrasound is used in industrial **quality control**

<u>Ultrasound waves</u> can pass through something like a <u>metal casting</u>, and whenever they reach a <u>boundary</u> between <u>two different media</u> (such as metal and air), some of the wave will be <u>reflected back</u> and <u>detected</u>.

The exact <u>timing and distribution</u> of these <u>echoes</u> provides <u>detailed information</u> about the <u>internal structure</u> of the metal casting (or whatever).

The echoes are usually <u>processed by computer</u> to produce a <u>visual display</u> of what the object must be like <u>inside</u>. If there are cracks where there shouldn't be, <u>they'll show up</u>.

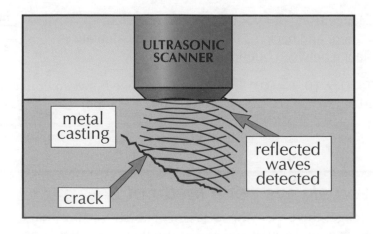

Ultrasound

Ultrasound imaging is used for **prenatal scanning** of a foetus

1) This follows the <u>same principle</u> as the industrial quality control. As the ultrasound hits boundaries between <u>different media</u>, some of the wave is <u>reflected</u> back.

2) In the uterus, there are boundaries between the <u>amniotic fluid</u> that the foetus floats in, and the <u>body tissues of the foetus</u> itself.

3) The reflected waves are <u>processed by computer</u> to produce a <u>video image</u> of the foetus.

4) The video image can be used to check whether the foetus is <u>developing correctly</u> — and sometimes what <u>sex</u> the foetus is too.

5) No-one knows for sure whether ultrasound is absolutely safe in all cases, but <u>X-rays</u> would definitely be dangerous to the foetus. (See page 42.)

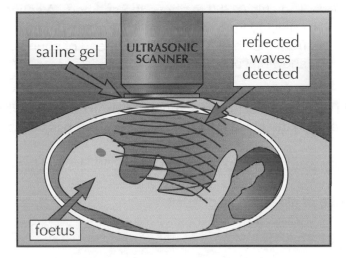

Bats use ultrasound to *sense* their surroundings

<u>Bats</u> use a similar technique. They send out <u>ultrasound squeaks</u> and pick up the <u>reflections</u> with their enormous ears. Their brains <u>process</u> the reflected signals, and turn them into a <u>picture</u> of what's around. So basically, bats '<u>see</u>' with sound waves.

This ultrasound technique lets bats 'see' in pitch dark conditions

Bats are amazing, really. They can 'see' with ultrasound well enough to <u>catch a moth</u> in <u>mid-flight</u> in <u>complete darkness</u>. It's a nice trick if you can do it. <u>Another nice trick</u>, and a much easier one, is to <u>learn everything on this page</u>. Cover up the page and scribble down a mini-essay on ultrasound scans.

Warm-Up and Exam Questions

There's been lots of stuff on CRO traces and ultrasound in the last few pages — it's not too bad really, but making it stick in your head can be a bit painful... So have a pop at these questions and see how you do.

Warm-Up Questions

1) What type of wave is a sound wave?
2) Would sound travel fastest in air, a copper bar or the sea?
3) Approximately what range of frequencies can humans hear?
4) How do the frequency and amplitude of a sound wave relate to the volume and pitch of a note?
5) Give the equation relating time, distance and velocity.

Exam Questions

1   A fishing trawler is searching for shoals of fish using ultrasound sonar. The ship sends pulses of ultrasound vertically downwards and 'listens' for the echo.

(a)   The ship is 360 m above the sea bed. A sound pulse reflected from the bottom is detected 0.48 s after it was sent from the ship. Calculate the speed of sound in sea water, showing your working.

(2 marks)

(b)   Another sound pulse is reflected off a shoal of fish. The echo is detected 180 ms after sending the pulse from the ship. How deep is the shoal of fish?

(2 marks)

(c)   Which frequency would the ship use to do this — 50 Hz, 5 kHz or 50 kHz?

(1 mark)

(d)   Give another use of ultrasound.

(1 mark)

2   Vicky is using a CRO to investigate the waveforms made by different musical instruments. She connects a microphone and amplifier to a CRO and plays the instruments in front of the microphone.

(a)   First she investigates a tuning fork. The trace on the left shows her results. Sketch the trace you would expect to see from a higher pitched tuning fork.

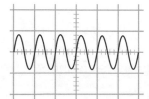 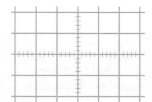

(1 mark)

(b)   Vicky now plays a note on a trumpet. The trace on the left shows her results. Sketch the trace you would expect to see if she played the same note on the trumpet, but louder.

(2 marks)

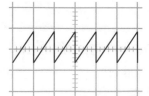 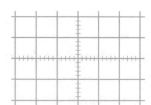

Revision Summary for Physics 3(i)

Phew, hurrah, yay — made it to the end of this section. A lot of tricky ideas to remember — especially all that stuff on drawing ray diagrams for different mirrors and lenses. So, get yourself stuck into these revision questions to find out how much you've learnt...

1) Sarah is levering the lid off a can of paint using a screwdriver. She places the tip of the 20 cm long screwdriver under the can's lid and applies a force of 10 N on the end of the screwdriver's handle as shown. Suggest two ways that Sarah could increase the moment about the pivot point (the side of the can).

pivot point

2) Describe two different ways of finding the centre of mass of a rectangular playing card.

3)* Arthur weighs 600 N and is sitting on a seesaw 1.5 m from the pivot point. His friend Caroline weighs 450 N and sits on the seesaw so that it balances. How far from the pivot point is Caroline sitting?

4) A cyclist is moving at a constant speed of 5 m/s around a circular track.

   a) Is the cyclist accelerating? Explain your answer.

   b) What force keeps the cyclist travelling in a circle? Where does this force come from?

   c) What will happen to the size of this force if the same cyclist travels at a constant speed of 5 m/s around a different circular track that has a larger radius?

5) Gravity is the force of attraction between two masses. What happens to the size of this force if the distance between the masses decreases?

6) Two identical satellites orbit at different distances from the Earth. Satellite A orbits the Earth at a distance of 10 000 km and satellite B orbits at 20 000 km. Which satellite has the smaller orbital period? Explain your answer.

7) Name four uses for artificial satellites.

8) State three differences between a low polar orbit and a geostationary orbit.

9) What is a real image? How is it different from a virtual image?

10) A ray of light hits the surface of a mirror at an incident angle of 10° to the normal. What is the angle of reflection for the ray of light?

11) Describe the steps you would take to draw a ray diagram for an image in a plane mirror. Draw diagrams to illustrate your method.

12) Explain how the following rays of light are reflected:

   a) an incident ray passing through the focal point of a concave mirror.

   b) an incident ray parallel to the axis of a convex mirror.

13) Draw a diagram to show the path of a ray of light as it passes from air → block of glass → air, meeting the block of glass at an angle.

14)* Peter measures the length of a seed to be 1.5 cm. When he looks at the seed through a converging lens at a certain distance, the seed appears to have a length of 4.5 cm. What is the magnification of this lens at this distance?

15) Describe how a sound wave travels through a medium. What is this type of wave called?

16) Explain why sound travels faster through an iron bar than through the air.

17) This is a diagram of a sound wave displayed on an oscilloscope.

   a) What is happening to the loudness of this sound wave?

   b) What is happening to the pitch of this sound wave?

	Time between reflected pulses
Location A	0.002 seconds
Location B	0.003 seconds

18)* An ultrasonic scanner above the ground is used to detect the depth of an underground water pipe at two different locations (A and B). For each location, the times between pulses reflected off the ground's surface and the top of the pipe are shown in the data table. The speed of the ultrasound is 2800 m/s. What is the depth of the pipe at its deepest point?

* Answers on p228.

Magnetic Fields

Electric currents can create magnetic fields. This turns out to be quite useful...

Magnetic fields are areas where a *magnetic force acts*

Loads of electrical appliances use magnetic fields generated by electric currents.

> A MAGNETIC FIELD is a region where MAGNETIC MATERIALS
> (like iron and steel) and also WIRES CARRYING CURRENTS
> experience a FORCE acting on them.

Magnetic fields can be represented by field diagrams.
The arrows on the field lines always point from the
North pole of the magnet to the South pole.

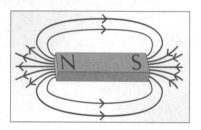

A current-carrying wire creates a *magnetic field*

There is a magnetic field around a straight, current-carrying wire.
The field is made up of concentric circles with the wire in the centre:

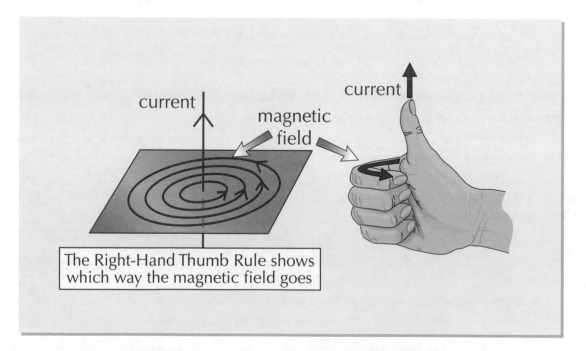

The Right-Hand Thumb Rule shows
which way the magnetic field goes

Just point your thumb in the direction of the current...

...and your fingers show the direction of the field. Remember, it's always your right thumb. Not your left, but your right thumb. You'll use your left hand on page 151 though, so it shouldn't feel left out...

Magnetic Fields

The magnetic field around a **solenoid**

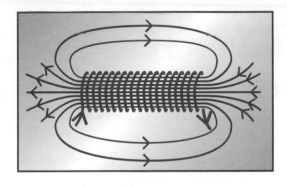

1) The magnetic field <u>inside</u> a current-carrying <u>solenoid</u> (a coil of wire) is <u>strong</u> and <u>uniform</u>.

2) <u>Outside</u> the coil, the field's just like the one round a <u>bar magnet</u>.

3) This means that the <u>ends</u> of a solenoid act like the <u>north pole</u> and <u>south pole</u> of a bar magnet.

4) Pretty obviously, if the <u>direction</u> of the <u>current</u> is <u>reversed</u>, the North and South poles will <u>swap ends</u>.

5) If you imagine looking directly into one end of a solenoid, the <u>direction of current flow</u> tells you whether it's the <u>N or S pole</u> you're looking at, as shown by the <u>diagrams</u> below.

6) You can increase the <u>strength</u> of the magnetic field around a solenoid by adding a magnetically 'soft' iron core through the middle of the coil. It's then called an <u>ELECTROMAGNET</u>.

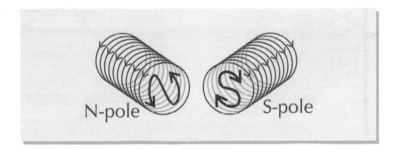

N-pole   S-pole

A <u>magnetically soft</u> material <u>magnetises</u> and <u>demagnetises</u> very easily. So, as soon as you <u>turn off</u> the current through the solenoid, the magnetic field <u>disappears</u> — the iron doesn't stay magnetised.

Iron, **steel** and **nickel** are **magnetic**

Don't forget that <u>all</u> other <u>common metals</u> are <u>not magnetic at all</u>. So a magnet <u>won't stick</u> to <u>aluminium ladders</u> or <u>copper kettles</u> or <u>brass trumpets</u> or <u>gold rings</u> or <u>silver spoons</u>.

Fields around electromagnets and bar magnets are the same shape

The <u>ancient Greeks</u> and <u>ancient Chinese</u> knew that lumps of magnetic rock would attract iron objects, and always point north-south — they could be used like a basic <u>compass</u>. But it took until the early 1800s before the links between electricity and magnetism were discovered.

The Motor Effect

Passing an electric current through a wire produces a magnetic field around the wire. If you put that wire into a magnetic field, you have <u>two magnetic fields combining</u>, which puts a force on the wire (generally).

A *current* in a *magnetic field* experiences a *force*

The two tests below demonstrate the <u>force</u> on a <u>current-carrying wire</u> placed in a <u>magnetic field</u>. The <u>force</u> gets <u>bigger</u> if either the <u>current</u> or the <u>magnetic field</u> is made bigger.

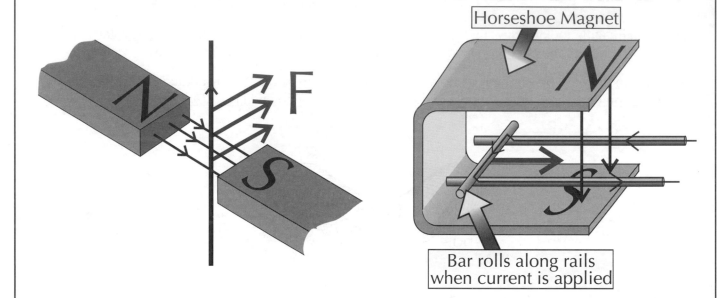

Horseshoe Magnet

Bar rolls along rails when current is applied

1) Note that in <u>both cases</u> the <u>force</u> on the wire is at <u>90°</u> to both the <u>wire</u> and to the <u>magnetic field</u>.

2) You can always <u>predict</u> which way the <u>force</u> will act using <u>Fleming's left hand rule</u> as shown on the next page.

3) To experience the <u>full force</u>, the <u>wire</u> has to be at <u>90°</u> to the <u>magnetic field</u>.

4) If the wire runs <u>along</u> the <u>magnetic field</u> it won't experience <u>any force at all</u>.

5) At angles in between it'll feel <u>some</u> force.

The Motor Effect

Fleming's left-hand rule tells you which way the force acts

1) They could test to see if you can do this, so <u>practise it</u>.

2) Using your <u>left hand</u>, point your <u>First finger</u> in the direction of the <u>Field</u> and your <u>seCond finger</u> in the direction of the <u>Current</u>.

3) Your <u>thuMb</u> will then point in the direction of the <u>force</u> (<u>M</u>otion).

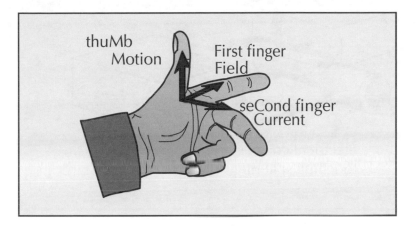

Example:

Which direction is the force on the wire?

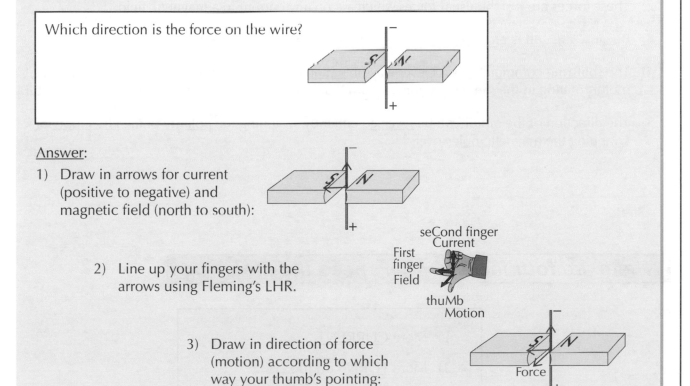

<u>Answer:</u>
1) Draw in arrows for current (positive to negative) and magnetic field (north to south):

2) Line up your fingers with the arrows using Fleming's LHR.

3) Draw in direction of force (motion) according to which way your thumb's pointing:

<u>F</u>irst finger = <u>F</u>ield, se<u>C</u>ond finger = <u>C</u>urrent, thu<u>M</u>b = <u>M</u>otion

See, I told you you'd need your left hand for this page. You might think thu<u>M</u>b = <u>M</u>otion is a bit of a tenuous link, but I bet you never forget it now. Anyway, learn the rule and <u>use it</u>.

The Simple Electric Motor

Aha — one of the favourite exam topics of all time. Read it. Understand it. Learn it.

The simple *electric motor*

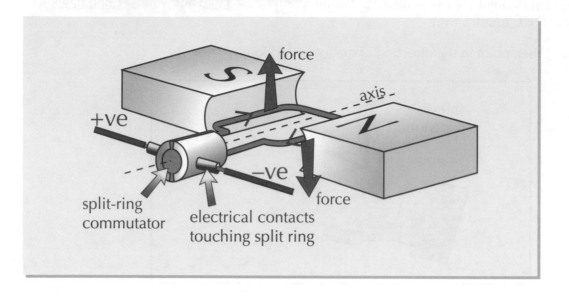

1) The diagram shows the <u>forces</u> acting on the two <u>side arms</u> of the <u>coil</u>.

2) These forces are just the <u>usual forces</u> which act on <u>any current</u> in a <u>magnetic field</u>.

3) Because the coil is on a <u>spindle</u> and the forces act <u>one up</u> and <u>one down</u>, it <u>rotates</u>.

4) The <u>split-ring commutator</u> is a clever way of '<u>swapping</u> the contacts <u>every half turn</u> to keep the motor rotating in the <u>same direction</u>'. (Learn that statement because they might ask you about it.)

5) The direction of the motor can be <u>reversed</u> either by swapping the <u>polarity</u> of the <u>DC supply</u> or swapping the <u>magnetic poles</u> over.

There are *four* factors which *speed the motor up*

> 1) More <u>CURRENT</u>.
>
> 2) More <u>TURNS</u> on the coil.
>
> 3) <u>STRONGER MAGNETIC FIELD</u>.
>
> 4) A <u>SOFT IRON CORE</u> in the coil.

The Simple Electric Motor

Answering <u>questions</u> on these might often involve using what you've learnt on earlier pages:

Is the coil turning clockwise or anticlockwise?

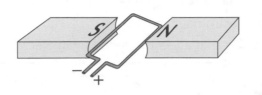

<u>Answer:</u>

1) Draw in current arrows (positive to negative):

2) Fleming's LHR on one arm (I've used the right-hand arm).

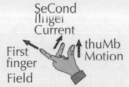

SeCond finger Current

First finger Field

thuMb Motion

3) Draw in direction of force (motion):

So — the coil is turning <u>anticlockwise</u>.

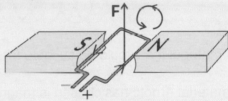

Electric motors *are used in:* **CD players, food mixers, printers...**

... fan heaters, fans, drills, hairdryers, cement mixers...

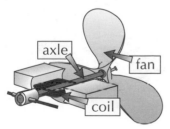

axle

fan

coil

1) Link the coil to an <u>axle</u>, and the axle <u>spins round</u>.
2) In the diagram there's a <u>fan</u> attached to the axle, but you can stick <u>almost anything</u> on a motor axle and make it spin round.
3) For example, in a <u>food mixer</u>, the axle's attached to a <u>blade</u> or whisks. In a <u>CD player</u> the axle's attached to the bit you <u>sit the CD on</u>. <u>Fan heaters</u> and <u>hairdriers</u> have an <u>electric heater</u> as well as a fan.

For example...

<u>Loudspeakers</u> also demonstrate the <u>motor effect</u>. <u>AC electrical signals</u> from the <u>amplifier</u> are fed to the <u>speaker coil</u> (shown in red). These make the coil move <u>back and forth</u> over the poles of the <u>magnet</u>. These movements make the <u>cardboard cone vibrate</u> and this creates <u>sounds</u>.

Warm-Up and Exam Questions

It's time for some questions — make sure you can do the warm-up ones first, then have a go at the exam questions below.

Warm-Up Questions

1) What does the right-hand thumb rule show?
2) In Fleming's left-hand rule, what's represented by the first finger? the second finger? the thumb?
3) Suggest two uses for electromagnets.
4) What are the four factors that affect the speed of an electric motor?

Exam Questions

1   Arnold is making an electromagnet using a current-carrying solenoid and a core.

   (a) Complete the following diagram of the solenoid to show the magnetic field around it.

       (2 marks)

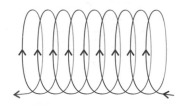

   (b) Suggest a material that would be suitable for the core.

       (1 mark)

   (c) The core material Arnold has chosen is magnetically soft.
        Explain what this means.

       (1 mark)

   (d) What effect will this core have on the magnetic field produced by the electromagnet?

       (1 mark)

2   Julia is designing a toy car with a small electric motor to drive the wheels.
    The diagram shows a simplified version of Julia's motor.

   (a) In which direction will the wheel turn?

       (1 mark)

   (b) Explain the purpose of the split-ring commutator.

       (1 mark)

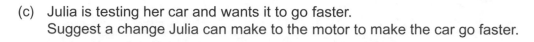

   (c) Julia is testing her car and wants it to go faster.
        Suggest a change Julia can make to the motor to make the car go faster.

       (1 mark)

   (d) Julia wants to make the car drive in forward and reverse.
        How can she reverse the direction of the motor?

       (1 mark)

Electromagnetic Induction

> ## ELECTROMAGNETIC INDUCTION
> The creation of a <u>VOLTAGE</u> (and maybe current) in a wire
> which is experiencing a <u>CHANGE IN MAGNETIC FIELD</u>

For some reason they use the word "<u>induction</u>" rather than "<u>creation</u>", but it amounts to the <u>same thing</u>.

Moving a magnet in a coil of wire induces a voltage

<u>Electromagnetic induction</u> means creating a <u>voltage</u> (and maybe a <u>current</u>) in a conductor.
You can do this by...

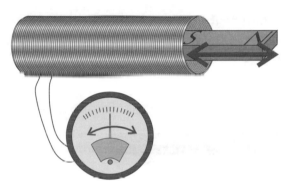

... <u>moving a magnet</u>
in a <u>coil of wire</u>...

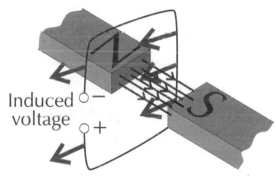

... or by <u>moving a conductor</u>
in a <u>magnetic field</u> ("cutting"
magnetic field lines)...

Induced
voltage

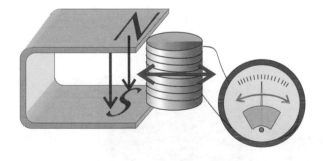

... or by shifting the magnet from
<u>side to side</u> to create a little
"<u>blip</u>" of current.

---

1) If you move the magnet in the <u>opposite direction</u>, then the <u>voltage/current</u> will be <u>reversed</u> too.
    Likewise if the <u>polarity</u> of the magnet is <u>reversed</u>, then the <u>voltage/current</u> will be <u>reversed</u> too.

2) If you keep the <u>magnet</u> (or the <u>coil</u>) moving <u>backwards and forwards</u>, you produce a <u>voltage</u>
    that <u>keeps swapping direction</u> — and this is how you produce <u>AC current</u>.

Electromagnetic Induction

A magnet *turning* end to end in a coil also *creates* a *current*

This current lasts as long as you spin the magnet. This is how generators work (see next page).

1) As you <u>turn</u> the magnet, the <u>magnetic field</u> through the <u>coil</u> changes — this <u>change</u> in the magnetic field induces a <u>voltage</u>, which can make a <u>current</u> flow in the wire.

2) When you've turned the magnet through half a turn, the <u>direction</u> of the <u>magnetic field</u> through the coil <u>reverses</u>. When this happens, the <u>voltage reverses</u>, so the <u>current</u> flows in the <u>opposite direction</u> around the coil of wire.

3) If you keep turning the magnet in the <u>same direction</u> — always clockwise, say — then the voltage will keep on reversing every half turn and you'll get an <u>AC current</u>.

Four factors affect the *size* of the induced *voltage*

1) If you want a <u>bigger</u> peak voltage (and current) you have to <u>increase</u> at least one of these four things:

> 1) The <u>STRENGTH</u> of the <u>MAGNET</u>
> 2) The <u>AREA</u> of the <u>COIL</u>
> 3) The <u>number of TURNS</u> on the <u>COIL</u>
> 4) The <u>SPEED</u> of movement

2) To <u>reduce</u> the voltage, you would <u>reduce</u> one of those factors.

3) If you <u>move</u> the magnet <u>faster</u>, you'll get a higher peak voltage, but also get a <u>higher frequency</u> — because the magnetic field is reversing more frequently.

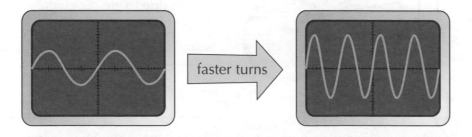

faster turns

EM Induction — works whether the coil or the field is moving

Who'd have thought you could make electricity from a magnet and a bit of wire — try it yourself if you don't believe it. While you're there try changing the magnet and the number of turns and things to see how the voltage changes. Once you get the hang of it, it'll stick in your head for the exam no trouble.

Generators

Think about the simple electric <u>motor</u> — you've got a current in the wire and a magnetic field, which causes movement. Well, a <u>generator</u> works the <u>opposite way round</u> — you've got a magnetic field and movement, which <u>induces a current</u>.

AC generators — *just turn the* **coil** *and there's a current*

You've already met <u>generators</u> and <u>electromagnetic induction</u> (see page 155-156) — this is a bit more detail about how a simple generator works.

1) Generators <u>rotate a coil</u> in a <u>magnetic field</u> (or a magnet in a coil... see below).

2) Their <u>construction</u> is much like a <u>motor</u>.

3) As the <u>coil spins</u>, a <u>current</u> is <u>induced</u> in the coil. This current <u>changes direction</u> every half turn.

4) Instead of a <u>split-ring commutator</u>, AC generators have <u>slip rings</u> and brushes so the contacts <u>don't swap</u> every half turn.

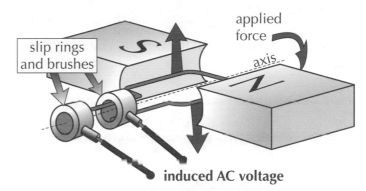

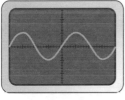 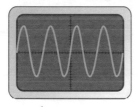

original   faster revs

5) This means they produce <u>AC voltage</u>, as shown by these <u>CRO displays</u>. Note that <u>faster revolutions</u> produce not only <u>more peaks</u> but <u>higher overall voltage</u> too.

6) All power stations use AC generators to produce electricity, they just get the energy needed to turn the coil or magnetic field in different ways.

Dynamos — *you* **turn** *the* **magnet** *instead of the coil*

1) <u>Dynamos</u> are a slightly different type of <u>generator</u>. They rotate the <u>magnet</u> instead of the coil.

2) This still causes the <u>field through the coil</u> to <u>swap</u> every half turn, so the output is <u>just the same</u> as for a generator.

3) This means you get the <u>same CRO traces</u> of course.

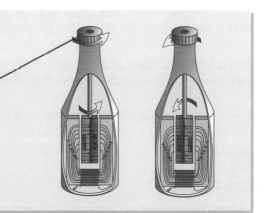

1) <u>Dynamos</u> are sometimes used on <u>bikes</u> to power the <u>lights</u>.

2) The <u>cog wheel</u> at the top is positioned so that it <u>touches</u> one of the <u>bike wheels</u>.

3) As the wheel moves round, it <u>turns</u> the cog which is attached to the <u>magnet</u>.

4) This creates an <u>AC current</u> to power the lights.

Transformers

Transformers use <u>electromagnetic induction</u>. So they will <u>only</u> work on <u>AC</u>.

Transformers change the voltage — but only AC voltages

There are a few different types of transformer. The ones you need to know are <u>step-up transformers</u> and <u>step-down transformers</u>. They both have two coils, the <u>primary</u> and the <u>secondary</u>, joined with an <u>iron core</u>.

<u>STEP-UP TRANSFORMERS</u> step the voltage <u>up</u>. They have <u>more</u> turns on the <u>secondary</u> coil than on the primary coil.

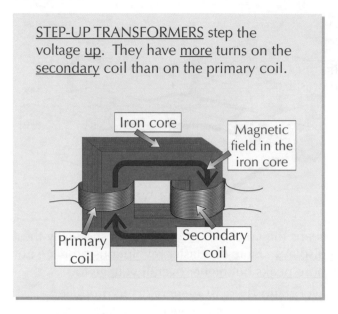

<u>STEP-DOWN TRANSFORMERS</u> step the voltage <u>down</u>. They have <u>more</u> turns on the <u>primary</u> coil than on the secondary.

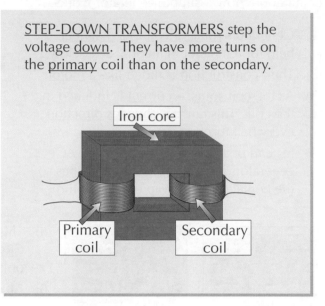

Transformers work by electromagnetic induction

1) The primary coil <u>produces a magnetic field</u> which stays <u>within the iron core</u>. This means <u>nearly all</u> of it passes through the <u>secondary coil</u> and hardly any is lost.

2) Because there is <u>alternating current</u> (AC) in the <u>primary coil</u>, the field in the iron core is constantly <u>changing direction</u> (100 times a second if it's at 50 Hz) — i.e. it is a <u>changing</u> magnetic field.

3) This <u>rapidly changing</u> magnetic field is then felt by the <u>secondary coil</u>.

4) The changing field <u>induces</u> an <u>alternating voltage</u> in the secondary coil (with the same frequency as the alternating current in the primary) — <u>electromagnetic induction</u> of a voltage in fact.

5) The <u>relative number of turns</u> on the two coils determines whether the voltage induced in the secondary coil is <u>greater</u> or <u>less</u> than the voltage in the primary.

6) If you supplied DC to the primary, you'd get <u>nothing</u> out of the secondary at all. Sure, there'd still be a magnetic field in the iron core, but it wouldn't be <u>constantly changing</u>, so there'd be no <u>induction</u> in the secondary coil because you need a <u>changing field</u> to induce a voltage.

So don't forget it —

> Transformers only work with AC. They don't work with DC at all.

Transformers

The *iron core* carries *magnetic field, not current*

1) The <u>iron core</u> is purely for transferring the <u>changing magnetic field</u> from the primary coil to the secondary.

2) No <u>electricity</u> flows round the <u>iron core</u>.

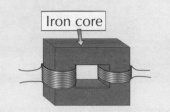

Iron core

The *transformer equation* — *use it either way up*

You can calculate the output voltage from a transformer if you know the input voltage and the number of turns on each coil.

$$\frac{V_P}{V_S} = \frac{N_P}{N_S}$$

or

$$\frac{V_S}{V_P} = \frac{N_S}{N_P}$$

$$\frac{\text{primary voltage}}{\text{secondary voltage}} = \frac{\text{number of turns on primary}}{\text{number of turns on secondary}}$$

Well, it's <u>just another formula</u>. You stick in the numbers <u>you've got</u> and work out the one <u>that's left</u>. It's really useful to remember you can write it <u>either way up</u> — this example's much trickier algebra-wise if you start with V_S on the bottom...

Example:

A transformer has 40 turns on the primary and 800 on the secondary. If the input voltage is 1000 V, find the output voltage.

<u>Answer:</u> $\frac{V_s}{V_p} = \frac{N_s}{N_p}$, so $\frac{V_s}{1000} = \frac{800}{40}$

$V_s = 1000 \times \frac{800}{40} = 20\,000 \text{ V}$

Or you can say that 800 is 20 times 40, so the secondary voltage will also be 20 times the primary voltage.

Transformers are nearly 100% efficient so 'power in = power out'

Transformers

Transformers are used on the National Grid

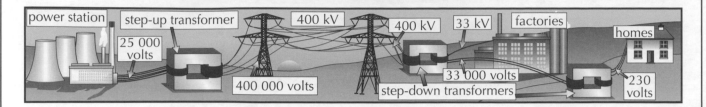

You get both step-up and step-down transformers on the National Grid:

1) To transmit <u>a lot of power</u>, you either need <u>high voltage</u> or <u>high current</u> (P = VI).

2) The problem with <u>high current</u> is the <u>loss</u> (as heat) due to the <u>resistance</u> of the cables.

3) The formula for <u>power loss</u> due to resistance in the cables is: $P = I^2R$.

4) Because of the I^2 bit, if the current is <u>10 times</u> bigger, the losses will be <u>100 times</u> bigger.

5) It's much <u>cheaper</u> to boost the voltage up to <u>400 000 V</u> and keep the current <u>very low</u>.

6) This requires <u>transformers</u> as well as <u>big pylons</u> with <u>huge insulators</u>, but it's still <u>cheaper</u>.

7) The transformers have to <u>step</u> the voltage <u>up</u> at one end, for <u>efficient transmission</u>, and then bring it back down to <u>safe, usable levels</u> at the other end.

Choose the right transformer — is it up or down?

Remember, it's <u>step-up</u> when you need to <u>increase</u> the voltage, and <u>step-down</u> to <u>decrease</u> the voltage.

<u>EXAMPLE</u>: A German tourist is visiting the United States. Domestic electricity supply in Germany is 230 V AC, and domestic electricity supply in the United States is 110 V AC.
The tourist is bringing a laptop which needs 230 V AC when it's plugged in.
State what kind of transformer the German tourist needs, and explain your answer.

<u>ANSWER</u>: The tourist needs a step-up transformer.
The 110 V supply needs to be stepped up to 230 V.

A high voltage is used in the cables and a lower one in your home

You'll need to <u>practise</u> with those tricky transformer equations. They're unusual because they can't be put into formula triangles, but other than that the method is the same — stick in the numbers.

Warm-Up and Exam Questions

It's that time again — check you can do the basics, then get stuck into some lovely exam questions. Don't forget to go back and check up on any niggling bits you can't do.

Warm-Up Questions

1) What are the four factors that affect the size of an induced voltage?
2) AC generators do not have a split-ring commutator. What do they have instead?
3) Write down the transformer equation.
4) Why is electricity distributed at high voltage?

Exam Questions

1   Explain how a generator produces an alternating current.

(3 marks)

2   Gordon is thinking of fitting a dynamo to his bicycle, to power its lights. He is investigating the voltage that might be produced when he cycles by connecting a dynamo to an oscilloscope.

(a)   Match the most appropriate CRO trace shown to the following conditions:

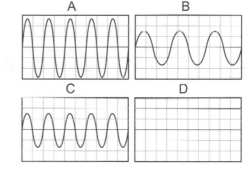

   (i)   The dynamo is turned slowly.

(1 mark)

   (ii)   The dynamo is turned quickly.

(1 mark)

(b)   (i)   What happens to the dynamo's output when it is not rotating?

(1 mark)

   (ii)   Why is this a disadvantage when a dynamo is used to power bicycle lights?

(1 mark)

3   A student is trying to test a transformer using a battery.

(a)   Explain why the voltmeter connected to the secondary coil reads 0 V.

(2 marks)

(b)   The student finds an AC power supply and reconnects the transformer. Her results are: V_P = 12 V, I_P = 2.5 A, V_S = 4 V (where V_P is the voltage across the primary coil, etc.).

   (i)   Calculate the power input to the transformer.

(1 mark)

   (ii)   Calculate the current in the secondary coil, I_S.

(2 marks)

   (iii)   The primary coil has 15 turns.
         How many turns must be on the secondary coil?

(2 marks)

Stars and Galaxies

There's all sorts of exciting stuff in the Universe... Our whole solar system is just part of a huge <u>galaxy</u>. And there are billions upon billions of galaxies. Yep, the Universe is pretty huge...

*Stars and **solar systems** form from **clouds of gas and dust***

1) Stars form from <u>clouds of gas and dust</u> which <u>spiral in together</u> due to <u>gravitational attraction</u>.

2) Gravity <u>compresses</u> the matter so much that <u>intense heat</u> develops and sets off <u>nuclear fusion reactions</u>. The star then begins <u>emitting light</u> and other <u>radiation</u>.

3) At the <u>same time</u> that the star is forming, <u>other lumps</u> may develop from the same <u>spiralling cloud</u>. These eventually gather together and form <u>planets</u> which orbit <u>around the star</u>.

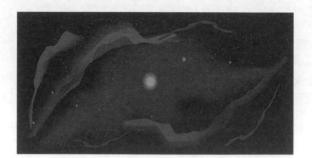

*Our **Sun** is in the **Milky Way galaxy***

1) The <u>Sun</u> is one of <u>many billions</u> of <u>stars</u> which form the <u>Milky Way galaxy</u>.

2) The <u>distance</u> between neighbouring stars is usually <u>hundreds of thousands of times greater</u> than the distance between <u>planets</u> in our Solar System.

3) <u>Gravity</u> is of course the <u>force</u> which keeps the stars <u>together</u> in a <u>galaxy</u> and, like most things in the Universe, the <u>galaxies all rotate</u>, kinda like a Catherine wheel only <u>much slower</u>.

4) Our Sun is about two thirds of the way out towards the <u>end</u> of one of the <u>spiral arms</u> of the Milky Way galaxy.

You are here

Stars and Galaxies

The **whole universe** has **billions of galaxies**

1) <u>Galaxies</u> themselves are often <u>millions of times further apart</u> than the <u>stars</u> are within a galaxy.
2) The Universe is <u>mostly empty space</u> and is <u>really really big</u>.

The **early universe** contained **only hydrogen**

1) At the very beginning, just seconds after the Big Bang, there was <u>only hydrogen</u> (with some helium forming very soon after). As the Universe expanded, these atoms clumped together to form stars.

2) In the cores of stars, hydrogen nuclei smash together to form <u>helium nuclei</u>.
   This is nuclear <u>fusion</u>. As a star grows older, all the hydrogen in the core turns into <u>helium</u>.

3) Once the hydrogen has run out, helium nuclei fuse to form other, heavier elements. Three helium nuclei can combine to form one <u>carbon</u> nucleus. More helium nuclei combine with carbon nuclei to make <u>oxygen</u> and <u>neon</u>. This all happens in <u>red giant</u> stars (see p164).

4) Eventually the helium in the core <u>runs out</u>, and some of the carbon, oxygen and neon combine to make <u>silicon</u>. In the very biggest stars, nuclei keep on combining by fusion until they've formed <u>iron</u>.

5) At the end of their lives, massive stars <u>explode</u>, flinging gas out into space. In these explosions, heavy nuclei combine with <u>each other</u> and with <u>neutrons</u> to make pretty much <u>all the elements in the Universe</u>.

6) The dust and gas from these <u>supernova</u> explosions can form <u>new stars</u> and planets (like ours). These <u>second</u> (or third, or fourth...) <u>generation star systems</u> contain heavier elements as well as hydrogen.

The Universe — it's impressive stuff

Just look at those numbers: there's <u>billions</u> of stars in the Milky Way, the Universe contains <u>billions</u> of galaxies... And <u>all</u> of the elements in the Universe were made in <u>stars</u> from hydrogen and helium...

The Life Cycle of Stars

Stars go through <u>many traumatic stages</u> in their lives.

Clouds of Dust and Gas

1) Stars <u>initially form</u> from <u>clouds of DUST and GAS</u>.

Protostar

2) The <u>force of gravity</u> makes the gas clouds come <u>spiralling in</u>. As they do, <u>gravitational energy</u> is converted into <u>heat energy</u> and the <u>temperature rises</u>.

3) When the <u>temperature</u> gets <u>high enough</u>, <u>hydrogen nuclei</u> undergo <u>nuclear fusion</u> to form <u>helium nuclei</u> and give out massive amounts of <u>heat and light</u>. A star is born. It immediately enters a <u>long stable period</u> where the <u>heat created</u> by the nuclear fusion provides an <u>outward pressure</u> to <u>balance</u> the <u>force of gravity</u> pulling everything <u>inwards</u>. In this stable period it's called a <u>MAIN SEQUENCE STAR</u>. Because the <u>balanced forces</u> stop everything exploding outwards or collapsing inwards, and because of the <u>huge amount of hydrogen</u> stars contain, this stable period can last <u>millions of years</u>.
(The Sun is in the middle of its stable period... or to put it another way, the <u>Earth</u> has already had <u>half its innings</u> before the Sun <u>engulfs</u> it!)

Main Sequence Star

4) Eventually the <u>hydrogen</u> begins to <u>run out</u> and the star then <u>swells</u> into a <u>RED GIANT</u>. It becomes <u>red</u> because the surface <u>cools</u>.

5) A <u>small star</u> like our Sun will then begin to <u>cool</u> and <u>contract</u> into a <u>WHITE DWARF</u> and then finally, as the <u>light fades completely</u>, it becomes a <u>BLACK DWARF</u>.

Red Giant

Small stars

White Dwarf

Black Dwarf

Big stars

6) <u>Big stars</u>, however, start to <u>glow brightly again</u> as they undergo more <u>fusion</u> and <u>expand and contract several times</u>, forming <u>heavier elements</u> in various <u>nuclear reactions</u>. Eventually they'll <u>explode</u> in a <u>SUPERNOVA</u>.

new planetary nebula... ...and a new solar system

Supernova

Neutron Star...

...or Black Hole

7) The <u>exploding supernova</u> throws the outer layers of <u>dust and gas</u> into space, leaving a <u>very dense core</u> called a <u>NEUTRON STAR</u>. Or if the star is <u>big enough</u>, a <u>BLACK HOLE</u>.

8) The <u>dust and gas</u> thrown off by the supernova will form into <u>SECOND GENERATION STARS</u> like our Sun. The <u>heavier elements</u> are <u>only</u> made in the <u>final stages</u> of a <u>big star</u>, many in the <u>supernova</u> itself, so the <u>presence</u> of heavier elements in the <u>Sun</u> and the <u>inner planets</u> is <u>clear evidence</u> that our beautiful and wonderful world, with its warm sunsets and fresh morning dews, has all formed out of the snotty remains of a grisly old star's last dying sneeze.

9) The <u>matter</u> from which <u>neutron stars</u> and <u>white dwarfs</u> and <u>black dwarfs</u> are made is <u>MILLIONS OF TIMES DENSER</u> than any matter on Earth because the <u>gravity is so strong</u> it even crushes the <u>atoms</u>.

Warm-Up and Exam Questions

Here are some nice warm-up questions to get you into the swing of things before you try the exam questions. If you find any of the questions difficult, take another look back at the section.

Warm-Up Questions

1) What is a galaxy?
2) What are stars formed from?
3) What type of star will form a black hole?
4) At the end of its main sequence state, what does a star become?

Exam Questions

1   Many stars in our galaxy are second generation stars.

(a)   What is meant by a second generation star?

(1 mark)

(b)   In which galaxy is our Sun?

(1 mark)

(c)   What keeps all the stars together in a galaxy?

(1 mark)

2   (a)   What was first element present in the Universe seconds after the Big Bang?

(1 mark)

(b)   How were most helium nuclei formed in the early Universe?

(1 mark)

3   Stars go through many stages in their lives.

(a)   Describe how a star is formed.

(3 marks)

(b)   Explain why main sequence stars undergo a stable period that can last millions of years.

(2 marks)

(c)   When main sequence stars begin to run out of hydrogen in their core, they swell and become Red Giants.

(i)   What happens to small stars after their Red Giant phase?

(2 marks)

(ii)   What happens to big stars after their Red Giant phase?

(3 marks)

Revision Summary for Physics 3(ii)

There's only one way to check you know it all...

current

magnetic field

1) In which direction is the magnetic field around this wire — clockwise or anticlockwise?

2) Name the three common magnetic metals.

3) Describe the three details of Fleming's left hand rule. What is it used for?

4) Sketch a diagram of a simple motor. Indicate the direction in which the motor spins.

5) The diagrams show a simple electric motor. The coil is turning clockwise. Which diagram, A or B, shows the correct polarity of the magnets?

A)

B)

6) What are the four factors that affect the speed of a motor?

7) Give the definition of electromagnetic induction.

8) What are the four factors that affect the size of the inducted voltage?

9) Sketch a generator with all the details. Explain how it works.

10) Describe how a dynamo works.

11) Sketch the two types of transformer and explain the differences between them.

12) An engineering executive is travelling from the USA to Italy and taking a computer monitor with him. In the USA, domestic electricity is 110 V AC, and in Italy it's 230 V AC. What kind of transformer would the engineering executive need to plug his monitor into?

13) Explain how a transformer works and why transformers only work on AC voltage.

14) Write down the transformer equation.

15)* A transformer has 20 turns on the primary coil and 600 on the secondary coil. If the input voltage is 9 V, find the output voltage.

16) Explain why transformers are used on the National Grid.

17) Describe the first stages of a star's formation. Where does the initial energy come from?

18) What process starts inside a star to make it produce so much light and heat?

19) Sketch the Milky Way and show the Sun in relation to it.

20) How far away are stars from each other, compared to the distances between planets in our Solar System?

21) How far away are galaxies from each other, compared to the distances between stars in a galaxy?

22) Shortly after the Universe began, what was the most common element?

23) Briefly describe how elements like carbon, silicon and iron were formed.

24) Briefly explain how a star can keep producing light and heat for millions of years.

25) Describe the full life cycle of a small star like the Sun.

26) Describe the full life cycle of a massive star.

27) How do we know that the Sun isn't a first generation star?

* Answers on page 229.

Answering Experiment Questions (i)

You'll definitely get some questions in the exam about <u>experiments</u>. They can be about any topic under the Sun — but if you learn the basics and throw in a bit of common sense, you'll be fine.

Read the question *carefully*

The question might describe an <u>experiment</u>, e.g. —

Roger had a toy diver and three different sized parachutes made from the same plastic.
He investigated which parachute was the most effective in slowing down the diver when falling through water.

Toy diver   Small parachute   Medium parachute   Large parachute

Roger timed the diver's fall to the bottom of a fish tank (without parachute). He did this three times. He then attached the smallest parachute to the toy and timed its fall, again three times. He did the same for the medium and the large parachutes.

1. What is the independent variable?
    The size of the parachute

2. What is the dependent variable?
    The time taken to fall

3. Give two variables that must be kept the same to make it a fair test.
    1. The distance the toy had to fall.
    2. The mass of the toy (ideally the same toy would be used)

4. What is the control in this investigation?
    The toy with no parachute

The <u>independent variable</u> is the thing that is <u>changed</u>.

The <u>dependent variable</u> is the thing that's <u>measured</u>.

To make it a <u>fair test</u> you've got to keep <u>all</u> other variables the same, or you won't know if the <u>only thing</u> affecting the dependent variable is the <u>independent variable</u>.

There are <u>loads</u> of other things that must be kept the same throughout this experiment. You could also have put <u>the shape of the parachute</u> or the <u>size of tank</u>, etc.

It's easy to keep the variables the same in this experiment as it's in a <u>laboratory</u>. But it can sometimes be <u>trickier</u>. E.g. if you were doing this in a <u>pond</u>, it'd be hard to ensure that you had exactly the <u>same conditions</u> each time — the <u>depth</u> may vary, the <u>water</u> could be <u>moving</u>, etc.

It's even harder to make investigations involving <u>people</u> fair. If, say, the effect of a person's age on their blood pressure was being investigated, there'd be <u>loads of other variables</u> to consider — weight, diet and whether someone's a smoker could make a <u>big difference</u> to their blood pressure.

To make it a <u>fairer</u> test, it would be better if just nonsmokers with a similar weight and diet were used.

A <u>control</u> isn't really part of the experiment, but it uses the <u>same conditions</u> as the rest of the experiment. You can compare the results of the experiment with those of the control group, and see if the same things might have happened <u>anyway</u>. Control groups make results <u>more meaningful</u>.

In this experiment the toy might <u>fall slower</u> without any parachute — unlikely, but with a control you can check for this.

Control groups are used when <u>testing drugs</u>. People can feel better just because they've been given a drug that they <u>believe</u> will work. To rule this out, researchers give one group of patients <u>dummy pills</u> (called placebos) — but they <u>don't tell them</u> that their pills aren't the real thing. This is the control group. By doing this, they can tell if the real drug is actually working.

Answering Experiment Questions (ii)

5. Why did Roger time each fall three times, instead of just once?

To check for anomalous results and make the results more reliable.

Sometimes <u>unusual results</u> are produced — <u>repeating</u> an experiment gives you a better idea of what the <u>correct result</u> should be.

6. The table below shows the times taken by the diver to fall to the bottom of the tank.

parachute size ↓	Time for Fall 1 (s)	Time for Fall 2 (s)	Time for Fall 3 (s)	Mean Time (s)
none	1.2	1.5	1.2	
small	2.1	2.4	2.4	2.3
medium	2.8	2.6	2.5	2.6
large	3.2	3.4	5.1	3.3

When an experiment is <u>repeated</u>, the results will usually be <u>slightly different</u> each time.

The <u>mean</u> (or average) of the measurements is usually used to represent the values.

The more times the experiment is <u>repeated</u> the <u>more accurate and reliable</u> the average will be.

To find the mean:

Add together all the data values and divide by the total number of values in the sample.

The <u>range</u> is how far the data <u>spreads</u>.

You just work out the <u>difference</u> between the <u>highest</u> and <u>lowest</u> numbers.

a) Calculate the mean time taken for the toy to fall without a parachute.

Mean = (1.2 + 1.5 + 1.2) ÷ 3 = 1.3 s

b) What is the range of the times for the fall without a parachute?

1.5 − 1.2 = 0.3 s

7. One of the results in the table is anomalous. Circle the result and suggest why it may have occurred.

The parachute may have had an air bubble trapped inside it.

If one of the results doesn't seem to fit in, it's called an <u>anomalous</u> result. You should usually <u>ignore</u> an anomalous result. It's been <u>ignored</u> when the mean was worked out.

This is a <u>random error</u> — it only happens occasionally.

If the same mistake is made every time, it's a <u>systematic error</u>, e.g. if you were looking at the tank from too high up, it might look like the toy hit the bottom before it actually did. So you'd stop the stopwatch too soon, meaning <u>all</u> your timings would be a <u>bit quick</u>.

8. What conclusion can you draw from these results?

Parachutes slow down the fall of the toy, and the bigger the parachute (made from this plastic) the slower the toy falls.

Be careful that your conclusions <u>match</u> the data you've got and <u>don't</u> go any further than your results actually show.

For example, you can't say that the bigger the parachute the slower the fall, because the results may be <u>totally different</u> with <u>another type of material, e.g. lace</u>.

These experiments are just examples — don't learn the details

The point of these pages isn't to remember the details of the experiments — they could ask these questions about <u>any</u> random experiment. You need to know what your different kinds of <u>variable</u> are, what's the <u>control</u>, how to make it a <u>fair test</u> and what to do with your <u>results</u> when you've got them.

Answering Experiment Questions (iii)

Use *sensible measurements* for your *variables*

Jamie did an experiment to see how the length of a wire changed depending on the weight hanging on it.

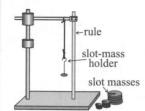

←rule

slot-mass holder

slot masses

He started off with just a slot-mass holder hanging on the wire and made sure that the starting length was 10 cm for each wire. He then gradually added slot masses until the wire broke. For each mass he added, he measured the new length. He did the experiment using iron, steel, aluminium, copper and brass wires.

Before he started, he did a trial run, which showed that most wires snapped under loads of between 10 kg and 30 kg and extended by lengths of between 2 cm and 4 cm.

1. What kind of variable was the list of metals?

   A A continuous variable ☐

   B A categoric variable ✓

   C An ordered variable ☐

   D A discrete variable ☐

Categoric variables are variables that can't be related to size or quantity — they're <u>types</u> of things. E.g. <u>names of metals</u> or <u>types of fertiliser</u>.

Continuous data is <u>numerical data</u> that can have any value within a range — e.g. length, volume, temperature and time.

Note: You <u>can't</u> measure the <u>exact value</u> of continuous data. Say you measure a height as 5.6 cm to the nearest mm. It's not <u>exact</u> — you get a more precise value if you measure to the nearest 0.1 mm or 0.01 mm, etc.

<u>Ordered variables</u> are things like <u>small, medium and large lumps</u>, or <u>warm, very warm and hot</u>.

<u>Discrete data</u> is the type that can be counted in chunks, where there's no in-between value, e.g. <u>number of people</u> is discrete not continuous because you can't have half a person.

2. Jamie should add masses in intervals of...

   A 0.5 g. ☐

   B 10 g. ☐

   C 1 kg. ✓

   D 10 kg. ☐

It's important to use <u>sensible values</u> for variables. It's no good using <u>really heavy</u> slot masses as the wire might snap immediately. But on the other hand, adding <u>really weedy ones</u> like 0.5 g one at a time could take ages.

3. The rule used to measure the wire length should be capable of measuring...

   A to the nearest mm. ✓

   B to the nearest inch. ☐

   C to the nearest 10 cm. ☐

   D to the nearest cm. ☐

A rule measuring only to the nearest cm, or bigger, would <u>not</u> be <u>sensitive enough</u> — the changes in length are likely to be quite small, so you'd need to measure to the <u>nearest mm</u> to get the <u>most precise</u> results.

The <u>sensitivity</u> of an instrument is the <u>smallest change</u> it can detect, e.g. some balances measure to the nearest <u>gram</u>, but really sensitive ones measure to the nearest <u>hundredth of a gram</u>. For measuring <u>tiny changes</u> — like from 2.00 g to 1.92 g — a sensitive balance is needed.

You also have to think about the <u>precision</u> and <u>accuracy</u> of your results.

Measurements (of the same thing) that are very <u>precise</u> will be close together. Really <u>accurate</u> measurements are those that have an <u>average value</u> that's <u>really close</u> to the <u>true answer</u>. So it's possible for results to be precise but not very accurate, e.g. a fancy piece of lab equipment might give results that are precise, but if it's not calibrated properly those results won't be accurate.

Answering Experiment Questions (iv)

Once you've collected all your data together, you need to <u>analyse</u> it to find any <u>relationships</u> between the variables. The easiest way to do this is to draw a graph, then describe what you see...

Graphs are used to show *relationships*

These are the results Jamie obtained with the brass wire.

Load (kg)	0	1	2	3	4	5	6	7	8	9	10
Extension (mm)	0	1	2	2	3	4	5	5	7	8	9

4. a) Nine of the points are plotted below.
        Plot the remaining **two** points on the graph.

    b) Draw a straight line of best fit for the points.

Scattergram to show the extension of a
brass wire with different amounts of load

anomalous result

To plot the points, use a <u>sharp</u> pencil and make a <u>neat</u> little cross.

nice clear mark   smudged unclear marks

A line of best fit is drawn so that it's easy to see the <u>relationship</u> between the variables. You can then use it to <u>estimate</u> other values.

When drawing a line of best fit, try to draw the line through or as near to as many points as possible, ignoring <u>anomalous</u> results. In this case, it's also got to go through the <u>origin</u> (0, 0) as you know there'd be no extension without any load.

This is a <u>scattergram</u> — they're used to see if two variables are <u>related</u>.

This graph shows a <u>positive correlation</u> between the variables. This means that as one variable <u>increases</u>, so does the other one.

5. Estimate the load you would need if you wanted the brass wire to extend by 4 mm.

    Estimate of load = ...4.5 kg (see graph)......

The other correlations you could get are:

<u>Negative correlation</u> — this is where one variable <u>increases</u> as the other one <u>decreases</u>.

<u>No correlation</u> — this is where there's <u>no obvious relationship</u> between the variables.

6. What can you conclude from these results?

    There is a positive correlation between the load and the extension. Each additional mass causes the wire to extend further.

In lab-based experiments like this, you can say that one variable <u>causes</u> the other to change. The extra load <u>causes</u> the wire to extend further. You can say this because everything else has <u>stayed the same</u> — nothing else could be causing the change.

Once you've been through all the questions in this book, you should feel pretty confident about the exams. As final preparation, here is a set of practice exams to really get you set for the real thing. The papers are designed to give you the best possible preparation for the AQA specification. If you're doing Foundation then you won't have learnt every bit — but it's still good practice.

General Certificate of Secondary Education

AQA GCSE Physics (Objective Test)

Unit Physics 1a – *Energy and Electricity*

Higher Tier

Time allowed: 30 minutes.

Centre name					
Centre number					
Candidate number					

Surname	
Other names	
Candidate signature	

Instructions to candidates

- Write your name and other details in the spaces provided above.
- Answer all the questions.
- Do all rough work on this question paper.

67

Information for candidates

- Marks will not be deducted for incorrect answers.
- In calculations show clearly how you worked out your answers.
- You may use a calculator.
- There are 9 questions in this paper.
  The maximum mark for this paper is 36.

Advice to candidates

- Do not choose more responses than you are asked to.
- Work steadily through the paper.
- Don't spend too long on one question.
- If you have time at the end, go back and check your answers.

For examiner's use							
Q	Attempt Nº			Q	Attempt Nº		
	1	2	3		1	2	3
1				6			
2				7			
3				8			
4				9			
5							
				Total 36			

SECTION ONE

Questions **ONE** and **TWO**.
In these questions, match the letters **A**, **B**, **C** and **D** with the numbers **1 – 4**.
Use **each** answer only **once**.

QUESTION ONE

Match the words **A**, **B**, **C** and **D** with the statements **1 – 4**.

A   Insulation

B   Conduction

C   Convection

D   Heat Radiation

	Term		Description
✗	1	B	This happens more slowly in liquids than in solids.
✗	2	D	This is the only way in which heat energy can pass through a vacuum.
✓	3	C	This cannot happen in solids.
✗	4	A	This slows down the rate of heat transfer.

QUESTION TWO

The diagram below shows a hydroelectric power station and part of the National Grid which distributes electricity to people's homes.

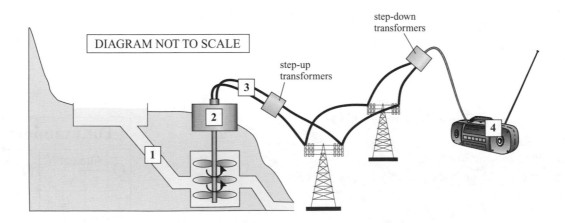

Match the energy transformations **A**, **B**, **C** and **D** to the stages labelled **1 – 4** in the diagram.

✗ 3   **A**   Kinetic energy to useful electrical energy

✓ 1   **B**   Potential energy to useful kinetic energy

✗ 2   **C**   Electrical energy to heat energy

✓ 4   **D**   Electrical energy to useful sound energy

SECTION TWO

Questions **THREE** to **NINE**.
Each of these questions has four parts.
In each part choose only **one** answer.

QUESTION THREE

Read the passage below about nuclear power.

Currently about 63% of the world's electricity is produced from fossil fuels (coal, oil and natural gas) and about 16% is produced from nuclear energy.

In the UK, the Government is thinking very seriously about how we are going to generate enough electricity in the future. The problem is that fossil fuel supplies won't last forever, and demand for electricity is rising. The burning of fossil fuels also releases lots of carbon dioxide into the atmosphere, which contributes to global warming. So the Government may decide that we need to start building more nuclear power stations now.

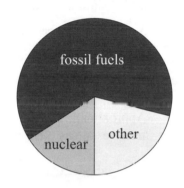

Nuclear fuels are a more concentrated source of energy than fossil fuels. 1 kg of uranium can give the same amount of energy as 17 000 kg of coal. Importantly, nuclear power doesn't release carbon dioxide into the atmosphere (although some is released in mining, processing and transporting the uranium, and in building a power station).

The main problem with nuclear power is that it produces waste which remains radioactive for thousands of years.

3A   Uranium is used as a fuel in nuclear power stations.
Which of the following is also a nuclear fuel?

1   Plutonium

2   Radium

3   Thorium

4   Tritium

Question 3 continues on the next page

Turn over

3B   What is the main environmental advantage of using nuclear
fuels rather than fossil fuels to generate electricity?

    1   Fossil fuels don't produce radioactive waste.

    2   Stocks of uranium will last longer than stocks of oil

    3   Nuclear power stations aren't expensive to decommission

    ✓ (4)   Using nuclear fuels to generate electricity doesn't release large quantities of carbon dioxide
           into the atmosphere.

3C   The methods of generating electricity in nuclear and oil-fired power stations are...

    1   similar because fuel is burnt to produce heat in both cases.

    2   similar because both use steam to drive a turbine.

    3   different because no heat is produced in a nuclear power station.

    ✗ (4)   different because no heat energy is wasted in a nuclear power station.

3D   Approximately what percentage of the world's electricity is produced
from resources other than fossil fuels and nuclear power?

    1   about 16%

    2   about 79%

    ✓ (3)   about 21%

    4   about 84%

QUESTION FOUR

Light bulbs are designed to transform electrical energy into light energy.
However, some of the electrical energy is wasted as heat energy.

4A An energy efficient light bulb is...

    1   a light bulb that's as bright as possible.

    2   a light bulb that only transforms a small proportion of electrical energy into heat energy.

    3   a light bulb that only transforms a small proportion of electrical energy into light energy.

    4   a light bulb that doesn't need much energy to make.

4B Here are some diagrams showing the energy transformations in four light bulbs.
Which light bulb is the least efficient? 4

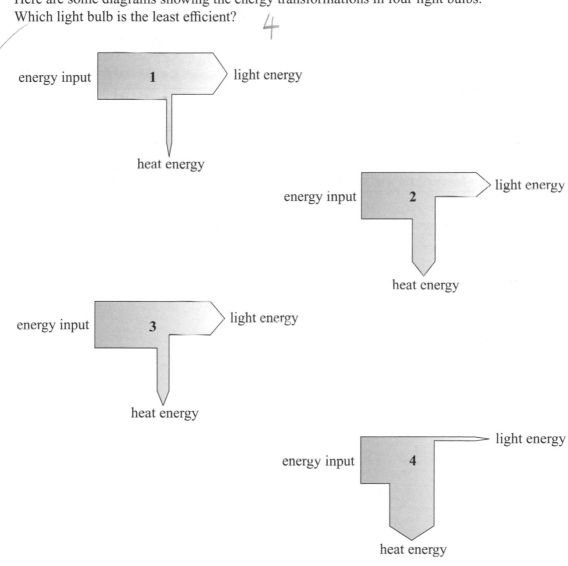

Question 4 continues on the next page

Turn over

176

4C A light bulb transforms 200 J of electrical energy into 150 J of heat energy and 50 J of light energy.

Efficiency = useful energy output ÷ total energy input

What is the efficiency of the light bulb?

$$\frac{50}{200} = \frac{1}{4} = 0.25$$

1 0.25

2 3

3 0.75

4 0.35

4D The table gives some data about one type of high efficiency light bulb.

Type of light bulb	Cost	Saving per hour (compared to a low efficiency bulb)
High efficiency	£3.75	0.75p

What is the payback time of this type of high efficiency light bulb?

1 5000 hours

2 50 hours

3 5 hours

4 500 hours

$U = kW \times (hours)$ *Time*

$E = P \times t$

$cost = no. units \times price$

$$\frac{3.75}{0.75} = units = 5$$

$5 = kW \times$

6

QUESTION FIVE

Below is a close-up of some metal cooling fins on a motorbike engine.

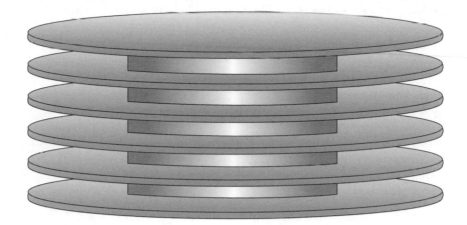

5A   The cooling fins are shaped like this so that they...

   1   have a large mass

   2   are very strong.

   3   have a large cross sectional area.

   (4)   have a large surface area. ✓

5B   The fins have a matt black surface because...

   1   that makes them good emitters of heat radiation.

   2   that makes them good reflectors of heat radiation.

   (3)   that makes them good absorbers of heat radiation. ✗

   4   that makes them good convectors of heat radiation.

5C   Why does heat conduct well through the metal fins?

   (1)   Because metals contain free electrons

   2   Because metal atoms are strongly bonded together

   3   Because metals have high melting points

   4   Because metals are shiny

5D   Which one of these effects would not increase the
      rate of heat transfer from the motorbike engine?

   (1)   Making the air flow faster through the cooling fins

   2   Riding the motorbike when the outside temperature is lower

   3   Increasing the temperature of the engine

   4   Polishing the cooling fins to make them as shiny as possible

Turn over

QUESTION SIX

This question is about energy and efficiency.

6A   Which option correctly shows two different units of energy?

1   joules and watts

2   watts and kilowatts

3   joules and kilowatt-hours

4   kilowatt-hours and watts

6B   Which of these statements about energy is incorrect?

1   Energy can change from one form to another.

2   Useful energy can be eventually transferred to the surroundings, which become warmer.

3   Whenever energy is transformed some of it disappears.

4   Heat energy is often difficult to use since it becomes very spread out.

6C   A device is efficient if...

1   it transforms input energy into useful energy very quickly.

2   it transforms a large proportion of input energy into useful energy.

3   over its lifetime it transforms a large amount of energy.

4   it doesn't produce very much heat energy.

6D   Why is electricity 'stepped up' to a higher voltage
before being transmitted through the National Grid?

1   It makes it safer.

2   It allows a higher current to be transmitted, so more electricity is delivered.

3   The voltage generated in power stations is too low for use in people's homes.

4   It reduces the current and therefore the heating effect of the electricity in the
power cables, so less energy is wasted.

QUESTION SEVEN

Vacuum flasks are designed to reduce the amount of heat transferred to (or from) the surroundings as much as possible. The diagram shows the structure of a vacuum flask.

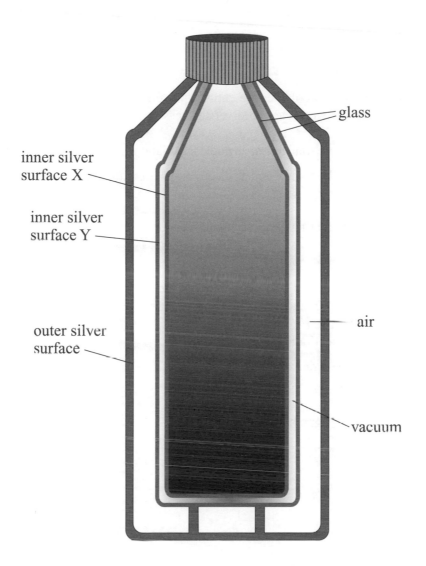

7A   Glass is used because...

    1   its particles don't collide with each other very easily.

    2   it allows electromagnetic radiation to pass through.

    3   it can be easily moulded into the right shape.

    4   it is a good conductor of heat.

Question 7 continues on the next page

Turn over

7B   A partial vacuum is used since it (very nearly) stops heat transfer by...

    1   conduction, convection and radiation.

    2   conduction and radiation.

    ③   conduction and convection.

    4   conduction only.

7C   If the vacuum was perfect, would heat be entirely prevented from passing across the gap between the two silver surfaces?

    1   No — heat would be transferred as nuclear radiation.

    ②   No — heat would be transferred as electromagnetic radiation.

    3   Yes

    4   No — heat would be transferred by water vapour.

7D   When a vacuum flask is used to keep something warm, the innermost silver surface, labelled X on the diagram, reduces heat transfer because it is a...

    1   poor absorber of heat radiation.

    2   good emitter of heat radiation.

    3   good reflector of heat radiation.

    ④   poor emitter of heat radiation.

QUESTION EIGHT

A farmer decides to generate some electricity for his farmhouse
using a small wind turbine mounted on the roof.

8A In a strong wind, the turbine generates enough electricity to power the farmer's
1.5 kW washing machine as well as all his lights. A cycle on the washing
machine takes 90 minutes. If electricity costs 18 pence per kilowatt hour, how
much does the farmer save each time he washes his clothes without mains electricity?

> energy transferred = power × time
> total cost = number of kilowatt-hours × cost per kilowatt-hours

1   27p

2   £1.35

③   40.5p $40.5p = 1.5 \times 27$

4   £2.43

8B Which of the following statements about the advantages
and disadvantages of wind turbines is true?

1   Wind turbines require expensive fuel.

②   Some people think wind farms cause visual pollution.

3   Wind turbines are silent.

4   The amount of carbon dioxide released by wind turbines is small.

8C The wind turbine costs the farmer £1800 to buy and install. Before he had the turbine, his
annual electricity bill was £900. He calculates that the turbine will pay for itself, through
savings on mains electricity, in five years. What percentage of his electricity
requirements does he expect to be supplied by the wind turbine?

1   50%

2   10%   £360 per year

3   20% $\dfrac{360}{900} = \dfrac{2}{5} = 0.4$

④   40%

8D The farmer is thinking about installing another six wind turbines. He thinks this would
reduce his electricity bill to zero with energy to spare. Why wouldn't this be the case?

1   There isn't enough wind energy available to power six wind turbines.

2   The electricity from six turbines would overload his electrical appliances.

③   He won't be able to generate electricity from the turbines all the time.

4   He needs to pay for the electricity that powers the wind turbines.

Turn over

QUESTION NINE

Kirsty carried out an investigation to see how the thickness of a cotton wool jacket affected its ability to insulate. She used the following apparatus and method.

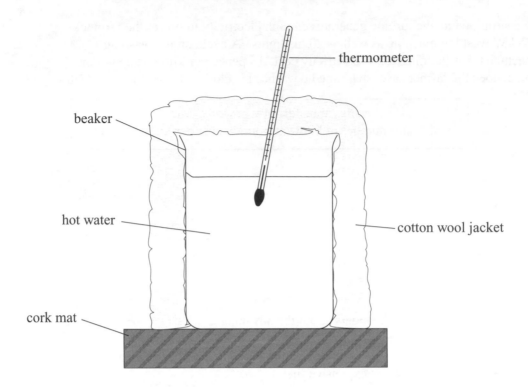

Put 200 cm³ of boiling water in the glass beaker.

Fit the 1 cm thick wool jacket over the beaker.

Start the stop clock when the temperature cools to 95 °C.

Record the temperature after three minutes.

Repeat the experiment using jackets of 2, 3, 4 and 5 cm thickness.

9A Which was the independent variable in this investigation?

    1   The final temperature of the water

    2   The original temperature of the water

    3   The time taken for the water to cool

    4   The thickness of the cotton wool jacket

9B What type of variable is thickness?

    1   A continuous variable

    2   A categoric variable

    3   A discrete variable

    4   A qualitative variable

9C   When Kirsty repeated the investigation she got very similar results.
It would therefore be reasonable to say that...

   1   she hasn't made any errors.

   2   her test was fair.

   3   any errors she has made are probably systematic ones.

   4   repeating the test would be pointless.

9D   Kirsty's results are shown in the graph below.

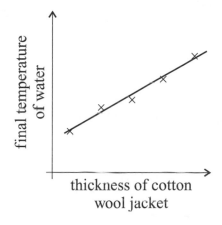

Which of the following conclusions can she draw from her graph?

   1   Cotton wool is the best insulator available.

   2   Increasing the thickness of cotton wool improves its ability to insulate.

   3   The temperature of the water changes how well the cotton wool insulates.

   4   There is a negative correlation between cotton wool thickness and insulating ability.

END OF TEST

General Certificate of Secondary Education

AQA GCSE Physics
(Objective Test)

Unit Physics 1b –
Radiation and the Universe

Higher Tier

Time allowed: 30 minutes.

Centre name					
Centre number					
Candidate number					

Surname	
Other names	
Candidate signature	

Instructions to candidates
- Write your name and other details in the spaces provided above.
- Answer all the questions.
- Do all rough work on this question paper.

66%

Information for candidates
- Marks will not be deducted for incorrect answers.
- In calculations show clearly how you worked out your answers.
- You may use a calculator.
- There are 9 questions in this paper.
  The maximum mark for this paper is 36. 32

21/32

Advice to candidates
- Do not choose more responses than you are asked to.
- Work steadily through the paper.
- Don't spend too long on one question.
- If you have time at the end, go back and check your answers.

	For examiner's use						
Q	Attempt Nº			Q	Attempt Nº		
	1	2	3		1	2	3
1				6			
2				7			
3				8			
4				9			
5				Total 36			

SECTION ONE

Questions **ONE** and **TWO**.
In these questions, match the letters **A**, **B**, **C** and **D** with the numbers **1 – 4**.
Use **each** answer only **once**.

QUESTION ONE

The diagrams show some ways we use electromagnetic radiation.

1. X-rays in hospital

2. laser light for laboratory experiments

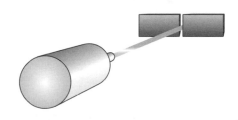

3. transmitting TV and radio signals

4. cooking burgers on a barbecue

The list gives examples of dangers to health that are associated with electromagnetic radiation.
Match **A**, **B**, **C** and **D** with the uses numbered **1 – 4**.

A   No known effect

B   Cancer

C   Skin burns

D   Damage to the retina

Turn over

2

QUESTION TWO

The diagram shows two isotopes of the same element.

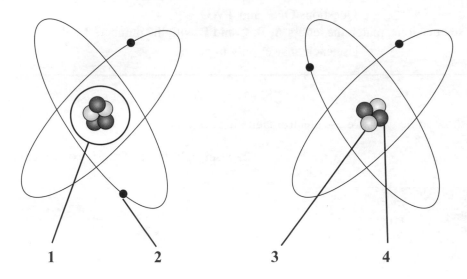

1   2   3   4

Match words **A**, **B**, **C** and **D** to the labels **1 – 4**.

✓1 **A**   nucleus

✗4 **B**   proton

✓2 **C**   electron

✗3 **D**   neutron

SECTION TWO

Questions **THREE** to **NINE**.
Each of these questions has four parts.
In each part choose only **one** answer.

QUESTION THREE

Read the passage below about the use of gamma rays to treat cancer.

Although gamma radiation can cause cancer, carefully controlled doses can actually be used to treat it.

Because cancer cells reproduce quickly, they can be killed much more easily by the gamma radiation than healthy cells.

A cancer patient attends several sessions of radiotherapy with time in between treatment sessions for their healthy cells to recover.

During the treatment, care is taken to minimise the harm done to healthy cells. One way of doing this is by changing the position of the radiation source so that gamma rays are sent from several different directions — while still being focused on the tumour.

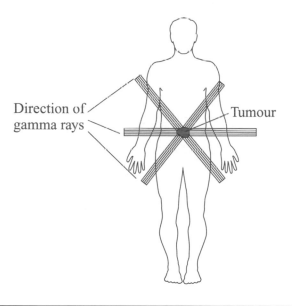

3A   Which of these statements is incorrect?

1   Gamma radiation is less strongly ionising than alpha or beta radiation.

2   Gamma rays travel at the same speed as X-rays in a vacuum.

3   Gamma rays are very high frequency electromagnetic radiation.

4   Gamma rays are reflected by skin.

Question 3 continues on the next page

Turn over

188

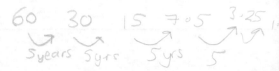

3B Cobalt-60 can be used as a gamma source for radiotherapy.
Its half-life is about 5 years, which means that...

1. the sample will have changed into cobalt-30 in five years.

2. the source will no longer be radioactive in 15 years.

3. about ¾ of the radioactive nuclei will have decayed in ten years.

4. the source should be replaced every six months.

3C The gamma ray beam is sent from different directions during each treatment session because...

1. all sides of the tumour need to be irradiated evenly.

2. the whole of the patient needs to be irradiated.

3. gamma rays coming from one direction might not irradiate the far side of the tumour.

4. the dose received by healthy cells needs to be as small as possible.

3D There is a risk of getting cancer from gamma radiation. This type of treatment is used because...

1. the benefits to the patient outweigh the risks.

2. it uses new technology.

3. the patient has cancer anyway.

4. it doesn't cost very much.

QUESTION FOUR

This question is about the three types of nuclear radiation.

4A Some engineers suspect that a metal pipe deep underground is cracked.
They plan to pass a radioactive tracer through the pipe to detect any leaks.

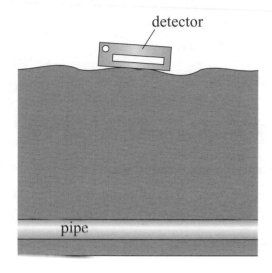

DIAGRAM NOT TO SCALE

Which of the following radioisotopes should they use?

   (1)   a beta emitter with a long half-life

   2   a gamma emitter with a short half-life

   3   an alpha emitter with a long half-life

   4   a beta emitter with a short half-life

4B A worker has to use an isotope which emits beta radiation. Which of the following safety precautions would protect the worker most effectively from the radiation?

   1   using tongs to handle the isotope

   2   wearing safety spectacles

   3   holding the sample at arm's length from the body

   (4)   wearing a lead lined suit

Question 4 continues on the next page

Turn over

4C The diagram shows the internal mechanism of a smoke detector.

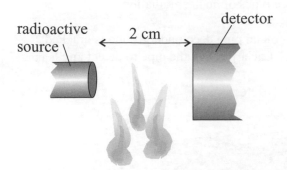

Which of these is the best explanation of why the detector works?

1 Alpha radiation can only pass through a few centimetres of air.

2 Beta radiation can pass through smoke in order to set off the alarm.

3 Alpha radiation is highly ionising, but is absorbed by smoke.

4 Beta radiation is highly ionising, but is absorbed by smoke.

4D The diagram below shows the paths of the three types of nuclear radiation through an electric field.

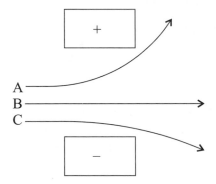

Which row in the table, 1 - 4, correctly describes the diagram?

	A	B	C
1	alpha	beta	gamma
2	beta	alpha	gamma
3	gamma	alpha	beta
4	beta	gamma	alpha

QUESTION FIVE

A digital DAB radio displays the following information: 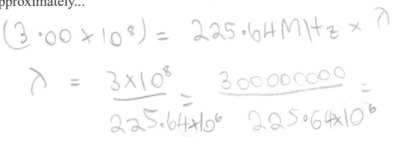 CGP Radio   225.64 MHz

5A   The speed of light in a vacuum is 3.00×10^8 m/s.

> wave speed = frequency × wavelength

The wavelength of these radio waves is approximately...

1   1.33 m

2 1.3×10^6 m

3 6.8×10^{10} m

4   0.75 m

$(3.00 \times 10^8) = 225.64 \, MHz \times \lambda$

$\lambda = \dfrac{3 \times 10^8}{225.64 \times 10^6} = \dfrac{300000000}{225.64 \times 10^6} = $

5B   Which of the following statements about radio signals is false?

1   Analogue signals have continuously varying values.

2   Digital signals are either on or off.

3   Analogue signals are harder to process in a computer than digital signals.

4   Digital signals travel much faster than analogue ones.

5C   The diagrams below show two analogue radio waves. Both waves travel at 3×10^8 m/s.
Which of the following statements is incorrect?

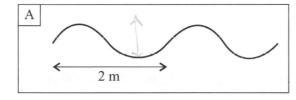

1   Wave B has twice the frequency of wave A.

2   The amplitude of waves A and B is the same.

3   The frequency of wave A is 6×10^8 Hz.

4   The wavelength of wave B is 1 m.

5D   DAB digital radios can produce better quality sound than analogue radios because...

1   Digital radio signals never pick up any interference.

2   Several signals can be transmitted at the same time using one radio wave.

3   Even if there is interference in the digital radio signal, the DAB radio can ignore this
interference when changing the radio signal back into sound.

4   The components used in digital radios are much better quality than those in analogue radios.

Turn over

QUESTION SIX

This question is about the Doppler Effect and the Big Bang Theory.

6A   The diagram below represents the sound waves produced by the siren of an ambulance.

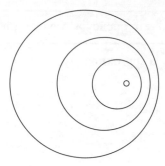

Which of the following statements best describes what's happening?

1   The ambulance's siren is pointing to the left.

2   The ambulance is moving quickly to the right.

3   The sound waves from the siren are bouncing off a wall to the right.

4   The sound waves are distorted because the air is denser on the right.

6B   The light we observe from most galaxies is shifted to the red end of the spectrum.
This is because...

1   they are colder than our galaxy.

2   they are moving towards our galaxy.

3   they are a long way away from our galaxy.

4   they are moving away from our galaxy.

6C   Galaxy red-shifts suggest that the Universe began as an explosion from a small initial point because...

1   red shift is more pronounced in galaxies that are further away from Earth.

2   everything is moving away from Earth at a constant speed.

3   red stars are older than white ones, so the stars furthest away are the oldest.

4   all observed galaxies are red shifted to the same extent.

6D   Most scientists accept the Big Bang theory because...

1   it is the only theory that describes how the Universe began.

2   it is the simplest theory that explains all the known facts.

3   it was proposed by a well respected scientist.

4   it has been proved to be true by scientific experiments.

QUESTION SEVEN

A teacher carried out an investigation to test different sunscreens using the apparatus below. The table show the results of the experiment.

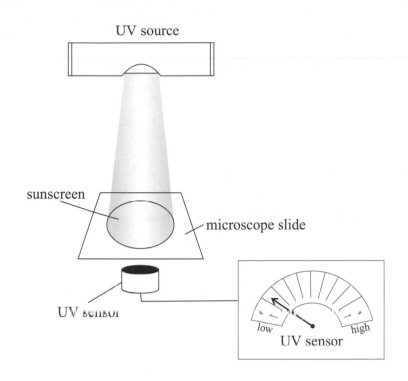

7A The results are shown in the table.
Which sunscreen sample provides the best protection from UV radiation?

1

Sunscreen sample	Reading on UV sensor in W/m^2
1	12
2	15
3	20
4	23

7B Which of these is the dependent variable in the experiment?

1 The type of sunscreen.
2 The thickness of sunscreen layer.
3 The intensity of UV light reaching the UV sensor.
4 The intensity of UV light reaching the sunscreen.

Question 7 continues on the next page

Turn over

7C   When UV radiation hits the sunscreen, it is...

1   reflected back towards the source.

2   diffracted, spreading out the rays to protect the material underneath.

3   absorbed — the energy it carried disappears.

 (4)   absorbed, transferring its energy to the sunscreen and increasing its temperature slightly.

7D   It is important to wear sunscreen...

1   to help prevent radiation sickness.

(2)   to help prevent skin cancer.

3   so that you can get a tan without absorbing any UV radiation.

4   to help keep your skin dry.

QUESTION EIGHT

This question is about the properties and uses of radioisotopes.

8A The graph below shows how the activity (count rate) of radon-220 varies with time. What is the half life of radon-220?

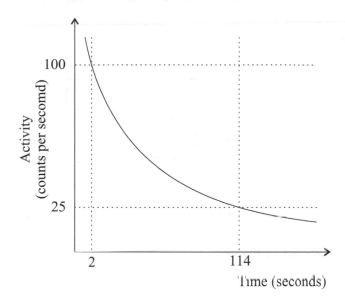

1 114 seconds

2 112 seconds

3 57 seconds

4 56 seconds

8B The radioisotope carbon-14 has a half life of 5730 years.
About 1 in 10 million carbon atoms in living organisms are carbon-14 isotopes.

The amount of carbon-14 in some human remains was found to be about 0.125 in 10 million. How long ago was the person alive?

1 1432.5 years

2 5730 years

3 17 190 years

4 22 920 years

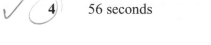

Question 8 continues on the next page

8C Which one of the radioisotopes in the table would be the most suitable for use as a medical tracer?

Radioisotope	Half-life	Type of radiation emitted
1	211 100 years	beta and gamma
2	8 days	beta
3	3 minutes	alpha
4	7340 years	alpha and gamma

8D The diagram below shows how a radioactive source can be used in a thickness gauge.

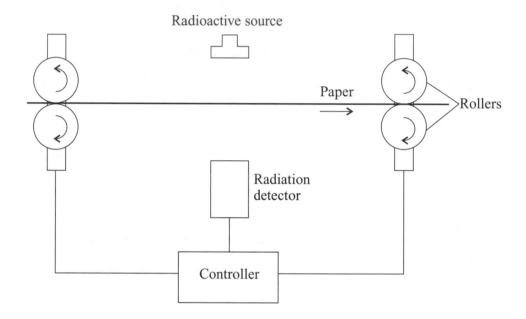

The radioactive source that's used emits...

1 all three types of radiation.

2 alpha radiation.

3 beta radiation.

4 gamma radiation.

QUESTION NINE

There are advantages and disadvantages of using different kinds of telescopes to find out about the Universe.

9A Optical telescopes give better images if they are in space rather than on the Earth because...

1   the temperature in space is much more constant than on Earth's surface.

2   telescopes can have larger mirrors in space because there's no gravity.

3   the light from astronomical objects is affected by the Earth's atmosphere.

4   astronomical objects look larger in space because you are nearer to them.

9B Which of the following statements is false?

1   Earth-based telescopes are cheaper and easier to maintain than telescopes in space.

2   X-ray telescopes only work from space because the Earth's atmosphere absorbs X-rays.

3   Optical telescopes in space need larger mirrors than similar Earth-based telescopes.

4   The best positions for Earth-based telescopes are away from cities or on top of mountains.

9C Radio telescopes need to have much larger reflecting dishes than the mirrors on optical telescopes because...

1   the energy from visible light is a lot less than the energy from radio waves.

2   the wavelength of radio waves is much larger than the wavelength of visible light.

3   the frequency of radio waves is much larger than the frequency of visible light.

4   objects which emit radio waves are much bigger than objects which emit visible light.

9D Data collected by a space telescope can be transmitted to Earth using microwaves. Microwaves are used for this because...

1   they travel at exactly the same speed whether they're in space or in the atmosphere.

2   they are reflected by the Earth's atmosphere.

3   they aren't likely to suffer from interference.

4   they can pass through the Earth's atmosphere.   4

END OF TEST

General Certificate of Secondary Education

AQA GCSE Physics

Unit Physics 2

Higher Tier

Time allowed: 45 minutes.

Centre name				
Centre number				
Candidate number				

Surname	
Other names	
Candidate signature	

Instructions to candidates

- Write your name and other details in the spaces provided above.
- Answer all the questions.
- Do all rough work on this question paper.

Information for candidates

- The marks available are given in brackets at the end of each question or part-question.
- In calculations show clearly how you worked out your answers.
- You may use a calculator.
- There are 7 questions in this paper. The maximum mark for this paper is 45.

63%

22/55

Advice to candidates

- Work steadily through the paper.
- Don't spend too long on one question.
- If you have time at the end, go back and check your answers.

	For examiner's use						
Q	Attempt Nº			Q	Attempt Nº		
	1	2	3		1	2	3
1				5			
2				6			
3				7			
4							
				Total 45			

Answer **all** questions in the spaces provided.

1   Rachel sets up two electric circuits as shown below.

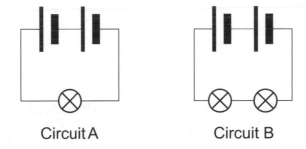

Circuit A   Circuit B

a)   All the lamps used are identical.
         Compare the resistance and current in circuit B with circuit A.

....

....

....
                                                                              (2 marks)

b)   Redraw circuit A to show how a voltmeter and an ammeter can be positioned to find the
         potential difference across the lamp and the current through it.

(2 marks)

Question 1 continues on the next page

Turn over

c) **i)** The equation linking potential difference, current and resistance is shown below. Rewrite the equation in terms of resistance.

$$\text{potential difference} = \text{current} \times \text{resistance}$$

resistance = ...

(1 mark)

ii) Rachel adds an ammeter and a voltmeter to the circuit. They show readings of 0.5 A and 3 V respectively. Calculate the resistance of the lamp. Give the unit.

....

....

potential difference = ...

(2 marks)

Rachel adds the following components to Circuit A.

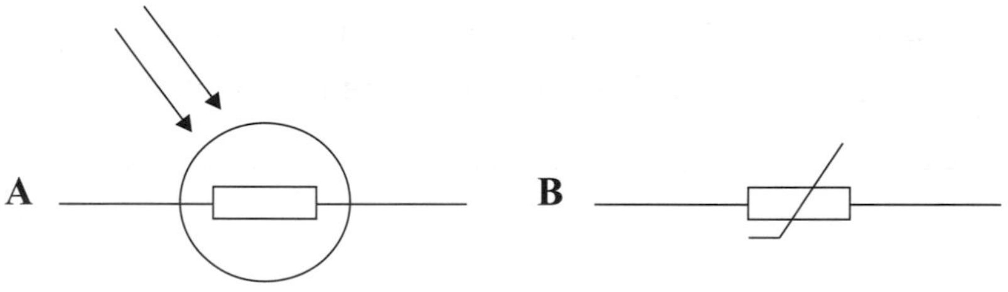

d) **i)** What are these components?

A ....

B ....

(2 marks)

ii) What happens to the resistance of component A as the intensity of the light that falls on it increases?

....

(1 mark)

2   Nuclear reactors in power stations and submarines release energy through nuclear fission.

a)   What is meant by nuclear fission?

The   Splitting of   an   atomic nuclei

(1 mark)

b)   Name two fissionable substances commonly used in nuclear reactors.

1.   Uranium

2.   plutonium

(2 marks)

Scientists are trying to develop reactors in which energy is released through nuclear fusion.

c)   What is meant by nuclear fusion?

The   joining   of small atomic nuclei of the

(1 mark)

d)   Where does nuclear fusion occur naturally?

air

(1 mark)

$\dfrac{4}{5}$

Turn over

4

3   Patrick is a free-fall skydiver. He jumps from an aeroplane and his motion is recorded.
     After his jump he looks at this velocity-time graph of his fall.

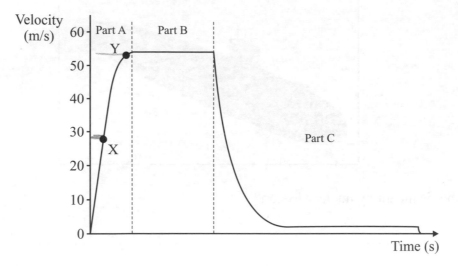

a) i) Is Patrick's acceleration greater at point X or point Y?
        Explain how you can tell this from the graph.

        ....Yes,....at....point...Y...he...is...starting........
        ....to...reach...a...constant...velocity.................
                                                                  (1 mark)

    ii) Is the resultant force acting on Patrick greater at point X or point Y?
        Explain why the resultant force changes magnitude in this way.

        ....Y,..because..it..forces..patrick..to..start........
        ....to..slow..down,..and..stay..a..constant.............
        velocity   *(2 marks)*

b) Part B of the graph is flat, showing that Patrick's velocity stayed constant for a time.
    Explain why his velocity stayed constant during this time.

        ....it.....wasnt..being..acting..on..by..a..............
        ....force...
                                                                  (1 mark)

c) Patrick's mass is 83 kg. Calculate his weight using the information given below.

        force = mass × acceleration   acceleration due to gravity = 10 m/s²

        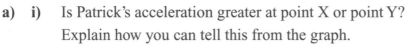

                                    Weight = ...830.........N
                                                                  (1 mark)

203

4   Dean and Natalie are ice dancers. During a dance display Dean skates up to Natalie and carries her away as shown in the diagram below.

360

| Mass = 60 kg | Mass = 40 kg |
| Velocity = 6 m/s | Not moving |

Dean   Natalie   Dean and Natalie together
       Before   **After**

360 kgm/s

a)   Calculate Dean and Natalie's total momentum as Dean approaches Natalie. Give the unit.

$$momentum = mass \times velocity$$

....

....

momentum = ...360 kgm/s....

(2 marks)

b)   What is their velocity immediately after they join together?

....

velocity = ...6 m/s....

(2 marks)

At the end of their routine, Dean lifts Natalie into the air.
When Dean lowers Natalie back down onto the ice, she bends her legs to avoid injury.

c)   Explain how bending her legs on landing will help Natalie avoid injury.

....She is refracting gravity causing....
....it to act at another place....
....reducing force to of impact....

(3 marks)

7

Turn over

6

5   Samantha is copper-plating a bracelet using electrolysis. She uses the circuit shown below.
    The circuit includes a lamp so that Samantha can easily see when current is flowing.

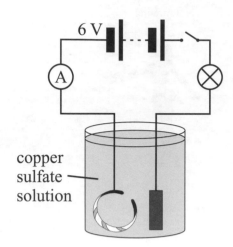

Samantha calculates that to plate the bracelet, she needs to pass 1000 C of charge through the
circuit. She decides to use a current of 0.5 A.

a) Use the equation below to calculate how long it will take to plate the bracelet.

charge = current × time

$$\frac{1000}{0.5} = 2000$$

time = 2000 .... s

(2 marks)

b) The potential difference across the lamp is 6 V. Use the equation below to calculate the
    energy transformed by the lamp during the time taken to copper-plate the bracelet.
    Give the unit.

energy transformed = potential difference × charge

VC   = 6V × 1000C

= 6000

energy transformed = 6000   VC

(2 marks)

6   Polonium-216 is a radioactive isotope.

$$\text{Mass number} \longrightarrow 216$$
$$\text{Atomic number} \longrightarrow 84 \quad \text{Po}$$

a)   How many protons does an atom of polonium-216 have?

84

(1 mark)

b)   How many neutrons does an atom of polonium-216 have?

1 3 2

(1 mark)

c)   Polonium-216 undergoes alpha decay to form a radioactive isotope of lead, Pb.
Write a balanced equation to show this event.

$$^{218}_{86}Pb \rightarrow {}^{216}_{84}PO + {}^{4}_{2}\alpha$$

(2 marks)

d)   The radioisotope of lead formed in **c)** decays by beta emission to form bismuth, Bi.
Write a balanced equation to show this event.

$$^{218}_{85}Bi \rightarrow {}^{218}_{86}Pb + {}^{0}_{-1}\beta$$

(2 marks)

6

Turn over

8

7   Suzi studies the motion of her dad's car as it moves away from a set of traffic lights.
     Using the speedometer and her watch she collects the following data:

Velocity (m/s)	0	3	6	9	12	12	12
Time (s)	0	1	2	3	4	5	6

a)   Draw a velocity-time graph for this data on the axes below.

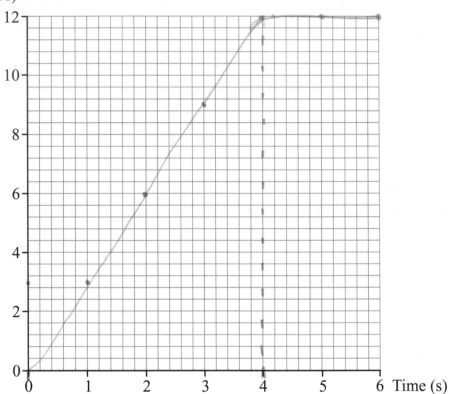

Velocity (m/s)

(2 marks)

b)   Using the graph, calculate the car's acceleration over the first 4 s.
     Show clearly how you used the graph to calculate the acceleration.

     acceleration = velocity / time = u+v / 12 = 3 / 4

     acceleration = 3 m/s²

(3 marks)

9

c) Use the graph to calculate the distance travelled by the car during those 6 s.

distance = $\frac{speed}{time}$ = $\frac{13}{4}$ + $\frac{12}{2}$ = 3 + 6

Distance travelled = 9 m

(3 marks)

8

END OF TEST

General Certificate of Secondary Education

AQA GCSE Physics

Unit Physics 3

Higher Tier

Time allowed: 45 minutes.

Centre name				
Centre number				
Candidate number				

Surname	
Other names	
Candidate signature	

Instructions to candidates
- Write your name and other details in the spaces provided above.
- Answer all the questions.
- Do all rough work on this question paper.

Information for candidates

45%

- The marks available are given in brackets at the end of each question or part-question.
- In calculations show clearly how you worked out your answers.
- You may use a calculator.
- There are 8 questions in this paper.
  The maximum mark for this paper is 45.

Advice to candidates
- Work steadily through the paper.
- Don't spend too long on one question.
- If you have time at the end, go back and check your answers.

For examiner's use

Q	Attempt Nº			Q	Attempt Nº		
	1	2	3		1	2	3
1				5			
2				6			
3				7			
4				8			
				Total 45			

1   James is riding his bicycle. He pushes down on the pedal with a force of 100 N.

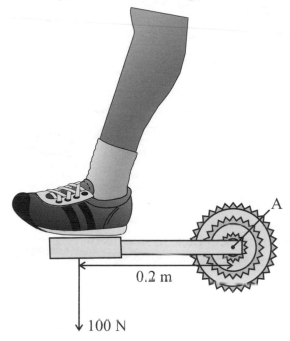

a)   Calculate the moment, about point A, that James exerts. Give the unit.

moment = force × perpendicular distance

moment = 100 N × 0·2 m

= 20 Nm

moment = 20 Nm

(2 marks)

b)   Explain what will happen to the moment about point A if James continues to push on the pedal with the same force while the pedal moves downwards.

The moment about point A will increase

(2 marks)

XX

Question 1 continues on the next page

Turn over

2

James has a little brother called Luke. Luke is just learning to ride a bicycle.
He has stabilisers fitted to his rear wheel.

c) Explain how the stabilisers help Luke to ride his bicycle.

The stabilisers make sure the stability
does not fall outside the base

(2 marks)

✓✓

6

3

2   Astronomers collect data about the planets.
     Here is some data about the 'gas giants' in our solar system.

Planet	Mean distance from the Sun (million km)	Mean orbital speed (km/s)
Jupiter	778	13.07
Saturn	1427	9.64
Uranus	2871	6.80
Neptune	4498	5.43

a)   What force keeps these outer planets orbiting the Sun?

...............Gravity...................................   ....   (1 mark)

b)   A year is defined as the time it takes a planet to complete an orbit of the Sun.
     Explain why a year on Neptune is longer than a year on Saturn.

...............It   take   Neptune longer   to orbit   the.......
...............Sun. ....
                                                                                        (1 mark)

c)   How does the force of attraction between the Sun and Earth differ from the force
     between the Sun and the gas giants? Give a reason for your answer.

...............The force in   outer   space..

....

....

....
                                                                                   (2 marks)   XX

4

Turn over

4

3   Amanda is looking at her reflection in a spoon.

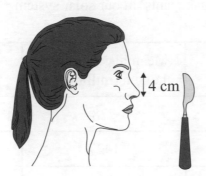

The spoon acts like a concave mirror.

a)   Draw a ray diagram on the grid below to construct the image of Amanda's nose.
Her nose is 4 cm long and 4 cm away from the spoon.

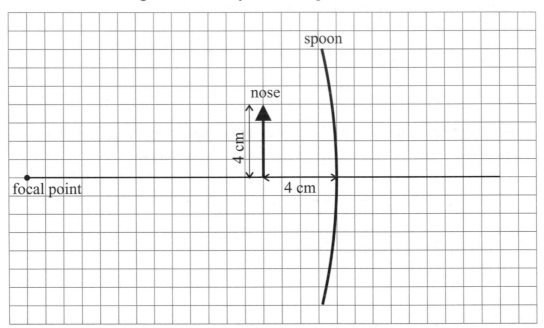

(3 marks)

b)   Use your diagram to calculate the magnification of the spoon at this distance.

....

....
(2 marks)

c)   Describe how the image of Amanda's nose would change if she turned the spoon over.

....

....
(1 mark)

4   The diagram below shows the oscilloscope traces made by sound waves from three different whistles — a referee's whistle, a toy whistle and a dog whistle.
The traces are all shown to the same scale.

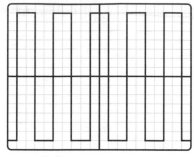 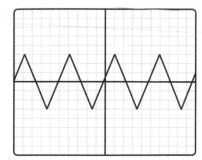 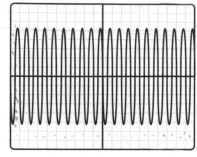

Referee's whistle   Toy whistle   Dog whistle

Scale: □ = 2.5 × 10⁻⁵ s

a)   The dog whistle has such a high pitch that it cannot be detected by the human ear.

   i)   Use the diagram to calculate the frequency of the dog whistle.

3905,

$$20 \times (2.5 \times 10^{-5}) = 5 \times 10^{-4} =$$

frequency = ~~0.005~~ 0.0005 ~~000.5~~ Hz

(2 marks)

XX

   ii)   What is the range of frequencies that can be detected by the human ear?

20 - 20,000 Hz

(1 mark)

b)   The referee's whistle was much louder than the toy whistle.

   i)   How is this shown by the oscilloscope traces?

The amplitude of the referee's whistle is bigger

(1 mark)

   ii)   How else do the oscilloscope traces show that the two whistles sound different?

The ~~does~~ have different wave patterns

- different pitches and amplitude

(1 mark)

5

Turn over

5   Louise is playing with an electric toy car. She has attached a piece of string to the car and pinned the string to the floor.

a)   When the car is moving it follows the circular path shown in the diagram below.
Draw and label an arrow on the diagram to show the force that makes the car follow this path.

(1 mark)

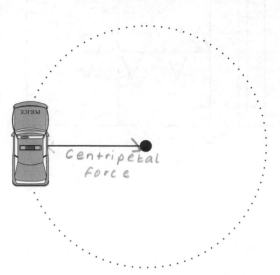

Centripetal force

b)   Louise is worried that the force on the string might cause it to snap. Describe two changes she could make to her apparatus to decrease the force on the string.

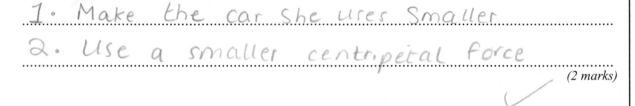

1. Make the car she uses smaller

2. Use a smaller centripetal force

(2 marks)

The car can be driven forwards at two speeds. The graph below shows the car's motion as it drives clockwise around the path shown in part a).

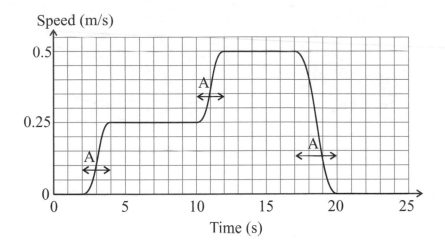

c)   Louise says that the car is only accelerating during the parts of the graph marked with an A (see graph).

Is she correct? Explain your answer.

Yes   because   the   other   parts
are   either   at a constant   velocity
or   at   rest

(2 marks)

☒

5

6   The diagram below shows a simple AC generator.

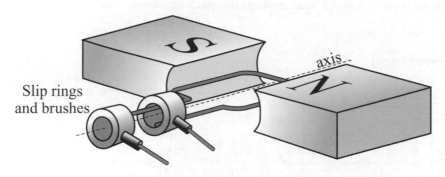

Induced voltage

a)   Use the diagram to explain how an AC generator produces an electric current.

....

....

....

The coil in the generator is turned using a wind turbine.
The output of the generator on a certain day is displayed on the oscilloscope trace below.

Voltage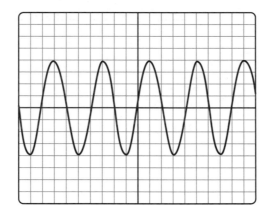

Time

b)   Sketch the trace you might expect to see if the wind blew faster.

(2 marks)

c)   Describe two ways in which the generator could be changed to increase the potential
difference induced at a given wind speed, when using the same wind turbine.

....

....
(1 mark)

5

7   Paul made a simple transformer from a laminated iron core and two lengths of wire, as shown in the diagram below. He connected a 12 V alternating power supply to one of the coils and a lamp and voltmeter to the other coil.

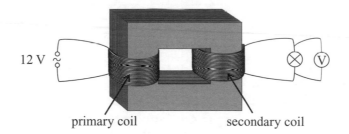

a)   Explain how a voltage is generated in the secondary coil.

....

....

(2 marks)

Paul experimented with the transformer by changing the number of turns on the secondary coil and measuring the voltage across the lamp each time. His results are shown below.

Number of turns on secondary coil (N_s)	Voltage induced in secondary coil (V_s)
5	3.8
10	7.5
15	1.3
20	15
25	18.8

Question 7 continues on the next page

Turn over

b) Plot Paul's results on the axes given and draw a line of best fit.

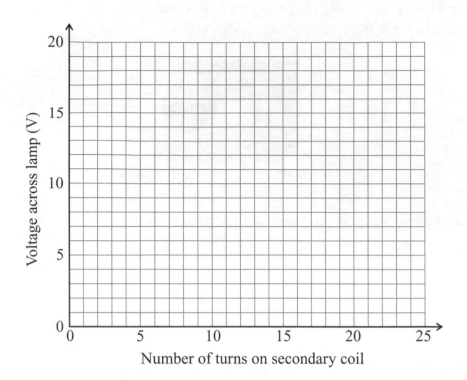

Number of turns on secondary coil

(2 marks)

c) Paul thinks he may have read the voltmeter incorrectly on one of the trials and recorded an anomalous result.

   i) Circle the anomalous result on the graph.

(1 mark)

   ii) Use your graph to estimate the actual voltage induced on this trial.

....

(1 mark)

6

8 The Milky Way galaxy contains many billions of stars, including the Sun.

a) How were the Sun and the planets in the Solar System formed?

....

....
(2 marks)

b) **i)** How is energy released inside the Sun?

....
(1 mark)

ii) Explain why the Sun has been stable for millions of years in its 'main sequence' stage.

....

....
(2 marks)

The diagram below shows the expected future of the Sun.

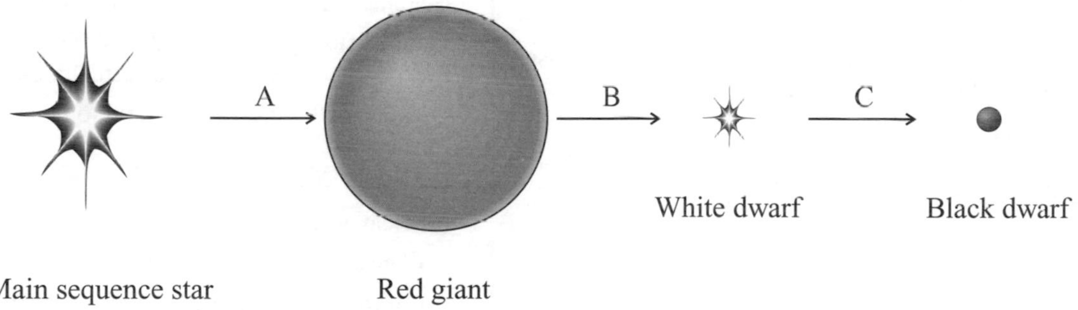

Main sequence star   Red giant   White dwarf   Black dwarf

c) Describe the changes that occur between each stage.

A: ....
(1 mark)

B: ....
(1 mark)

C: ....
(1 mark)

8

END OF TEST

Page 15

Warm-Up Questions

1) infrared (radiation)

2) E.g. make the surface darker in colour, make the surface rougher.

3) Particles that vibrate faster than others pass on their extra kinetic energy to their neighbours.

4) Heated air expands, so it becomes less dense than the surrounding cooler air and rises.

Exam Questions

1 D *(1 mark)*

2 D *(1 mark)*
   Light and shiny surfaces are best for reflecting heat radiation.

3 (a) (i) by (thermal) radiation *(1 mark)*

   (ii) by conduction through the metal pipe *(1 mark)*

   (iii) by convection currents in the water *(1 mark)*

   (b) Because black surfaces are good absorbers of heat radiation *(1 mark)*.

Page 22

Warm-Up Questions

1) chemical energy

2) Energy cannot be created or destroyed, only converted from one form to another.

3) More of the input energy is transformed into useful energy in modern appliances.

4) Some energy is always wasted and so all the input energy isn't transformed usefully.

5) E.g. wind-up radio, clockwork toy.

Exam Questions

1 B *(1 mark)*
   Efficiency = Useful energy output ÷ Total energy input.

2 A *(1 mark)*
   Each square represents 10 J. The bulb is 15% efficient, so when 100 J of energy are input, the useful output must be 1.5 squares wide.

3 (a) 1200 − 20 − 100 = 1080 J *(1 mark)*
   Energy cannot be destroyed or created, so the total energy output must equal the energy input.

   (b) By reducing the amount of energy wasted as sound / by having a quieter motor *(1 mark)*.
   Only the energy converted to sound is wasted — kinetic and heat energy are what you want from a hairdryer.

Page 25

Warm-Up Questions

1) kilowatt-hour (kWh)

2) No. of units (kWh) = power (kW) × time (hours)

3) Any three of, e.g. loft insulation / cavity wall insulation / draught proofing / double glazing / using thick curtains.

4) The amount of time it takes for the initial cost to equal the money saved.

Exam Questions

1 B *(1 mark)*

2 C *(1 mark)*

3 (a) 300 × 0.25 = £75 *(1 mark)*

   (b) 300 − 255 = £45 saved per year *(1 mark)*.
   Payback time = cost ÷ saving per year
   = 350 ÷ 45 = 7.8 years *(1 mark)*.

Page 35

Warm-Up Questions

1) Any two of, e.g. it releases greenhouse gases/contributes to global warming / it causes acid rain / coal mining damages the landscape.

2) Nuclear power stations produce radioactive waste, which is dangerous and difficult to dispose of / risk of a catastrophic accident.

3) Any two of, e.g. they're expensive to install / are inefficient / can only generate electricity when there is enough sunlight.

4) Pumped storage is a method of storing electricity whereas hydroelectric power schemes actually generate electricity.

5) Organic matter that can be burnt to release energy.

Exam Questions

1 (a) Heat energy from inside the Earth *(1 mark)*.

   (b) The source of energy will never run out *(1 mark)*.

   (c) Because there are no hot rocks near the surface of the Earth in the UK *(1 mark)*

2 A — 3 *(1 mark)*

   B — 4 *(1 mark)*

   C — 1 *(1 mark)*

   D — 2 *(1 mark)*

3 (a) 2 000 000 ÷ 4000 = 500 *(1 mark)*

   (b) If the wind isn't blowing strongly, the turbines will not generate as much as 4000 W each *(1 mark)*.

   (c) Any two of, e.g. they believe it would spoil the view (visual pollution) / cause noise pollution / kill or disturb local wildlife *(1 mark each)*.

4 (a) Any two of, e.g. wave / tidal / geothermal / biomass *(1 mark for each)*.

   (b) Any two of, e.g. set-up time / set-up costs / running costs / impact on environment / social impact *(1 mark for each)*.

Page 36

Revision Summary for Physics 1a — Energy and Electricity

10) 70%

12) a) 80 J

   b) 20 J

   c) 80% (or 0.8)

14) a) 2 years

   b) B (payback time is 1.5 years)

   c) $0.1 \times 5 \times 8 = 4$p

Pages 43-44

Warm-Up Questions

1) The number of complete wavelengths that pass a point within 1 second.

2) When light is travelling from a denser medium towards a less dense medium and its angle of incidence at the boundary is greater than the critical angle.

3) A thin glass or plastic fibre which is used to transmit light/IR waves. Because the light no longer hits the boundary within the optical fibre at a big enough angle, and so is not internally reflected (and transmitted along the fibre).

4) It causes heating / can cause burns.

5) They wear lead aprons and either stand behind a lead screen or leave the room when an X-ray is taken.

Exam Questions

1 C *(1 mark)*

2 A *(1 mark)* $\lambda = v \div f = 300\ 000\ 000 \div 100\ 000\ 000 = 3$ m. *Don't forget that you have to convert MHz to Hz before doing the calculation.*

3 (a) 5 cm *(1 mark)*

   (b) 1 complete wave would pass a point every 2 seconds, so $f = 1 \div 2 = \textbf{0.5 Hz}$ *(1 mark)*

   (c) It will halve. *(1 mark)*
   Because frequency and wavelength are inversely proportional.

4 (a)

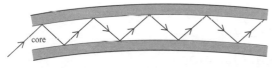

(1 mark)

   (b) The light ray meets the core/outer boundary at an angle greater than the critical angle, so is totally internally reflected, and this happens repeatedly. *(1 mark)*

5 C *(1 mark)*
No one knows for sure whether microwave radiation from phones and masts is causing any health problems.

6 A — 3 *(1 mark)*

   B — 4 *(1 mark)*

   C — 2 *(1 mark)*

   D — 1 *(1 mark)*

7 (a) Hazard: is absorbed by water molecules, causing heating which could damage living cells. *(1 mark)* Use: any one of, e.g. mobile phone signals / communication / cooking *(1 mark)*

   (b) Any one of, e.g. stay in the shade / wear sunscreen / keep covered up with clothing. *(1 mark)*

Page 47

Warm-Up Questions

1) Digital signals can only take two values, on and off, whereas analogue signals can take any values within a given range.

2) Any one of, e.g. dimmer switches, thermometers, speedometers, old-fashioned watches.

3) E.g. displays on digital clocks and meters.

4) Analogue signals

Exam Questions

1 D *(1 mark)*

2 B *(1 mark)*

3 (a) on or off (1 or 0) *(1 mark)*

   (b) Both types of signal will have lost energy and weakened. *(1 mark)*

   (c) Interference on digital signals can be much more easily filtered out by his radio. *(1 mark)*

Page 50

beta

Page 53

Warm-Up Questions

1) Atoms which have the same number of protons but different numbers of neutrons.

2) An unstable atom emits radiation and becomes more stable, often changing into a different element.

3) Alpha, beta and gamma

4) Gamma radiation

Exam Questions

1 A — 4 *(1 mark)*

   B — 1 *(1 mark)*

   C — 3 *(1 mark)*

   D — 2 *(1 mark)*

2 C *(1 mark)*

3 (a) The time taken for half of the unstable nuclei in a sample to decay / the time taken for the count rate to halve. *(1 mark)*

(b) one quarter / 25% *(1 mark)*

(c) beta *(1 mark)*

Page 58

Warm-Up Questions

1) A weak alpha source is used to ionise the air between two electrodes so that a current can flow. If the alpha radiation is absorbed by smoke, the current stops and the alarm sounds.

2) Because it is ionising and can damage cells.

3) Any one of, e.g. medical tracers / treatment of cancer.

4) Any two of, e.g. never look directly at the source / always handle a source with tongs / never allow the source to touch the skin / never have the source out of its lead-lined box for longer than necessary.

5) Any one of, e.g. wear lead-lined suits / work behind lead/concrete barriers / use robotic arms to do tasks in highly radioactive areas.

Exam Questions

1 A *(1 mark)*

2 B *(1 mark)*

3 a) Alpha radiation is stopped by the body's tissues and so wouldn't be detected externally. *(1 mark)* It is also strongly ionising which makes it dangerous inside the body. *(1 mark)*

b) So that the device lasts a long time and therefore doesn't need to be replaced as often. *(1 mark)*

c) So that the dose to the rest of the body is minimised, to reduce damage to healthy cells. *(1 mark)*

4 a) The radiation can collide with molecules in the body's cells, causing ionisation and damaging the cell. *(1 mark)* This can then result in mutant cells dividing uncontrollably, which is cancer. *(1 mark)*

b) It can kill cells, which causes radiation sickness if a large part of the body is affected. *(1 mark)*

Page 62

Warm-Up Questions

1) To minimise light pollution and pollution from dust, etc.

2) It increases the resolution of the images produced. / It allows fainter objects to be 'seen'.

3) The level of detail the images include.

Exam Questions

1 A *(1 mark)*

2 (a) All the matter and energy was in a very small space, then there was an explosion/a 'Big Bang'. *(1 mark)*

(b) The further the galaxy, the greater the red shift *(1 mark)*. This shows that the more distant the galaxy, the faster it's moving away from us. This must mean that the Universe is expanding. *(1 mark)*

3 (a) The Earth's atmosphere will not interfere with the view of a space telescope. *(1 mark)*

(b) It costs a lot more to build a space telescope *(1 mark)*. It's a lot harder to maintain / fix a space telescope *(1 mark)*.

4 (a) Linking up lots of smaller ones. *(1 mark)*

(b) To get good resolution the dish has to be large compared to the wavelength *(1 mark)* and radio waves have a longer wavelength than light waves *(1 mark)*.

(c) Because X-rays are absorbed by the Earth's atmosphere. *(1 mark)*

Page 63

Revision Summary Physics 1b — Radiation and the Universe

4 a) 500 000 Hz

b) 0.35 m

c) 4 600 000 Hz

d) 0.04 m/s

e) 150 s

5) $v = f \times \lambda = 50\ 000$ Hz $\times 0.003$ m $= 150$ m/s

10) A and D

20) (a)

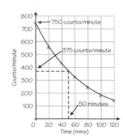

Count rate halves after 50 minutes, so half-life is 50 minutes.

Pages 69-70

Warm-Up Questions

1) 10 m $\div$ 5 s = 2 m/s

2) Acceleration — m/s², mass — kilograms (kg), weight — newtons (N)

3) Speed

4) $(30 - 0) \div 6 = 30 \div 6 = 5$ m/s²

5) Gravity

Exam Questions

1 (a) Because its direction is constantly changing. *(1 mark)*

(b) Time = distance ÷ speed = 2400 ÷ 45 = 53.3 s (to 1 d.p)
(2 marks, allow 1 mark for correct working)

(c) Acceleration = change in velocity ÷ time taken
= (59 – 45) ÷ 5
= 14 ÷ 5 = 2.8 m/s²
(2 marks, allow 1 mark for correct working)

2 (a) (i) 200 m *(1 mark)*
Read the distance travelled from the graph.

(ii) 200 ÷ 15 = 13.3 m/s (to 1 d.p.)
(2 marks, allow 1 mark for correct working)

(b) 13 s (allow answers from 11 s to 15 s) *(1 mark)*
The bus is stationary between about 33 and 46 seconds.

(c) The bus is travelling at constant speed (10 m/s) back towards the point it started from. *(1 mark)*

(d)

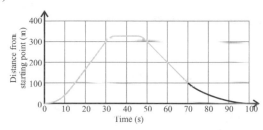

(1 mark)

3 (a) The cyclist is travelling at a constant velocity of 3 m/s. *(1 mark)*

(b) The cyclist's speed is constantly decreasing. *(1 mark)*

(c) (3 – 0) × (5 – 2) ÷ 2 = 4.5 m *(1 mark)*
Remember, distance travelled is the area under the graph.

4 (a) Acceleration due to gravity, g, is lower on Mars than on Earth *(1 mark)*, because Mars has a smaller mass than Earth. *(1 mark)* So the ball's weight is less on Mars than on Earth. *(1 mark)*

(b) 3 ÷ 1.1 = 2.7 (to 1.d.p) So, the spring extends 2.7 times as far on Earth, so g on Earth must be 2.7 times bigger than on Mars. *(1 mark)* 10 ÷ 2.7 = 3.7 N/kg (to 1.d.p) *(1 mark)*

5 (a) Acceleration = change in velocity ÷ time taken
= (10 – 0) ÷ 1 = 10 m/s² *(1 mark)*

(b) Change in velocity = acceleration × time = 10 × 3 = 30 m/s *(1 mark)*

(c) Assume g = 10 m/s².
Weight = mass × g = 0.12 × 10 = 1.2 N *(1 mark)*

(d) None — the stone's acceleration due to gravity is determined by the mass of the Earth, not the stone. *(1 mark)*

6 All of them. *(1 mark)*
Everything with mass exerts a gravitational force.

Page 76

Warm-Up Questions

1) 0 N

2) The acceleration also doubles.

3) 3 + 3 – 1 = 5 N towards the shore

4) Against motion.

Exam Questions

1 (a) (i) 900 N – 900 N = 0 N *(1 mark)*

(ii) Parachutist A is falling at a constant (terminal) velocity. *(1 mark)*

(b) (i) Terminal velocity is reached when the force of air resistance equals the parachutist's weight. *(1 mark)* Weight = mass × g = 70 × 10 = 700 N *(1 mark)*

(ii) Parachutist A would have a higher terminal velocity *(1 mark)* because he has a greater weight. *(1 mark)* This means the force of air resistance would need to be greater to balance his weight, and air resistance is greater at higher speeds. *(1 mark)*

(c) Because the parachute increases their air resistance/drag. *(1 mark)*

2 (a) The upwards force must be greater because Stefan is accelerating upwards. *(1 mark)*

(b) Assume g = 10 N/kg, Stefan's mass is 600 ÷ 10 = 60 kg *(1 mark)*
Force = mass × acceleration = 60 × 2.5 = 150 N *(1 mark)*

3 (a) Newton's third law says that if an object A exerts a force on another object, B, then object B exerts an equal but opposite force on object A. *(1 mark)* So if the bat exerts a force of 500 N on the ball, the ball also exerts a force of 500 N on the bat, but in the opposite direction. *(1 mark)*

(b) The ball's acceleration is greater *(1 mark)* because it has a smaller mass than the bat (F = ma). *(1 mark)*

Pages 83-84

Warm-Up Questions

1) The distance travelled in the time between a hazard appearing and the driver braking.

2) Braking distance

3) Because work done is a measure of energy transfer.

4) The energy an object has due to its height above the ground.

5) It increases by a factor of 3² or 9.

6) Momentum = mass × velocity

7) Any two of, e.g. seat belts / air bags / crumple zones.

Exam Questions

1 (a) (i)   Accept answers between 12 and 13 m *(1 mark)*

(ii) 35 m *(1 mark)*

(iii) 35 m – 12 m = 22 m *(1 mark)*

(b) Braking distance *(1 mark)*
Using the graph, thinking distance is about 15 m and braking distance about 38 m.

(c) No, *(1 mark)* if stopping distance and speed were proportional the relationship between them would be shown by a straight line. *(1 mark)*

2 (a) (i)   Momentum = mass × velocity = 100 × 6 = 600 kg m/s to the right *(1 mark)*

(ii) 80 × 9 = 720 kg m/s to the left *(1 mark)*

(b) (i)   Take left as positive, then the momentum of the two players is
720 – 600 = 120 kg m/s. *(1 mark)*
The mass of the two players is 100 + 80 = 180 kg, so the speed is
120 ÷ 180 = 0.67 m/s *(1 mark)*

(ii) Left *(1 mark)*
The two players travel in the direction player B was going because he had more momentum before the collision.

3 (a) 40 000 kg × 1.05 m/s^2 = 42 000 N
(2 marks, allow 1 mark for correct working)

(b) 42 000 N × 700 m = 29 400 000 J *(1 mark)*

(c) 29 400 000 J ÷ 29 400 N = 1000 m (1 km)
(2 marks, allow 1 mark for correct working)

(d) The train's kinetic energy would be reduced by a factor of 0.5^2 = 0.25, as would its braking distance, so the train would stop in 250 m. *(1 mark)*

(e) Heat/sound energy *(1 mark)*

4 (a) ½ × 2750 kg × (12 m/s)^2 = 198 000 J *(1 mark)*

(b) The van has the more energy as it has a bigger mass. *(1 mark)*

(c) The car's kinetic energy would be increased by a factor of 2^2 = 4. *(1 mark)*

(d) 550 000 J ÷ 25 m = 22 000 N
(2 marks, allow 1 mark for correct working)

Page 85

Revision Summary for Physics 2(i) — Forces and Motion

2) 0.09 m/s, 137 m

3) No

5) 35 m/s^2

15) 7.5 m/s^2

16) 5.7 kg

18) 1.33 m/s^2

25) 6420 J

26) 20 631 J

29) 1170 kg m/s

31) 700 N

Page 90

Warm-Up Questions

1) Positive and negative

2) Repel

3) Connect it to the earth with a metal strap.

4) Any one of, e.g. in a thunder storm / when refuelling a vehicle.

5) Electrons.

Exam Questions

1 (a) A *(1 mark)* The rod is negatively charged so would repel the negative charges in the balloon, making them move away from the rod. *(1 mark)*

(b) Because they are fixed in place so cannot move. *(1 mark)*

(c) The negative charges in the rod attract the positive charges in the balloon. *(1 mark)* As Jane brings the rod closer to the balloon this attraction gets stronger, causing the balloon to move. *(1 mark)*

(d) (i)   The negative charges flow through Jane to Earth. *(1 mark)*

(ii) Positively charged *(1 mark)*

2 (a) Electrons are scraped from the cloth onto the surface. *(1 mark)*

(b) The charged cloth attracts tiny neutral dust particles. *(1 mark)*

3 (a) Raindrops and ice particles bumping against one another. *(1 mark)*

(b) The top of the cloud becomes positively charged and the bottom becomes negatively charged. *(1 mark)*

(c) Lightning rods conduct the current from a charged cloud directly to Earth. *(1 mark)* The very high current doesn't pass through the fabric of the building, so there's less risk of fires starting. *(1 mark)*

Page 100

Warm-Up Questions

1) Ohms, Ω

2) It decreases.

3)

4) 50 Hz

5) 1 ÷ 100 = 0.01 s

Exam Questions

1 (a) (i) and (ii)

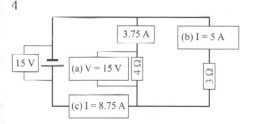

(1 mark each for the three components correctly drawn and placed)

(1 mark for correctly drawn arrows)

(b) Voltage = current × resistance = 0.3 × 5 = 1.5 V *(1 mark)*

2 (a) Diodes only allow current to flow in one direction. *(1 mark)*

(b) Resistance = voltage ÷ current = 6 ÷ 3 = 2 Ω
(2 marks, allow 1 mark for correct working)
Read the values from the graph, then use the formula R = V ÷ I.

3 (a) The trace shows an AC source so cannot be from a battery / must be from mains electricity *(1 mark)*

(b) 20 ms *(1 mark)*
The wave takes four divisions to repeat. 4 × 5 ms = 20 ms.

(c) 20 ms = 0.02 s. Frequency = 1 ÷ time = 1 ÷ 0.02 = 50 Hz *(1 mark)*

(d) The amplitude of the wave will be decreased so the peaks and troughs will be smaller. *(1 mark)*

4

	3.75 A		(b) I = 5 A
15 V	(a) V = 15 V	4 Ω	3 Ω
	(c) I = 8.75 A		

(a) 15 V *(1 mark)*
Voltage is the same across each branch in a parallel circuit.

(b) Current = voltage ÷ resistance = 15 ÷ 3 = 5 A
(2 marks, allow 1 mark for correct working)

(c) 5 + 3.75 = 8.75 A
(2 marks, allow 1 mark for correct working)

Page 107

Warm-Up Questions

1) The neutral wire (also accept the earth wire).
2) Plastic is a good insulator.
3) Electrical energy (to kinetic energy) to heat energy.
4) Current
5) E (energy) = Q (charge) × V (voltage).

Exam Questions

1 (a) (i) brown *(1 mark)*
(ii) blue *(1 mark)*
(iii) green and yellow stripes *(1 mark)*

(b) The live and neutral wires. *(1 mark)*

(c) A fuse. *(1 mark)*

2 (a) (i) Current flows in and out through the live wire and neutral wires. No current flows in the earth wire. *(1 mark)*

(ii) A large current flows in through the live wire and out through the earth wire. *(1 mark)*

(iii) No current flows until the fuse is replaced. *(1 mark)*

(b) It would flow from the live wire through the person to Earth. *(1 mark)*

3 (a) Power = current × voltage = 0.5 × 3 = 1.5 W
(2 marks, allow 1 mark for correct working)

(b) Charge = current × time = 0.5 × (30 × 60) = 900 C
(2 marks, allow 1 mark for correct working)

(c) Energy = charge × voltage = 900 × 3 = 2700 J
(2 marks, allow 1 mark for correct working)

Page 114

Warm-Up Questions

1) Any one of, e.g. cosmic rays, rocks, radon gas, food, building materials, human activity (e.g. fallout from nuclear bomb tests), living things.
2) E.g. uranium and plutonium.
3) It produces a lot of radioactive waste that must be carefully disposed of.
4) It would have made it possible to generate a lot of electricity easily and cheaply.

Exam Questions

1 (a) (i) -1 *(1 mark)*
(ii) +1 *(1 mark)*
(iii) 0 *(1 mark)*

(b) Protons *(1 mark)* and neutrons *(1 mark)*

(c) It increases by one. *(1 mark)*

(d) It decreases by four. *(1 mark)*

2 (a) U-235 is bombarded with slow-moving neutrons *(1 mark)*. A U-235 nucleus captures a neutron *(1 mark)* and splits into two smaller nuclei *(1 mark)*.

(b) The heat energy is used to heat water *(1 mark)* to drive a steam turbine *(1 mark)*.

3 (a) Deuterium *(1 mark)* and hydrogen *(1 mark)*
Fission uses heavy elements, whereas nuclear fusion uses light elements.

(b) Fusion power would allow a lot of electricity to be generated from a plentiful fuel *(1 mark)* without the large amounts of waste currently produced by fission. *(1 mark)*

(c) Fusion only works at such high temperatures that it uses more energy than it can produce. *(1 mark)*

Page 115

Revision Summary for Physics 2(ii) — Electricity and the Atom

6) 4.8 Ω

8) $A_1 = 0.2$ A, $V_1 = 1.4$ V, $V_2 = 0.4$ V, $V_3 = 10.2$ V, $R_1 = 51$ Ω

10) The wave should be drawn with one full wavelength (peak to peak) covering ten divisions of the screen.

13) a) 5 A

b) 13 A

14) 3180 J

18) 90 protons, 140 neutrons, 90 electrons.

20) a) $^{234}_{92}U \rightarrow ^{230}_{90}Th + ^{4}_{2}\alpha$

b) $^{230}_{90}Th \rightarrow ^{226}_{88}Ra + ^{4}_{2}\alpha$

c) $^{226}_{88}Ra \rightarrow ^{222}_{86}Rn + ^{4}_{2}\alpha$

21) a) $^{234}_{90}Th \rightarrow ^{234}_{91}Pa + ^{0}_{-1}\beta + ^{0}_{0}\gamma$

b) $^{234}_{91}Pa \rightarrow ^{234}_{92}U + ^{0}_{-1}\beta + ^{0}_{0}\gamma$

c) $^{14}_{6}C \rightarrow ^{14}_{7}N + ^{0}_{-1}\beta + ^{0}_{0}\gamma$

Page 120

Warm-Up Questions

1) Multiply the force by the perpendicular distance from the pivot.

2) Nm (newton metres)

3) The point where the object's whole mass can be considered to be 'concentrated'.

4) There is a resultant moment so it turns.

5) Because there is a resultant moment (caused by the weight acting out of line with the pivot).

Exam Questions

1 (a) (i) Moment = force × distance from pivot
= 15 × 0.03 = 0.45 Nm
(2 marks, allow 1 mark for correct working)

(ii) 15 × 0.12 = 1.8 Nm
(2 marks, allow 1 mark for correct working)

(b) End B should be put into the bolt *(1 mark)* because the same force exerts a larger moment (because it allows a larger distance between the pivot and the point where the force is applied). *(1 mark)*

2 (a) The decoration will hang with its centre of mass directly below the point of suspension. *(1 mark)*

(b) Maurice should suspend the decoration and a plumb line from the same point. *(1 mark)* When they stop moving, he should draw a line on the decoration where the plumb line lies. *(1 mark)* He should then repeat this, but with the shape suspended from a different pivot point. *(1 mark)* The centre of mass is where the two lines cross. *(1 mark)*

3 (a) No Robert is not correct. *(1 mark)* A seesaw will balance when the moments acting on each side of the pivot are equal (the masses only have to be equal when they are at the same distance from the pivot). *(1 mark)*

(b) (i)

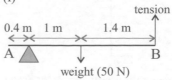

(1 mark for a correctly placed pivot, 1 mark for each correctly placed and labelled force arrow)

(ii) Clockwise moments = anticlockwise moments.
50 × 1 = T × (1.4 + 1). T = 20.8 N (to 1 d.p.)
(2 marks, allow 1 mark for correct working)

Page 125

Warm-Up Questions

1) Centripetal force

2) Gravity

3) Slightly elliptical (elongated circles)

4) Any two of, e.g. communication (telephone, television) / monitoring weather or climate / spying / navigation.

Exam Questions

1 (a) Any two of, e.g. driving force / friction / weight / air resistance. *(1 mark)*

(b) The forces must be unbalanced *(1 mark)* because the car is accelerating — its direction, and therefore velocity, is constantly changing *(1 mark)*.
Anything accelerating must have a resultant force acting on it.

2 (a) Geostationary/geosynchronous *(1 mark)*

(b) 24 hours *(1 mark)*

(c) (i) Satellite B sweeps over both poles while the Earth turns beneath it. *(1 mark)* So on each orbit the satellite 'sees' a different area of the Earth. *(1 mark)*

(ii) B — it must be in a low polar orbit because it is used to monitor the weather (it needs to be low to be able to take detailed pictures of the Earth). *(1 mark)*

3 (a) Venus travels faster *(1 mark)* because it has a larger centripetal force acting on it. *(1 mark)*

(b) Venus *(1 mark)*

Page 132

Warm-Up Questions

1) A real image can be captured on a screen. A virtual one can't.

2) Whether the image is real or virtual, which way up it is (the same way up as the object or inverted) and what size it is (bigger, smaller or the same size as the object).

3) Angle of incidence = angle of reflection

4)

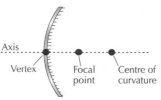

Exam Questions

1 (a) convex *(1 mark)*
   Convex mirrors make objects look smaller.

  (b) (i) 2 × 3 = 6 cm *(1 mark)*

   (ii)

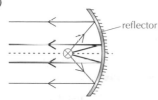

   (1 mark for two or more rays drawn correctly from bulb to reflector, and clearly showing parallel reflected rays. 1 mark for arrows on rays from bulb to reflector. 1 mark for arrows on reflected rays.)

  (c) The paintwork is a smooth/even surface, so parallel light rays all reflect at the same angle and Jennic's reflection is clear. *(1 mark)*

   The bumper is a rough/uneven surface, so parallel light rays reflect at different angles, giving a diffuse reflection. *(1 mark)*

2 As light reflected from the mobile phone leaves the pond it speeds up (because air is less dense than water) *(1 mark)*. This causes it to bend away from the normal, making the mobile phone (and therefore the bottom of the pond) appear closer than it actually is, i.e. shallower *(1 mark)*. The phenomenon is called refraction *(1 mark)*.

3

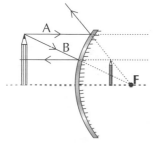

(1 mark for ray A and its reflected ray. 1 mark for ray B and its reflected ray. 1 mark for rays extended backwards (dotted lines). 1 mark for image in correct position.)

Page 138

Warm-Up Questions

1) Concave/diverging and convex/converging.

2) Convex lenses bulge outwards, concave lenses curve inwards.

3) Concave/diverging lenses always create virtual images. Convex/converging lenses can create real or virtual images (depending on the position of the object).

4) The point where the rays that hit the lens parallel to the axis appear to come from once they have passed through the lens.

5) Magnification = image height ÷ object height

6) E.g. magnifying glass, camera lens.

Exam Questions

1 (a) E.g. dispersion means the separation of white light/light from the Sun into its component colours/frequencies/wavelengths *(1 mark)*. Red light slows down the least / violet light slows down the most in glass *(1 mark)*, so red light is refracted the least / violet light is refracted the most *(1 mark)*.

   (1 mark for rays drawn correctly, showing red light refracted least and violet refracted most.)

  (b) The boundaries where light enters and leaves the block are parallel, so the colours recombine when they leave the block. *(1 mark)*

2 (a) A concave lens causes parallel rays of light to diverge (spread out) rather than converge (come together) *(1 mark)*. This means that Edward's lens cannot focus the sunlight to start a fire *(1 mark)*.

  (b) (i)

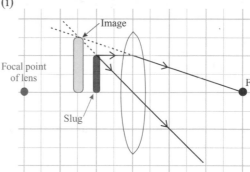

   (1 mark for showing a ray going to a correctly positioned focal point. 1 mark for showing a ray going through the centre of the lens. 1 mark for showing both rays extended backwards (dotted) and image drawn where they cross.)
   You sometimes need to draw another focal point on the opposite side of lens, the same distance away from the centre line of the lens.

   (ii) Magnification = image height ÷ object height
       = 3 ÷ 2 = 1.5
   (1 mark for answer between 1.4 and 1.6)
   Draw diagrams like this as neatly as you can so that you can measure the image and the object accurately.

228

Page 146

Warm-Up Questions

1) longitudinal
2) a copper bar
3) 20 Hz to 20 000 Hz
4) higher frequency = higher pitch
   larger amplitude = louder (higher volume)
5) distance = velocity × time

Exam Questions

1 (a) Distance = 2 × 360 = 720 m
   d = v × t, so v = d ÷ t = 720 ÷ 0.48 = 1500 m/s
   (2 marks for correct answer — otherwise 1 mark for correct formula)
   Don't forget to double the distance in echo calculations — the sound has to travel down to the sea bed and back again.

   (b) 180 ms = 0.18 s
   Distance = v × t = 1500 × 0.18 = 270 m
   So the fish are 270 ÷ 2 = 135 m below the ship.
   (2 marks for correct answer (based on the speed calculated in part (a)) — otherwise 1 mark for correct formula)

   (c) 50 kHz *(1 mark)*

   (d) Any one of, e.g. prenatal foetal scanning, cleaning delicate items/teeth/electronics, industrial quality control/crack detection. *(1 mark)*

2 (a) e.g.

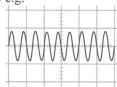

(1 mark for a sine wave with higher frequency)

   (b) e.g.

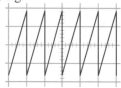

(1 mark for greater amplitude. 1 mark for the same frequency and shape)

Page 147

Revision Summary for Physics 3(i) — Forces and Waves

3) 1.5 × 600 = d × 450, so
   d = 900 ÷ 450 = 2 m

14) Magnification = image height ÷ object height
    = 4.5 ÷ 1.5 = 3

18) v = 2800 m/s and at the deepest point (B), t = 0.003 s.
    To find distance travelled to pipe and back, use d = v × t = 2800 × 0.003 = 8.4 m. So depth of pipe = 8.4 ÷ 2 = 4.2 m

Page 154

Warm-Up Questions

1) The direction of the magnetic field around a current carrying wire.
2) First finger — field
   Second finger — current
   Thumb — motion
3) Any two of, e.g. electric motors / speakers / generators / food mixers / CD players / locks / printers / fans / fan heaters.
4) Number of turns on coil, strength of magnetic field, amount of current, presence of magnetic/iron core.

Exam Questions

1 (a)

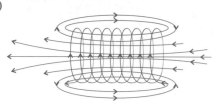

(1 mark for correct field shape, 1 mark for direction)

   (b) E.g. soft iron *(1 mark)*

   (c) A magnetically soft material loses its magnetism when the current is switched off. *(1 mark)*

   (d) It will increase the strength of the magnetic field produced by Arnold's electromagnet. *(1 mark)*

2 (a) Anticlockwise *(1 mark)*
   Use Fleming's left-hand rule on one of the arms of the coil.

   (b) The split-ring commutator keeps the motor turning in the same direction. *(1 mark)*

   (c) Any one of, increase the number of turns on the coil / increase the current flowing through the coil / use a stronger magnet / add an iron core to the coil. *(1 mark)*

   (d) By reversing the direction of the current / the magnetic field. *(1 mark)*

Page 161

Warm-Up Questions

1) Number of turns on coil, strength of magnet, area of the coil, speed of the movement.
2) Slip-rings and brushes.
3) $\frac{V_p}{V_s} = \frac{N_p}{N_s}$ or $\frac{V_s}{V_p} = \frac{N_s}{N_p}$
4) To transmit a lot of power efficiently (by keeping the current low).

Exam Questions

1 A coil of wire is rotated inside a magnetic field. / A magnet is rotated within a coil of wire *(1 mark)* As the coil/magnet spins a voltage is induced within the coil. *(1 mark)* This voltage and the resulting current reverse direction with every half-turn of the coil/magnet — resulting in an alternating current. *(1 mark)*

2 (a) (i) B *(1 mark)*

    (ii) A *(1 mark)*
       Turning the magnet faster increases the peak voltage as well as frequency.

  (b) (i) No voltage is induced. *(1 mark)*

    (ii) The lights would go out when the rider stops moving, e.g. at a junction. *(1 mark)*

3 (a) A voltage will not be induced in the secondary coil when using a DC supply *(1 mark)* because the magnetic field generated in the iron core is not changing. *(1 mark)*

  (b) (i) Power = current × voltage = 2.5 × 12 = 30 W *(1 mark)*

    (ii) Assuming that the transformer is 100% efficient, the output power is 30 W. *(1 mark)*
      Current = power ÷ voltage = 30 ÷ 4 = 7.5 A *(1 mark)*

    (iii) $\frac{V_s}{V_p} = \frac{N_s}{N_p} = \frac{4}{12} = \frac{N_s}{15}$. $N_s = 60 \div 12 = 5$ turns
      (2 marks, allow 1 mark for correct working)

Page 165

Warm-Up Questions

1) A very large group of stars/solar systems.

2) Clouds of dust and gas.

3) A very large/heavy star.

4) A red giant.

Exam Questions

1 (a) A star that is formed from material created in the supernova of a previous star. *(1 mark)*

  (b) The Milky Way. *(1 mark)*

  (c) The force of gravity. *(1 mark)*

2 (a) Hydrogen. *(1 mark)*

  (b) By nuclear fusion in the cores of stars (hydrogen nuclei smashed together to form helium nuclei). *(1 mark)*

3 (a) Stars form from clouds of dust and gas which spiral in due to gravitational attraction. *(1 mark)* Gravity compresses the matter so much that intense heat develops. *(1 mark)* When the temperature gets hot enough, nuclear fusion happens and huge amounts of heat and light are emitted. *(1 mark)*

  (b) The forces acting on a main sequence star are balanced, so it doesn't collapse or explode. *(1 mark)* The heat caused by nuclear fusion provides an outward force to balance the force of gravity pulling everything inwards. *(1 mark)*

  (c) (i) They cool and contract into white dwarfs *(1 mark)* and then as their light fades completely they become black dwarfs. *(1 mark)*

    (ii) They start to glow brightly again and undergo more fusion, and expand and contract several times. *(1 mark)* Heavier elements are formed and the star eventually explodes in a supernova. *(1 mark)* The supernova leaves behind a neutron star or a black hole. *(1 mark)*

Page 166

Revision Summary for Physics 3(ii) Magnetism and Stars

15) $V_s/V_p = N_s/N_p$ so $V_s = (600/20) \times 9 = 30 \times 9 = 270$ V

Exams

Unit 1a — Energy and Electricity

1) A — 4 *(1 mark)*

   B — 1 *(1 mark)* In solids, the particles are tightly packed in a rigid structure, so their vibrations are easily passed on.

   C — 3 *(1 mark)* In convection, the material itself moves — solids can't flow like liquids and gases can.

   D — 2 *(1 mark)* In a vacuum, there are no particles to transfer energy by conduction or convection.

2) A — 2 *(1 mark)* This is what generators do.

   B — 1 *(1 mark)* As water flows downhill, it loses gravitational potential energy and gains kinetic energy.

   C — 3 *(1 mark)* The cables heat up because they have resistance.

   D — 4 *(1 mark)*

3) A 1 *(1 mark)*

   B 4 *(1 mark)* 2 is also an advantage of using nuclear fuels, but not an environmental one.

   C 2 *(1 mark)*

   D 3 *(1 mark)* 63 (fossil fuels) + 16 (nuclear) = 79. So 21% of electricity is generated from other resources.

4) A 2 *(1 mark)* Only a small proportion is being 'wasted' (as heat).

   B 4 *(1 mark)* It's the thickness of the arrows that matters — number 4 has the thinnest 'light energy' arrow.

   C 1 *(1 mark)* 50 ÷ 200 = 0.25

   D 4 *(1 mark)* Payback time = cost ÷ saving = 375 ÷ 0.75 = 500 hours.

5) A 4 *(1 mark)*

   B 1 *(1 mark)* 3 is also true, but since they're hotter than the surroundings, they will emit more heat than they absorb.

   C 1 *(1 mark)*

   D 4 *(1 mark)* This would reduce the rate of transfer by making them poorer emitters of heat.

6) A 3 *(1 mark)* Watts and kilowatts are units of power.

   B 3 *(1 mark)* Energy can't disappear — it is transformed into other forms (such as heat).

   C 2 *(1 mark)*

   D 4 *(1 mark)*

7) A 1 *(1 mark)* This makes it a good insulator — kinetic energy isn't transferred easily from particle to particle.

   B 3 *(1 mark)* Conduction and convection require particles.

   C 2 *(1 mark)*

   D 4 *(1 mark)*

8) A 3 *(1 mark)* 90 mins = 1.5 hours. 1.5 × 1.5 = 2.25 kWh. 2.25 × 18 = 40.5p.

   B 2 *(1 mark)*

   C 4 *(1 mark)* 1800 ÷ 5 = £360 per year. 360 ÷ 900 × 100 = 40%.

   D 3 *(1 mark)* When it isn't windy, the turbine won't generate electricity, so he'll need to buy it from the National Grid.

9) A 4 *(1 mark)* This is the variable for which Kirsty set the value.

   B 1 *(1 mark)* The thickness could, theoretically, have any value.

   C 3 *(1 mark)* She might have made the same error both times, making the results wrong in the same way.

   D 2 *(1 mark)*

Unit 1b — Radiation and the Universe

1) A — 3 *(1 mark)*

   B — 1 *(1 mark)* X-rays are ionising, so they can cause mutations in cells which may cause cancer.

   C — 4 *(1 mark)* Heat (that cooks the burgers) is infrared radiation and can cause burns.

   D — 2 *(1 mark)* Laser light is very focused, so it can damage cells.

2) A — 1 *(1 mark)*

   B — 3 *(1 mark)* They're the same element so the number of protons must be the same.

   C — 2 *(1 mark)*

   D — 4 *(1 mark)* The number of neutrons is different in different isotopes.

3) A 4 *(1 mark)*

   B 3 *(1 mark)* After 5 years (a half-life), ½ the nuclei have not yet decayed. After another 5 years, ½ of these have decayed.

   C 4 *(1 mark)* The tumour receives radiation from several directions, but healthy cells don't, so their dose is much lower.

   D 1 *(1 mark)* The probability of being cured is higher than the probability of suffering serious damage.

4) A 2 *(1 mark)* Only gamma will pass through several metres of soil and rock.

   B 4 *(1 mark)* Of the four options, a lead lined suit is the only one that will stop beta radiation reaching the body.

   C 3 *(1 mark)* The circuit is broken when alpha radiation is absorbed by smoke — stopping it ionising the air.

   D 4 *(1 mark)* Gamma rays have no charge so aren't deflected. Alpha and beta particles are deflected.

5) A 1 *(1 mark)* Wavelength = speed ÷ frequency
= $(3.0 \times 10^8) \div (225.64 \times 10^8) = 1.33$ m

B 4 *(1 mark)* They travel at the same speed
(about 3.0×10^8 m/s).

C 3 *(1 mark)* Frequency = speed ÷ wavelength
= $(3 \times 10^8) \div 2 = 1.5 \times 10^8$ Hz

D 3 *(1 mark)*

6) A 2 *(1 mark)*

B 4 *(1 mark)* The frequency of light is lower than expected (i.e. red-shifted) because they are moving away from Earth.

C 1 *(1 mark)* Galaxies that are further away are moving away from us faster than those that are close.

D 2 *(1 mark)* There are other theories. 3 is not a good reason to accept a theory. Scientific theories cannot be proved by experiment.

7) A 1 *(1 mark)* The least radiation reached the detector so it must have absorbed or reflected most radiation.

B 3 *(1 mark)* This is the factor that is measured.

C 4 *(1 mark)*

D 2 *(1 mark)* Ultraviolet light has been linked to skin cancer.

8) A 4 *(1 mark)* The activity decreases to a quarter in 112 s, so will have decreased by half in 56 s.

B 3 *(1 mark)* It has been three half-lives since the human was alive ($5730 \times 3 = 17190$ years).

C 2 *(1 mark)* Alpha is strongly ionising and cannot pass out of the body (not 3 or 4). The half-life should be short.

D 3 *(1 mark)* Alpha would be stopped by any thickness. Gamma would penetrate any thickness.

9) A 3 *(1 mark)* The Earth's atmosphere absorbs (and reflects) a lot of light.

B 3 *(1 mark)* Optical telescopes in space don't need as big mirrors as Earth-based telescopes.

C 2 *(1 mark)* The longer wavelength means a larger telescope is needed for the same resolution of image.

D 4 *(1 mark)*

Unit 2

1 a) Circuit B has greater resistance *(1 mark)* and a smaller current *(1 mark)*.

b) Ammeter in series with the lamp *(1 mark)*, voltmeter in parallel with the lamp *(1 mark)*, e.g.

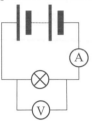

c) i) Resistance = potential difference ÷ current *(1 mark)*

ii) Resistance = 3 V ÷ 0.5 A = 6 Ω
(2 marks for correct value with unit, otherwise 1 mark for correct value.)

d) i) A — LDR / light dependent resistor *(1 mark)*
B — thermistor *(1 mark)*

ii) it decreases *(1 mark)*

2 a) The splitting of atomic nuclei *(1 mark)*.

b) plutonium-239 *(1 mark)*, uranium-235 *(1 mark)*

c) The joining together of atomic/light nuclei to form larger/heavier ones *(1 mark)*.

d) in stars/the Sun *(1 mark)*

3 a) i) Point X — the slope of the graph is steeper there *(1 mark)*.

ii) Point X — as Patrick's velocity rises the frictional forces acting on him increase *(1 mark)*, which means that the resultant downward force acting on him decreases *(1 mark)*.

b) Any one of, the forces acting on him were balanced / he had reached terminal velocity / the resultant force acting on him was zero *(1 mark)*.

c) Weight = 83 kg × 10 m/s² = 830 N *(1 mark)*

4 a) Total momentum
= Dean's momentum + Natalie's momentum
= (60 kg × 6 m/s) + (40 kg × 0 m/s)
= 360 kg m/s
(2 marks for correct value with unit, otherwise 1 mark for correct value.)

b) Total momentum after = total momentum before
= 360 kg m/s
Total momentum after = 100 × velocity = 360 kg m/s
So velocity = 360 ÷ 100 = 3.6 m/s
(2 marks for the correct answer, otherwise 1 mark for equating total momentum before and after.)
Momentum is conserved in any collision provided no external forces act on the bodies involved. The momentum immediately after is the same as Dean's momentum, since Natalie was at rest before the collision and so had zero momentum.

c) It increases the time taken to land *(1 mark)* and as force = change in momentum ÷ time *(1 mark)* increasing the time taken to change momentum will decrease the force, reducing the chances of injury *(1 mark)*.

5 a) Time = charge ÷ current
Time = 1000 C ÷ 0.5 A = 2000 s
(2 marks for the correct answer, otherwise 1 mark for correctly rearranging the equation.)

b) Energy transformed = 1000 C × 6 V = 6000 J
(2 marks for correct value with unit, otherwise 1 mark for correct value.)

6 a) 84 *(1 mark)*

b) 132 *(1 mark)*
Atomic number is the total number of protons. Mass number is the total number of protons and neutrons. So, number of neutrons = mass number − atomic number.

c) $^{216}_{84}\text{Po} \rightarrow \, ^{212}_{82}\text{Po} + \, ^{4}_{2}\text{He}$
(1 mark for Pb correct, 1 mark for He correct.)
An alpha particle is a helium nucleus.

d) $^{212}_{82}\text{Pb} \rightarrow \, ^{212}_{83}\text{Bi} + \, ^{0}_{-1}\text{e}$
(1 mark for Bi correct, 1 mark for e correct. (Allow for errors carried over from part c).)
A beta particle is an electron.

7 a)
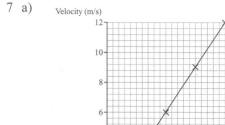
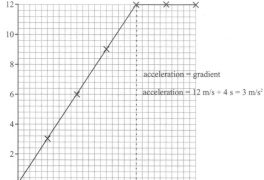

(1 mark for correctly plotted points, 1 mark for a line as shown.)

b) Indication on graph of how gradient was found *(1 mark)*.
Acceleration = 12 m/s ÷ 4 s = 3 m/s²
(2 marks for correct value with unit, otherwise 1 mark for correct value.)

c) Distance travelled in first 4 seconds
= ½ × 4 × 12 = 24 m *(1 mark)*
Distance travelled between 4 and 6 seconds
= 2 × 12 = 24 m *(1 mark)*
Total distance = 24 + 24 = 48 m *(1 mark)*

Unit 3

1 a) Moment = force × perpendicular distance
= 100 × 0.2 = 20 Nm
(2 marks for correct value with unit, otherwise 1 mark for correct value)

b) The moment will decrease *(1 mark)* because the perpendicular distance between the line of action of the force and the axis of rotation/point A will decrease *(1 mark)*.

c) The stabilisers increase the width of the base of the bike *(1 mark)*. The line of action of the weight of Luke and his bike is less likely to fall outside this wider base, so he is less likely to topple over. / The centre of gravity/mass is less likely to fall outside this wider base, so he is less likely to topple over *(1 mark)*.

2 a) gravity *(1 mark)*

b) Neptune is further away from the Sun and has a lower orbital speed than Saturn so its orbit is longer / it takes longer to complete an orbit *(1 mark)*.

c) There is a stronger force of attraction between the Sun and Earth than between the Sun and the gas giants *(1 mark)* because the Earth is closer to the Sun than the gas giants are *(1 mark)*.

3 a)
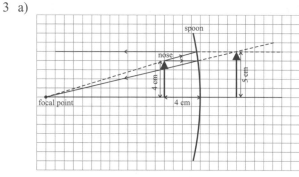

(1 mark for construction lines, 1 mark each for correct size and position of image)

b) Magnification = image height ÷ object height
= 5 ÷ 4 = 1.25
(2 marks for the correct answer, otherwise 1 mark for correct equation or substitution)

c) The image would be smaller (than 4 cm / her actual nose) *(1 mark)*.

4 a) i) Frequency = 1 ÷ time period
= 1 ÷ (2.5 × 10⁻⁵) = 40 000 Hz
(2 marks for the correct answer, otherwise 1 mark for correct substitution)

ii) around 20 – 20 000 Hz *(1 mark)*

b) i) The sound waves from the referee's whistle have a greater amplitude *(1 mark)*.

ii) The two wave forms are different shapes (which means the two whistles would have a different quality of sound) *(1 mark)*.

5 a)

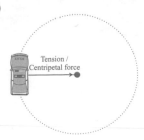

Tension /
Centripetal force

(1 mark)

b) Any two of, e.g. use a lighter car / use a car that travels
more slowly / increase the length of the string/radius of the
circle *(2 marks)*.

c) No, Louise is incorrect. Except when it's stationary, the
car is always accelerating *(1 mark)* towards the centre of
the circle / because it is constantly changing direction
(1 mark).
Acceleration doesn't have to involve speeding up or slowing
down. Acceleration means a change in velocity — and that
could just be a change in direction.

6 a) A coil of wire rotates in a magnetic field to induce a
voltage in the coil *(1 mark)*. The slip rings and brushes
connect the coil up to a complete circuit, allowing a
current to flow *(1 mark)*.

b) The trace should have a higher frequency and higher peak
voltage, e.g.:

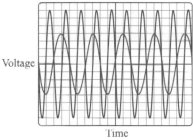

Voltage

Time

*(1 mark for a higher frequency, 1 mark for a higher peak
voltage)*

c) Any two of, e.g. increase the strength of the magnetic field
/ increase the number of turns on the coil / increase the
area of the coil *(1 mark for two correct suggestions)*.

7 a) The alternating current in the primary coil causes a rapidly
changing magnetic field in the iron core *(1 mark)*. The
changing magnetic field induces an alternating voltage in
the secondary coil *(1 mark)*.

b)

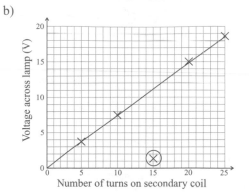

*(1 mark for all points correctly plotted, 1 mark for line of
best fit)*

c) i) The result using 15 turns on the primary coil should
be circled. *(1 mark)*

ii) 11 V (Accept values between 10.5 and 11.5 V)
(1 mark)

8 a) The Sun was formed from gas and dust pulled together by
gravitational attraction *(1 mark)*. The planets were formed
at the same time from smaller clumps of dust and gas
(1 mark).

b) i) By nuclear fusion / fusion of hydrogen nuclei *(1 mark)*

ii) The heat it generates provides an outward force
(1 mark) that balances the inward force of gravity and
stops it collapsing *(1 mark)*.

c) A The Sun's hydrogen begins to runs out and the Sun
swells and cools / its surface turns red *(1 mark)*.

B It contracts (to form a white dwarf) *(1 mark)*.

C It cools and fades (to become a black dwarf) *(1 mark)*.

Index

Index